R
An Altern

Simon Webb

Copyright Simon Webb 2014
All Rights Reserved
http://www.runningblindbook.com

"A fantastic insight into the experiences of
running the London Marathon as a blind runner
– wonderfully evocative language"
John Inverdale BBC Sport

"What Simon has achieved is incredible. His
story is truly compelling"
Michael Dobbs, author of House of Cards

Contents

Chapter 1: 'One Day Like This' 1

Chapter 2: 'Let's Work Together' 7

Chapter 3: 'Long May You Run' - Blackheath 22

Chapter 4: 'Up the Junction' - Blackheath to Woolwich 41

Chapter 5: 'Stroll On' - Woolwich to Greenwich .. 56

Chapter 6: 'It's About Time' - Greenwich 67

Chapter 7: 'Fun City, SE8' - Deptford 92

Chapter 8: 'Let's Go Down to the Water Line' - Deptford to Rotherhithe 106

Chapter 9: 'Caliban's Dream' - Rotherhithe to Tower Bridge 121

Chapter 10: 'Watching the River Flow' - Tooley Street to East Smithfield 139

Chapter 11: 'The Middle' - Sporting Greatness runs amongst us 154

Chapter 12: 'Highway to Hell' - Tower Hill to Limehouse along The Highway 163

Chapter 13: 'Limehouse Blues' - Narrow Street to Canary Wharf 176

Chapter 14: 'I Am the Resurrection' - Canary Wharf and the Isle of Dogs 194

Chapter 15: 'Morning Glory' - Isle of Dogs to Poplar 204

Chapter 16: 'The Road Goes on Forever' - what it's like to hit the wall 211

Chapter 17: 'A13, Trunk Road to the Sea' - Poplar to The Highway 221

Chapter 18: 'Towers of London' - Tower of London and the Ceremonial City 231

Chapter 19: 'I'm on Fire' - climbing the Monument to the Great Fire of London 248

Chapter 20: 'Run For Home' - Tower of London to Upper Thames Street 254

Chapter 21: 'Light at the End of the Tunnel' - Upper Thames Street to Temple 263

Chapter 22: 'Waterloo Sunset' - Somerset House to Westminster Bridge 270

Chapter 23: 'At the Chime of a City Clock' - Big Ben 281

Chapter 24: 'Home Town Glory' - Westminster Bridge to The Mall 289

Chapter Names Explained 297

Chapter 1: Elbow - 'One Day Like This' 297

Chapter 2: Canned Heat - 'Let's Work Together' 297

Chapter 3: The Stills-Young Band - 'Long May You Run' 297

Chapter 4: Squeeze - 'Up the Junction' 297

Chapter 5: Yardbirds - 'Stroll On' 298

Chapter 6: Lemonheads - 'It's About Time' 298

Chapter 7: Alternative TV - 'Fun City, SE8' 298

Chapter 8: Dire Straits - 'Let's Go Down to the Water Line' 298

Chapter 9: Underworld - 'Caliban's Dream' 298

Chapter 10: Bob Dylan - 'Watching the River Flow' 299

Chapter 11: Jimmy Eat World - 'The Middle' 299

Chapter 12: AC/DC - 'Highway to Hell' 299

Chapter 13: Django Reinhardt - 'Limehouse Blues' 300

Chapter 14: Stone Roses - 'I Am the Resurrection' 300

Chapter 15: Oasis - 'Morning Glory' 300

Chapter 16: High Contrast - 'The Road Goes on Forever' 301

Chapter 17: Billy Bragg - 'A13, Trunk Road to the Sea' 301

Chapter 18: XTC - 'Towers of London' 301

Chapter 19: Bruce Springsteen - 'I'm on Fire' 301

Chapter 20: Lindisfarne - 'Run For Home' 301

Chapter 21: Half Man Half Biscuit - 'Light at the End of the Tunnel' 302

Chapter 22: The Kinks - 'Waterloo Sunset' 302

Chapter 23: Nick Drake - 'At the Chime of a City Clock' 302

Chapter 24: Adele - 'Home Town Glory' 302

Acknowledgements **304**

Research and other Assistance 304

Additional Thanks 305

About the Author **306**

Chapter 1: 'One Day Like This'

As race day dawned and my alarm went off at 6 am, the sun was already streaming through my bedroom window. Clear skies meant a chilly morning that would become pleasantly warm later in the day. I had that tangible feeling of anticipation in my stomach which had me up and in the shower in minutes. I'd been looking forward to this day for weeks, and this time I wasn't even running!

It wasn't long before I heard someone on the radio enthuse "where else would you rather be on London Marathon Day?" Standing on The Highway close to Tower Bridge, bacon roll in hand, soaking up the sun and waiting for the first elite runners to pass, the answer to that question was "nowhere".

The London Marathon is one of the key fixtures in the UK's sporting calendar, alongside FA Cup Final day, the Grand National and Wimbledon.

Football supporters dream of going to Wembley to support their team in the Cup Final. People feel part of the Grand National by placing their one bet for the year on a horse with a vaguely amusing name. Britain becomes a nation of tennis fans each summer during Wimbledon fortnight; you might even have picked up a racket, although it went back in the cupboard as soon as the rain started. Three occasions which transcend their sports' fan base boundaries; but unless we're talented enough to be a professional footballer, tennis player or jockey, or rich enough to own a race horse, our participation is generally limited to being in the crowd, watching on TV at home, in the pub or the betting shop.

The London Marathon has the crowds, the cameras, the atmosphere, the hopes of the elite and the disappointment of those who don't quite succeed, but it has something that the Cup Final, Grand National and Wimbledon do not. It has a member of your family, a friend, neighbour, work colleague, the person in the pub you never thought could be a runner. It might even have had you.

For the vast majority, running a marathon is a personal challenge and not something we do as a professional or international athlete and it's rather comforting that the London Marathon, as we know it, was born from a conversation in a pub. It was the Dysart Arms just outside Richmond Park, where Chris Brasher first considered the idea of a marathon through the streets of London.

Brasher was one of the pacemakers helping Roger Bannister become the first man to run a mile in less than four minutes in 1954. He went on to enjoy his own success two years later, winning gold in the 3000m steeplechase at the Melbourne Olympics.

After returning from completing the 1979 New York Marathon, he, along with friend John Disley, secured sponsorship which enabled the staging of the first London Marathon on March 29th 1981. Their objectives were to promote long-distance running, raise money for charity and create a feeling of community - without question a mission well and truly accomplished.

Seven thousand runners took part in the first London Marathon in 1981. Thirty years on, filling in the online application simply to be in the ballot from where lucky names are drawn, is a race for the prize similar to buying a ticket for a major music or sports event. In 2013 the 125,000 ballot places were filled in less than eleven and a half hours, a record time five hours quicker than the previous year.

In his book 'From Last to First', 1984 London Marathon winner Charlie Spedding talks of going for dinner in a Central London Italian restaurant the night before his victorious run. Sitting on his own, he was able to overhear his fellow diners on next door tables complaining about this wretched run which was causing so many roads to be shut the next day. You can just imagine what they were saying:

"Who do these runners think they are?"

"Aren't there enough parks for them to run in?"

"Don't they know some of us have church to get to, and how are we supposed to drive when all the roads are closed?"

Times have changed since the mid 80s, Time Out, for example, lists running, or at least watching the Marathon as one of the essential things to do in London. A record 36,705 finished the event in 2012. In 2013 organisers estimated another record was broken as 700,000 people gathered along the route, many brought onto the streets in a show of solidarity following the bombing of the Boston Marathon earlier that week.

At key points like Canary Wharf and the Cutty Sark, sport and entertainment collide to create an atmosphere that is a cross between the Notting Hill Carnival and the free events which saw thousands line the streets during the 2012 Olympics.

The carnival atmosphere is replicated on the road with the world's best runners followed over the finish line (albeit several hours later) by a collection of cartoon characters, zoo animals and half the fruit and veg aisle at Tesco.

For the professionals, this is one of the key events in their race calendar; elite runners will only complete a couple of marathons a year, so for the athletics enthusiast this is an opportunity to see world class sport for free. For those further down the pecking order, be they the club runner who can pull out a sub 3 hour performance, or the charity runner looking for a life-changing experience, this is a rare chance to line up in the same field as Olympians, even if in reality they're likely to finish nearer the bloke dressed as a pineapple than Paula Radcliffe. And, the fun runner enjoys that special experience, usually only reserved for the elite, being cheered on by thousands!

In 2002 I was lucky enough to be part of the England team at the Manchester Commonwealth Games, competing in the visually impaired 100 metres. The stadium wasn't full for the morning session my race was part of, but by being the English competitor in front of an English crowd, for that brief moment the biggest cheer was for me – the fact that only four people in the crowd of over 30,000 had any idea who I was made no difference at all.

A friend from the Richmond Athletics Club, where I was a member at the time, made everyone in a TV shop stop what they were doing to watch my race, no doubt holding court with pre and post race analysis.

"If he gets a great start here this could be an impressive run."

I didn't, and it wasn't. I did have a microphone shoved in my face as I walked off the track at the City of Manchester Stadium so was able to give a breathless and unintelligible interview to add to my 15 minutes of fame experience.

It's the potential for the Sunday morning jogger to have their moment in the spotlight which makes the London Marathon such an appealing prospect. For those taking part, or perhaps more so for the friends watching at home, being spotted on the TV, or better still, interviewed by one of the many reporters dotted around the route adds to the excitement.

Nine years after my Commonwealth Games moment, I made my debut as a marathon runner. So, whilst the 2011 London Marathon wasn't my first experience of running in front of thousands of people, the atmosphere was certainly something I was looking forward to as I waited to cross the start line. This was not only my first time running a marathon but my first experience of the London Marathon. How could I have been a living Londoner since two years before the debut of this great event and never actually been to sample the atmosphere? In fact, until the latter point of my training, I wasn't even sure what the actual route was. I knew about Tower Bridge and the finish in Westminster but my knowledge of the rest was fairly vague.

As I familiarised myself with the course, I

did so partly with preparation in mind: where would I be taking on water or energy drink; what landmarks could be recommended for anyone planning to try and spot me; but also I was looking for interesting facts about the route that might distract my brain from extreme fatigue.

I am a registered blind runner, and not being able to appreciate the aesthetic quality of London on marathon day was one of the reasons why I developed a strong interest in the route. Whilst I could never take my mind off the physical challenge of running by admiring the view, knowing about the history of Cutty Sark, or that we'd just run past an especially interesting pub, and being able to talk to my guide runner about it, I hoped would pass the time.

From the start in Blackheath, where the people of London welcomed a victorious Henry V back from Agincourt in 1415, to the finish line outside the Queen's front door, there's much of historical and cultural significance to admire and enjoy, something which presumably is hard to do when pounding the streets dressed as a vegetable.

Whilst I'd never attempt a marathon dressed as anything other than a runner, I too was in no mood for sightseeing as I undertook that famous tour of London. As I hope to run the course again one day, I'm going back for a second look. Only this time, it'll take a bit longer than 3 hours 43 minutes and 40 seconds to get round.

Chapter 2: 'Let's Work Together'

Before I dive into my exploration of sections of South and East London, I want to answer the question I get asked the most when I tell people I run, which is, not unreasonably, "How?"

My sight level, or lack of it, amounts to only light and dark perception. This means I can wake up in the morning and see how light it is outside - always useful if I've overslept in the winter. If a light in a room is especially bright, then I can pick that out, and on a particularly bright day I can make out shadows and large objects, such as buildings, although only if I'm close up.

I especially like being in the countryside away from light pollution on clear nights. When the moon is full I find myself releasing my inner werewolf by staring up at the sky.

I can appreciate sunrises much more than sunsets, as it's easier for me to make out the change from dark to light, or perhaps it's just that if I'm still awake at sunrise I've usually had a very good night!

What I can see is no use when it comes to running – so I run by having a guide runner with me.

Take one sweatband bandana, tie a knot in the middle to create two smaller loops, hold one end, give the other to your guide, and off you go. By tying a knot in the middle of something which is large enough to go round a person's head, this allows the guide to retain control, whilst giving enough room for the arms of both runners to move in a relaxed way. I've no idea whose idea the knotted bandana was - whoever they are, they're a genius! I know of blind runners who prefer to hold the elbow of the person guiding them. Personally, I find this limits arm movement, something which is likely to make you run slower, but it's all down to what you feel most comfortable with.

There's no specific rule about what person A and person B can be attached to one another with. The International Blind Sport Federation states that "Whether or not a tether is being used, the athlete and the guide shall be no more than 50cm apart at all times".

Rule 7.4.5 instructs "At no time may the guide pull or propel the athlete forward by pushing. Infringement of this rule shall lead to disqualification" (Rules courtesy of 'Guide Running, A Practical Guide' produced by British Blind Sport's Youth Athletics Development Officer and senior coach Sheila J. Carey).

If the guide crosses the finishing line ahead of the runner, even if only by a fraction of a body part, as I have found out through experience, you're disqualified.

That's the short answer, and something that is often followed up with further questions about how it feels, what it's like, and the observation that "it must be really difficult".

At primary school I was always one of the quicker runners. Whilst the traditional sports day events of egg and spoon, sack and three legged races were good fun, I especially looked forward to what I think they used to call the 'running race'. This usually presented something of a challenge as it was difficult to find an adult that was quick enough to keep up with me. One year they came up with a plan. A ball of string long enough to stretch the length of the course was found, and staff members stood holding each end. I was then to run, holding onto the string. If only they'd considered the rope burns I'd get and suggested I wore a glove, I might not have stopped half way!

My primary school actually handled the needs of a child with rapidly deteriorating sight extremely well. When I joined as a seven year old, I could read normal books. By the time I left at the age of eleven, I could barely read large words on a CCTV screen.

I was born long sighted, with my sight level reaching the point it's at now at around the age of fifteen. This deterioration was caused by an eye condition called Retinitis Pigmentosa, a Latin sounding scientific term which took me years to remember.

Retinitis Pigmentosa is an eye disease where there is damage to the retina, the layer of tissue at the back of the inner eye that converts light images to nerve signals and sends them to the brain.

Symptoms often first appear in childhood, but severe sight issues tend to develop in early adulthood. These can include the loss of peripheral sight resulting in tunnel vision, something my parents identified in the 4 year old me when I thought I could hide behind a drain pipe in the back garden!

In advanced cases, which I became, central vision also goes. All of this is as a result of expanding dark spots on the retina.

Scientific research is developing at such a

rate that there is now a chance that, in my lifetime, some form of treatment may become available. It goes without saying that I'm not clinging onto hope of a medical breakthrough, as I have more important things to occupy my mind like having marathons to run. Never has the phrase "I'll believe it when I see it" been more relevant.

Having been in mainstream education until the age of eleven, I was dispatched to a boarding school for blind and partially sighted people where P.E., in particular, benefited from specialised teaching. I soon realised that 'track and field' was the sport for me. This led to me being invited to train with the Great Britain blind athletics team, and subsequently shortlisted for places at international championships. The closest I came to representing Great Britain was in 2001, where I was told that, as long as I continued to match the standard I was training and competing at, I'd be in the team for the European Championships in Poland. Disaster struck in the form of a torn hamstring, and the plane left for Eastern Europe without me.

My fifteen minutes of fame came the following year, when I learnt that the Commonwealth Games were including a small number of disabled sports to count towards the medals table which had previously only been part of the programme as demonstration events. As one of the quickest blind 100 metre runners in England at the time, there was me, suddenly a team mate of Paula Radcliffe, Jonathan Edwards, Mark Lewis–Francis and countless more famous people off the telly.

I do have a recording of the BBC TV

coverage of my race somewhere. I can't remember anything of the event, other than being excited to discover that Steve Cram had commentated on me.

Too many injuries and the need for a new challenge meant I was never likely to move up to Paralympic level as a sprinter, so, soon after the Manchester experience, I took up distance running.

Whilst there are some differences between how to guide a sprinter and a long distance runner, the basic principles remain the same. A guide running partnership is all about teamwork, relying on confidence, communication, understanding, anticipation and practise. Like a sprint relay team, tennis or badminton doubles pair, or defensive unit in football, when you don't have these principles your chances of success become much harder.

Above all, though, trust is absolutely crucial if the blind runner is going to perform to the best of their ability, and that's on both sides. The runner has to have one hundred percent confidence that the guide is going to do everything they can to ensure accidents are avoided. The guide has to be confident that they have the blind runner's trust and that the runner will respond to instructions quickly, as well as having trust in themselves to make the crucial calls at the right time, not to be overly protective, whilst not taking unnecessary risks. Both people have to understand that a problem may occur and work hard to prevent this from happening or minimise the impact; but when something doesn't go to plan it must not be allowed to have a negative effect on the bigger picture. A jockey will come off their horse, a cyclist will crash, a footballer will miss an open goal, a cricketer will drop a catch they should hold - the strong minded don't let these things affect them.

Anticipation becomes more of a factor the faster you run, something I experienced during my twelve years on the track. Regardless of your level of sight, reaction times are vital; how fast you come out of the blocks can be the difference between winning and losing. I was always among the fastest starters in groups I would train with, beating people to the 30 metre mark even though they could run a 100 metre race considerably quicker than me.

I am able to run fast on roads or paths now, safe in the knowledge that I can respond, even if a warning is late. Whilst training for the London Marathon, I ran a race called Tadworth Ten, a ten miler based on Epsom Downs. This event was a perfect example of where the runner/guide relationship working well results in a strong performance. There were stretches of off road terrain with many a bump in the ground where a sighted person could twist an ankle if they weren't concentrating. Where we ran on road, it was mostly down hill, and pretty steep. Jim, my guide on that occasion, told me afterwards: "The courage that you showed on those fast descents was remarkable, or foolhardy - I can't decide which".

Truth be told, it was probably a bit of both, but I'm only ever going to try something like that if I have faith in the person I'm attached to.

How much information I like to be given does depend on the situation. There are the obvious things like kerbs, tree roots, people and so on, but in a race situation I may ask the guide to tell me things which might help when fatigue becomes an issue.

"There are ten people ahead and I believe we can catch them" they might say. This is a judgement I'm unable to make but is exactly the sort of thing which I would use to drive me on. There remains a sprinter hiding inside me and my competitiveness means I get a kick out of the knowledge that I'm picking people off.

Sometimes, no matter how much information I'm given, not being able to focus on a target, or look at what's around me, can present a challenge. Fighting fatigue becomes an issue as the body and brain get tired and thoughts lurking in my subconscious take over. Think of it as like daydreaming in boring meetings, or thoughts keeping you awake at night. Often this takes the form of songs going round and round my head; frustratingly they're usually ones I hate. My desire to research locations of significance from the London Marathon route was, in part, preparation for this. I hoped that being told the name of a pub, or that a certain tourist attraction was now in view would be of help.

It's said that boxers go to some dark places in the mind when pushing themselves to the limit and beyond. I'm no psychologist, but I do know that if I feel I'm not running well, this thought can easily get tangled up with any other negative ones which might be lurking in my subconscious. Of course this can happen to anyone, and dealing with this is all part of toughing it out - a challenge I'd like to think I rise to. A word from the guide about how they think I'm running, a comment about whom or what is around us, or an update on mile splits, and the brain is focused on the job again.

How to guide is another common question I am asked. Having never done it, it's impossible for me to explain what it's like from the guide runner point of view. Luckily, I know three people who can.

I've been extremely lucky in recent years as I've rarely been in a situation where I can't go for a training run or enter a race due to lack of guides. In fact, there was as much enthusiasm for my graduation to marathon distance from my running friends as in my own head. "Every distance runner should attempt a marathon at least once", they kept telling me as I entered yet another 'half'. I'm reminded of this good fortune when inevitably things get in the way of running for my group of guides. Injuries and busy work schedules for all of us mean the best made plans sometimes don't work out. Being injured and unable to run is one of the biggest frustrations a runner can experience, but I would say being fit and free but unable to train because there is nobody to assist is worse and I've had my share of injuries to be able to make this comparison.

The reason I describe it as luck is how I came to be in the Kingston-based Stragglers Running Club. I used to run with a couple of friends, both of whom moved away. Whilst one was in North London, and occasionally available, the other being in Australia made going out of a Sunday morning rather difficult. Seeking Google's assistance, I looked up running clubs in South West London. The Stragglers were top of the results list. The fact they were close to where

14

I live, and a slogan on their website claimed they were a "drinking club with a running problem" had me firing off an email to the club secretary asking if I might come down.

When Simon hit reply to say I was "more than welcome", he can't have expected to be guiding me through the streets of London for my marathon debut a couple of years later.

To give you an idea of what guiding a blind runner is really like, I asked for the thoughts of three of my most regular training partners. Alongside Simon and Jim who I've already mentioned, there's Andrew, who has become the 'go-to man' for guiding in marathons. Who wouldn't want to stand on the start line alongside someone that has over thirty to his name?

As well as sharing names, Simon and I are also the most similar in running styles especially over shorter distances such as 5 or 10K. Our approach is to start hard, give it everything we've got, and hope for the best in the closing stages. We've both experienced the bad side of this, as well as the good, finding there's no energy left and still some distance to run.

Andrew on the other hand will start more conservatively, even over 5K. This tactic is something I've tried hard to learn from him for longer races. None of my partners impose their running style on me. If I start too hard and blow up that's my problem; however you don't run regularly with someone and not learn from their experience.

Andrew is an accountant by trade and that methodical nature has translated to his running. We once discussed what kind of runner your work might make you. I, at the time working in marketing, would spend as much time selling the idea of running to others as actually doing it myself – probably why I'm writing a book about running. When we asked Simon, the Council employee, what he'd be like he replied: "one step forward, two steps back".

To some blind runners, the guide is merely providing a service, but I've always thought of them as training partners who just happen to be making sure I don't have any accidents, a view that Simon, Andrew and Jim all acknowledge is a great benefit to both runner and guide. As Andrew says: "It has given me another regular running partner". Some people can happily go for a three hour training run by themselves, but, as Piglet said when wishing Pooh was with him as he was totally surrounded by water, "it's much more friendly with two". Andrew suggests two ways in which guiding has benefited his own running. "It puts a commitment in the diary which I would be reluctant to break. Secondly, it encourages me to keep fit. It is necessary to be about 30 seconds per mile quicker than a blind runner. This is because we then don't need to think about our own pace too much and can concentrate on guiding."

There are those within our club that have suggested that the benefit of being a guide runner to 'the other Simon' has been a significant one physically. Having had a lengthy lay-off, due to a serious knee injury a few years ago, the fact that not every run he now does is at the higher tempo that comes naturally to him, because he's guiding me, may well have contributed to protecting against any relapse. He rather modestly claims: "If I can do it, anyone can". Actually, it's this kind of laid back approach which makes someone good guide runner material. Simon says: "I do not think guiding is very different from running normally. I find that when I run on my own I can switch off and think of things other than running, but still manage to look out for hazards. I think the same applies to guiding. We often chat about stuff whilst running but subconsciously are still looking out for potential dangers. Who said men can't multi-task? The main difference I think (between guiding and running unattached) is of a technical nature. For example the arm that is holding the band is restricted in movement. When running on my own it helps to pump the arms to generate momentum, particularly running uphill. This is not so easy when guiding. Apart from that I have found that running as a guide has the same natural feeling as running on my own."

"The message we all try to get across when asked about the guide running experience is that there's far less to it than people might think."

Jim points out: "A sighted person anticipates there will be all sorts of problems to overcome that simply do not exist. One might imagine that the blind runner needs to know about all kinds of things related to the surface, surroundings or characteristics of the course to enable them to run free, when in reality you seem to need little more than being told when to go, keeping up with you and advising when a turn is required".

"An old friend of mine, Mike Peters,

used to guide Britain's greatest ever blind runner Rob Matthews, until Rob emigrated to New Zealand. They had quite a successful time together at the Sydney Paralympics, 10,000m (Gold), 5000m (Silver) and marathon (Silver). I remember running behind them in the London Marathon one year, until I got dropped, and the whole process of guiding seemed effortless. It has to be said that they were running a fair pace which meant there was plenty of space around them (the faster you run, the less crowded the road is). Also, Mike was very direct and assertive in his communication which seemed to be the key with all the noise going on."

In addition to having confidence in your own ability to enable that assertiveness, what other advice do all three of my guides offer for potential guide runners? As well as claiming anyone can do it if he can, Simon recalls our first time running together.

"We had a five minute practice within the safe surroundings of a car park, before venturing out onto the mean streets of Ham. Before I knew it, we were speeding along negotiating kerbs, lamp posts and road humps without any difficulty. I also remember one of the first things you said to me was, if you feel there is any chance of an accident, just grab my arm and stop. Simple advice I know but reassuring to me. Beforehand I was slightly apprehensive because I had not guided anyone before, and was obviously keen not to mess it up or fall over in a heap! That said I had seen other blind runners take part in races and clearly it was something that can be achieved and looks fun. So, although a little nervous, I was also looking forward to giving it a go."

Similarly to Simon's recollection of laps of a car park, Andrew suggests, "Choose a relatively easy stretch to run for the first time, such as a wide path or road in a park, rather than a crowded urban route. Talk to your runner first to see how much commentary they want or need, probably less than you expect, and relax and enjoy the run - it is very rewarding".

And, by way of proving a point, Jim's thoughts are along the same lines: "Just chill out and enjoy the experience. Take the cue from the blind runner regarding how they want to operate and then go with the flow. Make sure that you're at least half a minute per mile quicker than the blind runner as things are a lot harder when you're running close to the red-line".

It can be tough for the guide if the blind runner is faster than they are. In the first couple of months with the Stragglers I experimented with any willing volunteer, one of whom described the experience as like taking a dog for a walk.

In helping me write this, Simon, Andrew and Jim have all related comments to experiences they have had with me, most of which have been very complimentary. I have deliberately left many of these out, since the purpose of my writing this was to give a general overview of what guiding is like, rather than a beginner's lesson in what to do when attached to me. I believe that blind runners have a responsibility to make the experience for the guide as easy and enjoyable as possible, and on a selfish note, I'd be stuck without them. The wider point is that people are more likely to offer to help if they're confident they can make a difference whilst enjoying what they're doing, or at least not screw things up.

The level of confidence that people with disabilities have, and the contributing factors thereof, is an issue which, to be properly addressed, needs a book of its own. For some, just being given the chance to take part in sport at all will have invaluable benefits, be they physical, or in terms of mental wellbeing. However, at the sharp end, or certainly where running is done for the thrill of taking on a significant challenge, Jim feels self-belief on the part of the runner can make a massive difference to the guide: "A confident blind runner like you is relaxed and hence responsive to the smallest adjustment or instruction, and this makes it very easy to lead".

Through The Stragglers I've developed a love for running tourism, where events are entered as much for *where* they are, as *what* they are. Another reason for my taking such a keen interest in what the London Marathon route has to offer on the other 364 days of the year. So far I've competed in relay events in Norfolk and Wales, and spent excellent weekends running marathons in both Berlin and Inverness. None of which would be possible without fellow runners that understand guide running and what's in it for them. I know there are running clubs in the UK where this open mindedness doesn't exist.

If you wish to find out more about the subject of guide running, British Blind Sport should be your first point of contact. In addition to the practical guide I referenced earlier, they have an excellent leaflet produced by blind runner Hazel McFarlane and two of her guide runners, Anne Noble and Graeme McKenzie, all from the Troon Tortoises Athletics Club. It details advice for both the guide and the runner, and emphasises many of the points Simon, Andrew, Jim and I have made in this chapter.

Chapter 3: 'Long May You Run' - Blackheath

London isn't the original big city marathon. Of the five which made up the initial World Marathon Majors - a group of races where points are awarded for top five finishes with the winner of the most points receiving half a million pounds – London was the most recent to be founded with its first running in 1981. Chicago, Berlin and New York all began in the 1970s; 1977, 1974 and 1970 respectively. The fifth, Boston, is the world's oldest road marathon, first run in 1897 inspired by the success of the event at the first modern Olympics the previous year. Tokyo, which was added to the 'Majors' list in 2013, made its debut in 2007.

Athletics Weekly columnist and author of 'The 50 Greatest Marathon Races of All Time', Will Cockerell, a man who has completed nine London Marathons gave me his take on the route in comparison to Boston, which has a number of books tracking its points of interest.

"Boston is a considerably more stimulating course than London. It weaves through eight different towns and cities, and is undulating the whole way. London's course is, in comparison, rather banal and uninspired for the most part, especially the somewhat featureless first half. But of course it has its moments - Cutty Sark, Tower Bridge, some parts of Canary Wharf, the Embankment when you first see Big Ben looking oh so tiny, and Buckingham Palace; but they constitute only around a fifth of the race".

England's capital city's contribution to this challenging event is one of the most significant though. The early Olympic marathons weren't over a fixed distance, varying from one host city to the next, depending on the chosen route with a 'give or take a mile either side of 25' approach to course planning. It wasn't until the 1924 games in Paris that the current distance of 26.2 miles was adopted as the standard measurement.

There had been one 'running' of 26.2 miles prior to this at the London Olympics in 1908. This was so that the King, who didn't have a TV in those days, could view the start from the comfort of his own home and so the Marathon, which finished at White City, began at Windsor Castle. Originally the route was planned to be 25 miles long. However, protests over the course taking in cobbled streets with tram lines in the closing miles prompted a rethink, with an extra mile being added taking runners over rough ground at Wormwood Scrubs.

The 25 mile distance dates back to Greece in 490 BC. The legend of Marathon is a story of triumph over adversity and absolute bloody-minded determination to succeed.

A massive army of 50,000 Persians crossed the Aegean Sea, landing on the coast of Greece with the intention of capturing the city of Marathon, before moving on for the ultimate prize, Athens. The Greeks could only respond with 9,000 of their own warriors, and as reinforcements were urgently needed, the 490 BC equivalent of the 999 call was made, asking someone to run to the next city to get help. Messages were either sent via professional runner or horseman, but with the rocky mountainous terrain being unsuitable for horses, off went a chap called Pheidippides on a 150 mile round trip scamper to the southern Greek city of Sparta.

He found that the unhelpful Spartans would only come when the moon was full. "We'd love to, but it's against our religion you see" they would have explained. Whether or not they were all werewolves I can't say. Pheidippides returned to Marathon without reinforcements and was pitched straight into battle - a task made somewhat easier for the Greeks as, on learning that his opposition was considerably smaller than expected, the commander of the Persians sent half of his troops round the coast ready for the assault on Athens. He hadn't reckoned on the toughness of the Marathon army, for the Persians were defeated, losing over 6,000 men to a mere couple of hundred Greeks.

With good news to spread, and clearly a shortage of other runners to carry the message, off went Pheidippides again, this time to run the 25 miles from Marathon to Athens. He made it, but collapsed and died having managed to shout his victorious words.

Military historian Sir Edward S. Creasy, author of 'Fifteen Decisive Battles of the World: from Marathon to Waterloo', describes the day of Marathon as "The critical epoch in the history of the two nations. It broke forever the spell of Persian invincibility, which had previously paralyzed men's minds… It secured for mankind the intellectual treasures of Athens, the growth of free institutions, the liberal enlightenment of the western world, and the gradual ascendancy for many ages of the great principles of European Civilization."

Having run four marathons myself, I'm not sure Creasy's analysis of the importance of 490 BC comes as much of a consolation at mile 23 as tiredness takes over in a way only the ultimate running challenge can induce. Although clearly the people to blame for the last agonising stretch are actually our own royal family, so should you ever run London, don't feel bad about throwing a sneaky V sign in the direction of Buckingham Palace when you cross the finish line. As you'll already have noticed when running past the Tower of London, they're hardly likely to chuck you in it these days.

As the marathon is a sporting event of endurance direct from the battle field, where victory was secured by an army with significantly fewer resources in manpower, it seems appropriate that the London Marathon should begin at Blackheath. Here the people of London welcomed a victorious Henry V back from Agincourt in 1415, a decisive moment in the Hundred Years' War, although not decisive or important enough to interest Sir Edward. The English army, tiny in number, and weary from seventeen days marching with only one day's rest, came face to face with a French force far superior in size. Combat was brief as the French cavalry became stuck in the mud - on a site, it should be noted, of their choosing - making them mere target practice for the English archers. Around 10,000 French warriors were killed and 1,000 taken prisoner, whilst the English losses ran to just a few hundred.

It took Henry and his troops a month to

return home; if they'd sent a runner on ahead to break the good news of their victory it's just as well *this* wasn't taken as the blueprint for the London Marathon!

In other battle-based historical news, Blackheath was a rallying point for Walter (Watt) Tyler's Peasants' Revolt in 1381. In protest at Richard II's Poll Tax, which was the same rate for both rich and poor, Tyler assembled a crowd of over 50,000 people on the heath. They marched unopposed over London Bridge and on to the Tower of London. With things getting lively in the City, Richard agreed to meet Tyler at Mile End to discuss the grievances of his followers. For some reason Tyler rode alone and unarmed, and during the meeting with the King he was attacked and killed by the Lord Mayor of London.

Another notable gathering came in 1450, as Jack Cade's Kentish Revolt assembled on the heath. Unhappy at perceived corruptions in King Henry VI's regime, 5,000 Kentish folk descended on London, causing the King to retreat to the countryside. Whereas London Bridge had been no trouble for Tyler's Peasants, Cade's Kentishmen were defeated here and sent packing back to the sticks.

On a chilly November morning, I made what turned out to be a simple and relatively short, at just over an hour, train journey from South West to South East London to experience what 21st century Blackheath had to offer. Despite having run the race once, this was to be my first time on the heath itself for one third of the competitors get their race underway from across the road in Greenwich Park.

The London Marathon has three starting points: codes blue and green are on Blackheath, and red is a stone's throw away in Greenwich Park. The idea being that, with nearly 40,000 runners, they don't all have to try and cross the same start line. Runners follow one of three routes until around three miles into the race, by which time the field should be spreading out and there's room for everyone on one course. However, it can still take over half an hour before those near the back of each group can start running.

Each competitor has a timing chip fastened to their running shoe and their time is measured from the point they cross a mat at the start line. This means that there is no loss in recorded time for those starting near the back who take longer to cross the mat. The start is made smoother by runners choosing a time category relevant to their expected performance level, for example those expected to finish in between 3 hours 15 minutes and 3 hours 30 minutes begin from the same point. The faster you expect to run the further forward you are able to start. It's not an issue if you run faster or slower than you predict; the aim is to have people who are likely to want to run at the same speed starting together in the crowded early miles.

During the administration process I was given a starting position in Blackheath blue. Imagine our surprise when Simon, my guide runner, was placed in Greenwich red. Fortunately we were able to explain the impracticality of this to the organisers, not least as the International Blind Sport Federation states 50cm as the maximum length for a guide rope and we'd have struggled to stretch that over the wall of Greenwich Park. So I started on red too.

One thing which is striking about Blackheath, which perhaps isn't so noticeable when 40,000 people are hanging around, is how high up it is. Depending on where you stand it's possible to get a clear view northwards across to Canary Wharf. The 244 metre high tower of One Canada Square comprises 50 floors. From the start point on the marathon route it looks as if you're in line with the top. By mile 15, runners pass the front door at ground level.

Despite the Surrey Hills on the horizon to the south, and many a church spire within a 360° radius, London landmark spotters may prefer Primrose Hill to the north of the city, or out west, the highest point of Richmond Park. Plane spotters will not be disappointed, with aircraft on Final Approach to Heathrow passing overhead at 90 second intervals and those leaving City airport in the docklands clearly visible as they climb into the sky to the north.

I'd planned to leave the heath by going out onto Shooter's Hill Road, as the runners would have done, but the other event which draws mankind to this patch of grass in their thousands was being set up. Blackheath hosts London's largest free fireworks display, an occasion which attracts up to 40,000 people on the Saturday night nearest to November 5th.

I'd achieved my first objective though, to experience the calm and peaceful side to the heath. Well, as calm and peaceful as is possible with traffic thundering past on one of the major roads to Kent. During the Middle Ages this was a dangerous place to be as highwaymen lay in wait for wealthy folk enroute to and from the capital. Dick Turpin was one, it is said, who would prey on the vulnerable unsuspecting traveller, not far from where I now stood.

Just as I require assistance when running, the nature of my sight loss means all research trips for this book have been carried out with friends or family members – Blackheath was a family affair.

Standing on the heath, my challenge is this: to explore what the London Marathon route has to offer throughout the rest of the year and to dispel a view held by many runners that this 26.2 mile course is rather dull. When giving me his opinion on the course, Will Cockerell told me: "Ironically, I think you'll have more to say about it than a sighted person, as the atmosphere and noise is more about what makes the London Marathon great". What I hope to convey, which I feel my sight loss may prove advantageous in achieving, is the idea that just because you can't see it, doesn't mean it's not of interest. I can't see the Cutty Sark, Tower Bridge, Canary Wharf or Buckingham Palace, but I'm still interested in their existence and story. Anyone who runs the London Marathon, or happens to visit a section of the course, may see a building which doesn't appear to stand out from its surroundings, but what it might lack in appearance, it may make up for in origin, history or present day use. And if I discover something of note off the beaten track, I'll take a look; maybe one day you will too. I won't necessarily walk the whole course – public transport is allowed for this challenge. Whilst I'll tell the story of the course in the order which it appears on a map, I certainly won't explore in a logical order - at the moment of researching Blackheath I'd already crossed Greenwich, Deptford, Poplar and the Tower of London off the list.

Blackheath was the symbolic start to my journey, though. As I took the first steps of revisiting one of the most important moments in my personal running career, I was focused on one very important goal: lunch!

Retracing our walk across the heath, away from the start and towards Blackheath village, we passed one of the area's notable landmarks.

The Princess of Wales pub is a major part of English sporting history. In front of you as you walk in the door is a display cabinet of trophies and other memorabilia for the Blackheath Hockey Club. They were founded in 1861 with a motto "be proud, be worthy".

Defining what makes the oldest hockey club in the world depends on who you ask, and how you view the variations in the game during the 1860s and 1870s, as Teddington Hockey Club in South West London also lays claim to being the world's first. Their website tells it thus: "In 1871 members of the Teddington Cricket Club, who had recently moved to play in Bushy Park, were looking for a winter activity. They experimented with a 'stick' game, based loosely on the rules of association football. The TCC members rejected a game played by a Blackheath club that involved a 7oz (200g) rubber cube; catching, marking and scrimmaging; generally based on rugby football. The Teddington club chose to limit the number of players per side to eleven, and preferred to play with old cricket balls. They also introduced the idea of the striking circle ('The D'). In defining the rules this way, Teddington were the first to play the game that became modern hockey."

The cabinet in the Princess of Wales contains a number of photos from the Blackheath centenary celebrations in 1961, and a shield called the Princess of Wales trophy, which from the look of the winners engraved on it, was only played for twice, in 1990 and 1991.

The connection between Blackheath hockey and rugby is hardly a surprise, since the heath, and the pub played a key part in the development of that sport too.

Founded in 1858, Blackheath is the oldest *open* rugby club in the world. Anyone could join, whereas existing clubs at the time required those who played for them to either be current or previous attendees of a certain institution, such as a school or university.

Blackheath helped organise the first international rugby match, Scotland V England played in Edinburgh in 1871. The Club also hosted England's first home rugby international, a match against Wales in 1881. The Princess of Wales was used as changing facilities, and no doubt also did a fine trade at the bar.

Blackheath, along with a team representing the Civil Service are one of two clubs who are founder members of both the Rugby Football Union (RFU) and the Football Association (FA). In 1863, twelve clubs met with the aim of drawing up a set of rules that would combine the best elements of the various forms of football which were currently being played. By the sixth meeting, Blackheath withdrew; believing the new set of rules would destroy the game and would result in people losing interest. In other words, this no shin kicking, or picking the ball up and running with it will never catch on. They may actually have been proved right had the RFU, which was formed in 1871 and included a number of clubs that joined Blackheath in protest at the FA's view of football, not been so determined to keep the sport of rugby an amateur game.

By the end of the 19th century, a number of clubs from the north of England had broken ranks in protest at not being allowed to pay their key players in acknowledgement of the money they weren't earning in factories, mills and mines on game day. Henceforth the sport of rugby was divided: rugby league existed in the north, and union continued in its amateur tradition until turning professional in 1995. As rugby existed in different forms either side of the north/south divide, teams playing association football emerged across England making that the country's dominant sport.

When researching Blackheath Rugby Club, I noted with interest that they use a facility owned by Greenwich University, home also to the Greenwich Admirals Rugby League Team. The Admirals are considered one of London's leading grass roots rugby league clubs, and have produced two players who have gone on to represent England while playing for London Broncos before moves to St Helens and Wigan. So the rebel sport of rugby league, which broke away over a century ago, has a presence close to one of rugby union's spiritual homes.

I'd have happily stayed in the Princess of

Wales for the afternoon - what's not to like about a pub which has fish finger sandwiches and apple crumble on the menu, not to mention presenting me with the first of many opportunities to highlight the fine beer-making skills of local brewery, Meantime. A pint of their pale ale goes down a treat.

I decided to begin my exploration of the London Marathon course as I would have run it, following the red route from Greenwich Park. On race day Simon and I, and Jim (mentioned in the previous chapter who had decided to run with us instead of running his own race) arrived with an hour and a half to spare. There was much anxiety on show, the realisation hitting many that this was the moment they'd been building up to for months. I actually felt more relaxed and awake than I do before most morning runs, even though my alarm did shatter my sleep at 5:45 am!

I'm not sure what the collective noun for portaloo is, but whatever it might be, it needs to be used to describe the London Marathon start. Early morning visits to a bog-in-a-box in a field does put me in mind of music festivals. Memories of many a Reading or Leeds Festival weekend came flooding back. Fortunately hangovers, sleep deprivation, mud, and that lingering question about whether the late night burger was a good idea, are not an issue at the start of a marathon, however.

The bloke charged with making announcements appeared to be ambushing participants, asking them to pick from one of two songs that were lined up to be played over the PA system. When you're psyching yourself up for one of the biggest runs of your life, naturally the question that should be uppermost in the mind is, would I like to hear 'Sex on Fire' by the Kings of Leon or some rubbish from Lady Gaga?

Among the runners we saw that fell into the "this was a great idea in the pub but you're totally going to regret it by the 5 mile point" category were a man carrying a model Spitfire on his back, a full brass band, and of course numerous animals. I heard there was a picture of Dangermouse in the paper the following day; sadly I didn't get to meet him.

Every year thousands take on the London Marathon for the first time. The website for Runner's World magazine has an advice section for marathon debutants where others contribute tips and thoughts on how to prepare. One post, from a user whose name of Ouch Ouch suggests an indication of what might be to come, offers these excellent words of wisdom: "Be prepared for the mental 'rush' of the crowds, the noise, the colour and the excitement. Some runners find it vastly encouraging – first time round it just stunned me".

It took us about six minutes to get over the start line. An extraordinarily excitable Geordie fella who had been shouting into a microphone for what seemed like hours, yelped at the mass throng of runners as we went over the starting mat: "Give Jonathan Edwards a wave, he's on the BBC!"

We didn't. I shouldn't think he minded.

A long lunch meant it was now a November afternoon. Picking up the course at a large roundabout at the junction of Maze Hill

34

and Charlton Way, we were able to get a close look at the bandstand which could be seen from the heath. Tucked underneath was a seating area and water fountain. The inscription on it reads: "This monument was erected in 1931 in memory of Andrew Gibb, one of the first Aldermen of the Metropolitan Borough of Greenwich. As well as being a philanthropist, he presented the borough with one of its mayoral chains. The monument fell into disrepair but was restored to its former glory in 2003". So, not a monument to the lesser known Bee Gee as I'd hoped.

At the moment we were looking at the Gibb memorial, the No. 53 bus to Whitehall and Horseguards went by. All these years runners have been slogging it out over 26.2 miles when a perfectly adequate bus service runs from Blackheath to the finish! That thought reminded me of the widely-reported incident where a marathon runner took third place in a race held in Kielder, Northumberland, but didn't do so by fair means.

The Northern Echo reported: "Rob Sloan, 31, became tired at the 20 mile mark and hopped on the free spectator bus. Instead of telling marshals what he had done, Mr. Sloan, a former army mechanic, left the bus near the end and emerged from a wood to rejoin the course, crossing the line to accept the accolades of the spectators who had gathered at the finish."

The Echo, along with numerous national press reports, went on to explain how the athlete was exposed by several witnesses who had either seen him catch the bus, or who were suspicious of the significant improvement in his personal best.

I'm not sure that trick would work with the No 53 - with so many roads shut it's quicker to run to Westminster. Maze Hill, the road heading north away from the roundabout does lead directly downhill to Greenwich, but if you need to take a short cut this early in the race, you've probably entered the wrong event!

Being the furthest north of the three, the red route does offer runners the best opportunity to enjoy the views from the heights of Blackheath. Immediately after the Maze Hill roundabout is the wildest part of the heath. London Marathon runners get to see the Vanbrugh Pits, former gravel pits reclaimed by nature, at their best, for the many gorse bushes are in blossom in late spring. Further along, what would until recently have been an uninspiring bridge across the A2, is now a fantastic vantage point to look north to the Olympic Stadium, the ArcelorMittal Orbit (that tower thing in the Olympic Park which looks like a broken rollercoaster) and the O2 Arena.

Prior to the bridge is Blackheath High School for Girls, notable as one of the places where Blackheath Hockey Club now play home matches. A short distance further on, is the final location for my historical sporting tour of South East London: Rectory Field, home of Blackheath Rugby Club.

Walking up the drive, you come first to the courts for the Blackheath Lawn Tennis Club. Squash is also available here. On this Friday afternoon, the excitable shrieks of little people told us it was playtime at the day nursery.

Rectory Field was developed in the 1880s by Blackheath Cricket and Rugby Clubs, and the

Lawn Tennis Company, a pitch invasion during a rugby match on the heath between Blackheath and Richmond having prompted the development of a proper ground.

Kent enjoyed considerable success on the cricket pitch of the Rectory Field, their first county championship title win coming in 1906. Not especially noteworthy in itself, but the description from the history section of the Kent County Cricket Club website of how points were awarded throughout the season did catch my eye.

"In those years, the determining of the County Championship was based on an entirely different formula to that which is now the case. Counties did not all play the same number of games. In 1906 Northamptonshire played the lowest number (16) whilst Surrey and Yorkshire both played the highest (28). The M.C.C. laid down that one point would be awarded for each win, and one deducted for each defeat. Drawn games were not counted for points. Consequently, the side which obtained the greatest proportion of points, in effect losing the least number of matches, would be the champions."

Kent used Blackheath for matches until 1971. Noteworthy names to walk to the crease, from the classic English cricket pavilion which remains today, include: Bryan Valentine, Colin Cowdrey and, at the start of his career, Bob Woolmer. The latter will have only have made a small number of appearances at Blackheath, for a reduction in car parking spaces and concern about the quality of the outfield meant the ground was only occasionally used in the late 60s, usually for the home fixture against Surrey.

Born in Blackheath, Valentine played during the 1930s and ended his career with a test match batting average bettered only by the great Donald Bradman. It should be noted this came from only seven England appearances, his career cut short by the outbreak of the Second World War. So whilst his average may well have gone down had he played for longer, and were it not for the war, would we be mentioning him alongside the greats of the game more often?

Colin Cowdrey is one of the iconic names of the sport. He captained England and became the first cricketer to play in 100 test matches. He also held the record for most runs scored by a batsman and most catches taken in the field. Cowdrey's 22 centuries stood as an England record jointly held with Geoff Boycott and Wally Hammond. Boycott, the most recent addition to that trio, scored his final century in 1982. It took 30 years for another player to join that elite club with Alastair Cook and Kevin Pietersen succeeding within 10 minutes of each other in a test match against India in November 2012.

Bob Woolmer made his debut for Kent in 1968. He went on to play for England, and to coach both South Africa and Pakistan as well as spending time as a TV commentator. He was considered one of the game's great tacticians.

The cricketing world was rocked when news broke that Woolmer had been found dead in his hotel room a matter of hours after his Pakistan team had been knocked out of the 2007 World Cup by minnows Ireland. What followed was a media circus that simply was just not cricket. Initially treated as suspicious by the

Jamaican Police, his death was rumored to be murder or suicide but was eventually confirmed by three independent pathologists to be due to natural causes.

The Blackheath ground today is everything the grass roots cricket enthusiast would love. A pitch surrounded by trees with space to watch a game stretched out on the grass. It boasts a traditional pavilion complete with manually-operated scoreboard - a row of oblong-shaped metal numbers hung on hooks which can be flipped over to show the current score. The two on the left were missing, but the third column for the run total, and the fourth which showed how many wickets had been taken, both had numbers available to alter. As we moved on to take a look at the rugby pitch the scoreboard indicated that Blackheath were batting and in some difficulty, having only scored a mere seven runs for the loss of seven wickets.

Incredibly, anyone is free to walk around the pitch at Blackheath Rugby Club. Had I thought to bring a ball and a few mates there would have been nothing to stop us climbing over the barrier which surrounds the playing surface to have a game of our own!

The puntastic slogan "Swing low sweet Marriott" catches the eye, as all good adverts should, hoping to convince supporters of teams from rugby union's National League 1 that their next holiday destination should be Bexley Heath.

The stand runs along one side of the pitch, with covered seats for between five and six hundred people in the centre, and uncovered terracing either side of that. On the other three sides, supporters are free to lean on the barriers.

Presumably, when Richmond come to town now it's a more mild-mannered occasion as there's nothing to prevent a pitch invasion here.

As we passed the cricket pitch on our way out, our fictitious game appeared to have reached something of a stalemate with the score remaining 7 for 7. Some dogged defending from the Blackheath tail-enders, no doubt infuriating their unnamed opponent's bowlers!

Chapter 4: 'Up the Junction' - Blackheath to Woolwich

The first few miles of a marathon should feel like the easiest run you've ever done. You'll be fresh after minimal running during the previous week and, if you're sensible, you'll be saving as much energy as possible. It's important to decide a race strategy before the morning of the event, for example run every mile in around 8 minutes, then stick to it. This also allows for you to soak up the atmosphere and enjoy the thought that the hard months of training are over; now you just have to finish the job.

For me this part was about enjoying the thought that I was running in the actual London Marathon, that thing I'd watched at home for years and always wanted to be a part of. I had this crazy idea I would try and count the number of things or people playing music, street performers or sound systems booming out at what seemed like every few hundred metres. I quickly lost count and interest, but at least in London most of the time you've a reasonable chance of recognising what the songs are. The year I ran the Berlin Marathon the best I could manage was to say to my guide runner: "Was that meant to be 'Whatever You Want' by Status Quo?".

One of my pet hates is people who run in races with headphones on. When you're running with a guide it can take a little more work to get through a crowded field. Being the width of two people you need more space, plus, the guide has to work harder to steer the blind runner through gaps and round other runners. Usually a shout of "blind runner behind you" and space is made, but if the person you want to pass is lost to the world of their iPod there's a risk the first they'll know about you is when they get a kick on the back of the leg.

I've always believed that running to music is a bad idea. Aside from the obvious point that the beat of what you're listening to might, even subconsciously, alter the pace at which you run, if you train using headphones should you then enter races where they're not allowed I would imagine it's harder if you're used to passing the time by the distraction of music.

In an event like the London Marathon, I've no idea why someone would want to miss out on the fantastic atmosphere, but in the first few miles we did have a few near misses where there were too many headphone wearers for my liking. Gyms, with pounding music for people to work out to, have a lot to answer for.

After leaving Blackheath and Greenwich Park the marathon continues in its early miles as three separate courses, blue and green from the heath, red from Greenwich Park. Blue and green merge after a mile or so, joining up with red runners after three miles. Having passed through part of Charlton, close to Charlton House before Woolwich, once all runners are together on one course they then begin the run west, through the north side of Charlton before heading towards Greenwich.

Some months had passed since I visited Blackheath on a chilly November Friday in the previous chapter. Back in November, having left

Blackheath Rugby Club and returned to the red route, attention was drawn to a blue plaque on the other side of Charlton Road marking the former home of William Henry Barlow. A civil engineer, born in Woolwich and who died in Charlton (in 1902 aged 90), Barlow designed St Pancras station. Following the death of Isambard Kingdom Brunel in 1859, he was commissioned, along with John Hawkshaw, to complete the building of Bristol's Clifton Suspension Bridge.

Sir John Hawkshaw's influence can be found throughout the London Marathon course. He was engineer for the railway which ran through the Brunel Tunnel under the Thames between Wapping and Rotherhithe, now London Overground; he was involved in the construction of the tunnel which connects Aldgate and Mansion House, now the Circle Line, and he constructed the bridges which runners see adjacent to Cannon Street and Charing Cross stations.

On the right hand side of the Charlton Road stands the impressive sight of Charlton House: "The finest and best preserved Jacobean mansion in the London area", even if they do say so themselves. It's not open to the public; instead it can be hired for events, so I've no idea what it's like inside. I can tell you that: the Orangery is now a public toilet, one of the spaces in the grounds is given to an Amnesty International peace garden, and the land is home to what is said to be the oldest mulberry tree of its species in Britain.

As I discover later, you can walk from here, via Charlton Park, to meet the marathon course on the edge of Maryon Park a few miles further along the route.

Once this area was covered in forest, known as Hanging Woods. Highwaymen would hide here before attacking travellers on their way to or from Kent via Shooter's Hill. We can only imagine what a dangerous and spooky place this must have been, for the victims caught would be hung from trees - not for the faint hearted.

The history of this area is fascinating, underground as well as above. Numerous caves, shafts and holes criss-cross beneath Blackheath and Charlton. With conflicting research, newspaper archives and accounts of what these might have been used for and how they may have come to be there at all, the line between mythology and fact is somewhat blurred. Were they dug by the Romans? The suggestion that many were chalk mines would appear to be a logical thought. One large cavern is often referred to as Jack Cade's Cavern, he of Kentish Revolt fame, the assumption being that around this time it may have been used as an underground hideaway – how very cartoon villain.

In the 19th century the cavern became the home of a nightclub. Who knows whether parties held here were widely advertised, or were the Victorian equivalent of an illegal rave. It certainly must have provided an exhilarating location as clubbers descended the stairs into a hot, smoke-filled, dimly-lit place, where rules and inhibitions did not apply.

Parties appear to have featured much nudity and binge drinking, something which the fun-spoiling Victorian authorities didn't approve of, with the meanies shutting the club down in the 1850s. When the cavern was reopened as a potential air raid shelter in the Second World War, relics from those hedonistic days were discovered. A detailed description was published following an inspection by Greenwich Council in 1946 telling of carvings and graffiti from revellers found in the walls, and even left-overs from the last time a bar was operating. That must have been an astonishing, intriguing and slightly eerie exploration. Sadly it's no longer possible for us to see any of this for ourselves, as the entrances are long since closed.

Another interesting historical account connected to Charlton concerns the infamous Horn Fair, given this description in the 1720s by Daniel Defoe:

"Charleton, a village famous, or rather infamous for the yearly collective rabble of mad people at Horn Fair; the rudeness of which I cannot but think, is such that aught to be suppressed, and indeed in a civilised, well governed nation, it may well be said to be unsufferable. The mob indeed at that time take all kind of liberties, and the women are especially impudent for that day; as if it was a day that justify'd the giving themselves a loose to all manner of indecency and immodesty, without any reproach, or without suffering the censure which such behaviour would deserve at another time."

Not sure what he'd have made of modern day music festivals, or in fact, the 19th century underground nightclub.

The Horn Fair lives on today but only really by name. Reborn in 1973, and taking place in the grounds of Charlton House, it sounds like a suburban equivalent of a county show, with a dog show, community-run stalls, and school sports-day-style competitions. Presumably any drunken falling-over from Defoe's day is now replaced by the much more civilised behaviour of tripping up during the three-legged race.

The London Borough of Greenwich appears to be very good at memorials. The Council website has a handy list of locations honouring dead people with a varied collection of back stories. The Andrew Gibb memorial, which I discovered after leaving Greenwich Park, is one of the many you can read about. War veterans to local dignitaries, and even a 19th century world champion bare-knuckle fighter, are all honoured somewhere in the borough. To guide you through this next part of the course I went on my own monument tour of South East London.

Alighting at Woolwich Arsenal train station - Charlton v Arsenal, the great local rivalry that never was, more on that later - we headed uphill in search of plaques and inscriptions. This research day, like Blackheath, was another family affair. It's pretty knackering walking up that hill! Had Brasher and Disley decided to have the finish line in Blackheath I'm not convinced their marathon idea would have ever taken off. Who would want to run up that at 23 miles?

As blue and green runners head towards Woolwich along Grand Depot Road, they do so with Woolwich Common stretching away to the right, and Barrack Fields to the left. Charlton Athletic played matches on the Common for one season - 1907 to 1908. More recently, both the

Barracks and Common were used for the temporary shooting venues during the 2012 London Olympic and Paralympic Games. One of the game defining moments came as Peter Wilson clinched gold in the Double Trap at Woolwich, meanwhile at Lee Valley White Water Centre on the London/Hertfordshire border Tim Baillie and Etienne Stott were winning Britain's first ever canoe slalom gold. During a magical half hour of gripping sports coverage, Radio 5 jumped back and forth between venues, with commentators, who normally describe football, sounding as if they'd made a career out of covering two minority sports that were fully capitalising on their moment in the sun to really stamp their mark on the memory of the British public.

Away to the left through the trees stands the imposing sight of the Royal Artillery Barracks, and on their right, a runner might care to glance at a marble column, surrounded by trees. The Boer War Memorial is a monument which doesn't look unlike Cleopatra's Needle on the Embankment, but as that's close to the finish line, and the marathon is barely three miles old at this point, perhaps that's not the most helpful comparison to draw.

The inscription on the obelisk reads: "Erected by the officers, non-commissioned officers and men of the 61st Battery Royal Field Artillery in memory of the non-commissioned officers and men of the Battery who lost their lives in South Africa, December 1899 - May 1902".

My circuit of local memorials was to take me back along the blue route in the opposite direction which runners head in. An inviting Green Chain sign advertised walking routes across the common, towards the Thames Barrier or on to Barracks Field. As this one sign was heavily outnumbered by numerous notices along the fence of Barracks Field, with the intimidating warning of "guard dogs on patrol" who presumably wouldn't need telling twice to take a chunk out of your leg if you strayed on to the wrong patch of grass, we decided to stick with the road and go the long way round.

Further back along Grand Depot Road, at the point at which it becomes Ha-Ha Road, we discovered a bonus memorial which wasn't on my list to look out for.

"This fountain is designated for public use as a memorial to Robert John Little, a retired officer of the Royal Marines who died in October 1861."

It went on to tell us that Little had been "sustained by the fountain of living water and had devoted himself to the honour of God and the relief of human suffering".

So an all-round good egg then! Sadly his legacy doesn't provide an endless supply of water, living or otherwise, for the fountain bit had been removed.

Walking from the blue to the red route we passed a collection of large stables, an important part of the military base here in Woolwich. My great grandad served in the Royal Horse Artillery in World War I. As we walked along I was reminded of the story of one occasion when, startled by shrapnel, his horse reared up breaking his nose. He was ordered to get treatment by his commanding officer, but on arrival at the field hospital was, perhaps unsurprisingly, informed he should consider himself lucky he was still in one piece and they had far more urgent cases to attend to!

On the corner of Repository Road and Artillery place, we're on the red route now, is Mallet's Mortar. A 36-inch mortar weighing 42 tonnes, it's the largest ever built in this country. Designed in 1854 by Robert Mallet for use in the Crimean War, during tests it fired a shell weighing 2359 pounds, sending it a distance of 2750 yards. The Crimean War ended before the mortar could be used in anger and, stuck for what else to do with it, someone had the idea of sticking it on the side of a road in Woolwich.

And there it remains, a whacking great black metal cylinder which looks like a launch pad for a rocket, standing on a brick plinth complete with imitation shells. So, to my disappointment, Mallet's Mortar is nothing to do with Timmy, although if they never came and filmed a feature for Wacaday here they definitely missed a trick. I could just imagine him standing there with one trouser leg rolled up shouting Blaaaa! at a giant 19th century bomb. They don't make 'em like they used to, Wacaday that is, I'd say killing machines have evolved somewhat since the 1850s. That said it's an impressive lump, as are the barracks next door.

Built between 1776 and 1802 on a site overlooking Woolwich Common, The Royal Artillery Barracks has Britain's longest Georgian façade, more than 1000 feet (300 metres) in length.

Among those based at the Barracks is the King's Troop, formed in 1947 by George VI.

After 65 years of being based in St John's Wood in North London, February 2012 saw the Troop's relocation to Woolwich, where the Royal Artillery has been based since 1716.

The King's Troop consists of the people you'll have seen firing gun salutes on royal anniversaries and state occasions. The number of shots fired depends on the event and location. When William and Kate's son was born the Troop fired a 41 gun salute in Green Park - 21 for a member of the royal family, and 20 as it was a royal park. Meanwhile at the Tower of London as well as the 21 for a royal and 20 for a royal location, an additional 21 shots were fired to mark that they were on the site of the Tower of London.

BBC London News' footage from the day of the King's Troop's arrival in Woolwich shows them parading through the streets, resplendent in their ceremonial dress of all black, with gold braiding across the chest and black hats with a red plume. Groups of six horses pull thirteen pound field guns, many of which were used in the First World War.

A well spoken chap, minus his hat, tells the camera what a great privilege it is for the Troop to be welcomed back to the Borough of Greenwich by such large crowds. They were, after all, "Returning to the spiritual home of The Gunners".

Whilst undoubtedly a connection that generates enormous military pride, The Gunners' spiritual home is also a contentious football issue, especially in one corner of North London. The rivalry between Tottenham and Arsenal is partly geographical, but is also rooted in actions which took place a century ago.

By the 1912-1913 season, Woolwich Arsenal's crowds were declining and the club was in financial trouble. Chairman Sir Henry Norris sought a new home and identified Highbury as his preferred location. Despite objections from local residents and nearby teams, Tottenham and Clapton Orient, the move was approved, thus ending any potential rivalry between Charlton and Arsenal. Incidentally, whilst Charlton played matches on Woolwich Common for one season, Woolwich Arsenal never did, instead moving around the local area with the Manor Ground in Plumstead as their most regular home.

Arsenal compounded the unhappiness of their new neighbours Tottenham in the way they came to return to division 1. After their first season in North London The Gunners had finished 5th in division 2 and it was assumed this would be where they would remain once football resumed after the First World War.

Sir Henry had other ideas and saw an opportunity when it was announced that division 1 would be expanded to 22 teams. It was expected that the teams which finished bottom of the last pre-war season would be retained, as had happened in 1905 the last time the league was expanded, and joined by the top two from division 2. The bottom two clubs in division 1 were Chelsea and Tottenham.

The football league was at the time almost exclusively made up of teams from the North and the Midlands. Arsenal had been the first Southern club to join the league in 1905. It is believed this formed a part of Norris' campaign amongst his fellow chairmen to

51

engineer a vote in favour of his team's election to division 1, with Tottenham not retaining their place.

The club history section on the Arsenal website states that Norris neither confirmed nor denied his questionable actions. They concede that: "Whatever the truth, more than 90 years on Arsenal are the only club with continuous top flight membership since the Football League resumed, and the only club not to have been promoted on footballing merit".

And the spirit of Norris lives on, as Arsenal continually secure Champions League football ahead of Tottenham.

It could be argued that Arsenal's relocation from Woolwich to Islington makes them the first franchise football club. When Wimbledon were plucked from London, and dropped 60 miles away in Milton Keynes in 2003, that too was a move prompted by finances and low attendances at games. Just as Wimbledon fans who were left without a football team to support then founded AFC Wimbledon, a new team was formed in Woolwich, but unlike the Dons, they didn't survive long.

With soldiers and police on duty, not to mention the previously frequently advertised guard dogs, the closest look we would ever get of the barracks was through the fence, so we moved on.

John Wilson Street is a significant point in the London Marathon course as it's where the two routes meet. Just as you've got yourself nicely positioned with a bit of room to run, thousands more join the fun meaning you suddenly have to watch out for yet more headphone wearers and try and avoid being cut up by the person in a teddy bear costume who's gone off way too fast. It was at about this point that I ran past someone who was running backwards. Why would you do that?

It's just as well your mind is occupied by what's happening on the road, for John Wilson Street is not what you would call eye-catching. Grey lumps of concrete which might have been flats, or possibly offices; I didn't stop to ask. The John Wilson in question was a local Baptist preacher in the 1930s, who served a congregation of around 3000 people.

I looked for something to remember John Wilson Street by. It is an important part of the marathon course after all, but the dead-looking half tree trunk and CCTV camera were about all I could find. A few days later this street was global news, the location for events which would never be forgotten.

On May 22nd 2013, drummer Lee Rigby was targeted by two men, close to the Woolwich Barracks where he was based. His killing was brutal; amongst the weapons used was a meat cleaver, with the incident quickly being labelled as an act of terrorism.

Reflecting on an event like this isn't easy. I wasn't there, so I can only use accounts and analysis put forward through media outlets. Even in the UK, this is never a guaranteed way of getting the best and most accurate picture of an event like this, and the complex issues which relate to it.

One of the most shockingly iconic parts of the story was how, immediately after they'd carried out their attack, the two men encouraged members of the public to film them on their phones, leading to graphic images being transmitted into homes across the country on rolling news channels. This generated numerous complaints to the media watchdog Ofcom; but surely, to have censored this would be to censure reality, removing a crucial aspect of the story and not presenting it in its most accurate form.

Whilst the visual immediacy provided by TV news and social media was undoubtedly difficult for people to watch, for me the most powerful eye witness account came from a caller to LBC Radio, describing in vivid detail how he'd seen the victim being hacked at "like he was a piece of meat", his voice cracking up as he struggled to get his head round what he'd just seen. Pictures paint a thousand words, but the feeling in a human voice can convey so much more, taking you to emotional places an image cannot reach.

Events like the London Marathon are a fantastic example of how this city can unite, finding ways to make our world that little bit better, be that by raising money for charity, boosting well-being through improved fitness, or simply coming together as one, in order to support others to achieve a significant personal goal. With over seventy nations represented on the road - both running and supporting - it's unquestionably a global celebration of all that is good about the human spirit.

Sadly the aftermath of one man's tragic loss of life at the three mile point on that May Wednesday highlighted society's darker side. The English Defence League was quick to appear on the scene, showing their displeasure at the death of a member of the British military by chucking bottles at the British police - go figure.

This was no great surprise, nor was how expressing opinions, that ranged from unpleasant to blatantly racist and hateful, suddenly became fair game, especially on social media sites. A sobering reminder that the technological age is allowing people to publicly speak their mind, before that mind has been used to consider the consequence of what it is they're about to say.

Chapter 5: 'Stroll On' - Woolwich to Greenwich

St Mary Magdalene Church is on the left hand side as runners make the left turn from John Wilson Street into Church Street. Stepping away from the road into the church yard we found ourselves in a small, well-kept public park which boasts a great vantage point to look down towards the river. With the sun out and a surprising amount of tranquillity, given the busy road close by, you could do worse than spend time here.

We'd come in search of a memorial to 19th century bare knuckle boxing world champion Tom Cribb, who moved to Woolwich after his sporting career had ended and who appears to have been taken to the hearts of the locals.

The bloodthirsty sport of bare-knuckle boxing had few rules, with bouts often lasting for hours at a time. If there was no knock out, a winner would only be decided when their opponent was unable to give any more.

Cribb's career-defining fights came against an American named Tom Molineux. Firstly, in 1810, the pair fought to the point of exhaustion with Molineux forced to admit defeat after thirty two, count them, thirty two rounds!

A year later Cribb and Molineux were in the ring once again, this time the bout lasting a mere nineteen rounds, with the American once again the loser after having his jaw broken.

Scanning the grass we found numerous

graves; we could have been there all day reading their inscriptions. Then our attention was grabbed by a large stone lion; closer inspection found nothing to tell us what it was. Admitting defeat, and faced only with the alternative of searching for a plaque by crawling through the grass and scraping the mud away from the wall which surrounded the church yard, we headed off in search of lunch instead. That evening, reading articles about Tom Cribb's boxing career, I learnt that the lion would have watched our hunt with as knowing a look in its eye as is possible for an ancient stone statue to have, for it was he we had been looking for all along. Doubtless both the lion and Cribb himself would not have been impressed at the ease with which we gave up!

I could have had lunch in Britain's first McDonalds. However, since I figured that the Woolwich branch would have nothing to set it apart from the hundreds of other McDonalds which have sprung up across the UK since it opened in November 1974, I felt it wouldn't be an especially noteworthy experience.

The Woolwich Wimpey is also worth a mention, although for the less desirable claim to fame of being smashed up during the London riots of August 2011. It wasn't the only building to be targeted, of course, but it does make you wonder what the looters hoped to achieve by nicking a load of those bendy sausages.

Many people in Woolwich felt the trouble in their part of town was overlooked by the media in favour of reporting the carnage in Tottenham and other enduring images, such as the collapsing furniture store in Croydon. I wonder whether this was partly as the nearest tube station to Woolwich is some distance away in North Greenwich, by the O2 Arena, and TV crews and newspaper photographers could get sufficient material to tell the story of trouble sweeping across the capital without having to get on a South Eastern train or the Docklands Light Railway (DLR)?

We're on the Woolwich Road now and stop for lunch at the Millennium Café. The Albion pub which we passed on the way had a sign encouraging us to "watch the London Marathon here". It's good to put the idea into people's minds forty nine weeks early!

I consider myself something of a connoisseur of the English fry up, and our café of choice did it rather well. It's evidently popular, for as I worked my way through egg, bacon, sausage, mushrooms, beans, bread and butter and a mug of tea for not much more than a fiver, a steady stream of office workers and builders in high vis jackets came and went, greeted by the staff as if they were best of friends.

The Woolwich Road runs to the edge of East Greenwich, I'm about to spend my afternoon walking along it. I confess that, although I have a list of things to find which I hope will provide interesting material to write about, part of me is wondering how much this stretch will offer? Just before the change to Woolwich Road is a reminder of what's to come when we reach Greenwich, as a mural on the wall, close to a parade of shops and yet another ugly block of flats, shows sailing ships, rowing boats and the Cutty Sark, with a backdrop of significant buildings which are just a couple of miles down the road.

Perhaps the office workers who've collected their lunch from the Millennium Café take it across the road to one of the picnic benches in Maryon Park. Runners pass the entrance on the left hand side. As the park seemed far more enticing for us to walk through than along a busy road, we went in.

Crossing the railway line we find ourselves in a leafy, well-kept park with a children's playground, and basketball and tennis courts.

Many scenes from the 1960s Michelangelo Antonioni cult film 'Blow Up' were shot here, and a sign in the park tells us that it has changed little since then. In 'Blow Up' fashion photographer Thomas, who is very much an active participant in swinging 60s London, abandons a photo shoot and visits the park. He spots two lovers, one of whom is played by Vanessa Redgrave, and takes photos of them. Later in the day, having avoided giving the film to Redgrave who is angered by his intrusion, Thomas discovers a body lying in the background of one of his pictures with what appears to be the killer lurking in the trees!

A pre-Python Michael Palin, who in 1966 was presenting a music TV show called 'Now', makes a brief cameo appearance in a night club scene where the Yardbirds are performing 'Stroll On'. They and Herbie Hancock contribute to an excellent soundtrack album.

A sign in the park advertises the Green Chain Walk, part of Walk London's network of routes across the capital. "Please follow the Explore Charlton logo on metal finger posts and wooden posts along the trail", they politely request. This section of the walk begins on the opposite side of the Woolwich Road at the Thames Barrier, "The world's largest movable flood defence, built to save London from disastrous flooding and completed in 1984". So no longer would Joe Strummer have had to worry that "London is drowning and I live by the river". I always think it a little ironic when songs like 'London Calling', with its dark, apocalyptic subject matter, become a flag-waving anthem for this city.

The walk continues through Maryon Park to Gilbert's Pit, a sand pit which, according to the notice board, "provided sand for parlour floors before carpets came into fashion". Further south is Maryon Wilson Park, part of the area once called Hanging Woods which were mentioned in the previous chapter as the hide out place for Shooter's Hill and Blackheath highway men. Those who diligently follow the Explore Charlton signs would eventually find themselves at Charlton House, so in theory a handy short cut for a marathon runner, should they fancy a bit of trail running.

This does present a great option for a long training run, or long walk if you're not the running type, as the Thames Path starts at the Thames Barrier. I once walked from there to Tower Bridge, something well worth doing. The Thames Path and marathon route only meet once before Tower Bridge, at the Cutty Sark in Greenwich, so an exploration of that route will have to be for another book.

The information board we read on entering Maryon Park concludes by saying

60

"Charlton is one of a few inner London communities to retain its village features. Referred to in the Domesday Book, Charlton means peasants' farmstead".

Among those village features are cottage-like houses, corner shops, a local school and, for nearly a decade until 2007, Premier League football. The reclaimed Charlton sand pits which now contain Maryon Park, are also the home to, and the name origin for The Valley, Charlton Athletic's football ground.

Built on a former chalk quarry, then known as The Swamps, which opened after World War I, the stadium can be seen from the Woolwich Road as you leave Maryon Park behind you.

Charlton's recent successful period came under the guidance of former player Alan Curbishley, appointed as manager in 1995 after a period as joint boss with Steve Gritt. The pair took charge of the team during the Addicks wilderness years, forced to play games away from The Valley following safety concerns raised by the Football League that were prompted by the 1985 Bradford City fire which saw 56 fans lose their lives. Charlton played games at both Crystal Palace and West Ham and it was only through selling players that they could raise sufficient funds to return home. One such sale was of Rob Lee to Newcastle. The story, which may well have some artistic license, is that Lee was tempted to join Kevin Keegan's side as he was told it was closer to London than Middlesbrough who were also interested in signing him!

Under Curbishley, Charlton were promoted to the Premier League via the play-off

61

final at Wembley in 1998. I still vividly remember sitting in my bedroom listening to Jonathan Pearce's excitable commentary on Capital Radio, describing a thrilling 4-4 draw with Sunderland, Charlton progressing to the big time after a penalty shoot out that ended 7-6. Without question one of the greatest football matches of all time - do yourself a favour, look up the highlights on YouTube.

Charlton were relegated after one season in the top league but made an immediate return and became a consistent mid table finisher.

After fifteen years as manager, Curbishley left Charlton in 2006. In a classic case of 'be careful what you wish for', the Club followed this long period of stability with three managers in one season, which ultimately saw the end of their time in the Premier League.

We took a walk up to the stadium, once again crossing the railway line to leave the main road. With houses tightly surrounding the ground it must be the highlight of these people's year when Milwall arrive for a South London derby. I was slightly disappointed that there wasn't a Clive Mendonca statue in recognition of his hat-trick in the 1998 play-off final.

While I was writing this book another former Charlton player was confirmed as one of the most significant names in English football history. For over thirty years Laurie Cunningham has been known as the first black player to represent England at any level, making his debut for the under 21s in 1977, scoring in a match against Scotland at Sheffield United's Bramall Lane.

However, six years earlier, Nigerian born

Benjamin Odeje, who was raised in Charlton and played for the Addics, pulled on an England shirt in a school boys' international match against Northern Ireland, walking out at Wembley in 1971 in front of 70,000 fans.

Even though Odeje's first international game is a few years ahead of Cunningham's, 1971 is still ridiculously recent to be the time before which no black person had ever played for the England football team.

Back on the Woolwich Road, yes, we're still walking along that one, we're flanked by residential property on the left, and industrial and retail units on the right. Suddenly we caught sight of Canary Wharf, peering over the roof of a giant Macro supermarket - a timely reminder for runners of where the three quarter point of the marathon course is.

Passing under a flyover taking traffic to and from the Blackwall Tunnel, the smell of engine fumes was broken by a far nicer, enticing scent; the Meantime Brewing Company was calling me. However I had one final memorial from the Borough of Greenwich to find.

The East Greenwich Pleasaunce Royal Hospital Pensioners Memorial is located in a small park behind a row of Victorian houses. From the main road you'd never know it was here, and so is not something a marathon runner will see, however it's definitely worth telling you about.

The park is surrounded by a high brick wall, creating a secluded, peaceful atmosphere. The traffic noise was distant and the only break to the calm came from building work on a loft conversion in one of the houses overlooking the park.

63

The sun was hot now, so we paused for a chocolate and water break on one of the many benches before exploring the graves which were set apart from the rest of the park and surrounded by fruit trees forming a community orchard. Most of the grave stones were so old it was difficult to read their inscriptions, with dates ranging from 1871 to 1976. Following the path around the park, through numerous blossom trees which do wonders for the hay fever, we came to a collection of plain white graves, marked only by an anchor symbol and their inscriptions, for men who died serving in the navy during World War I.

Able seaman, 29th November 1918 aged 25;

Able seaman, HMS Gainsborough, 29th November 1918;

Seaman, 19th November 1918;

Seaman, HMS London Bell, 19th January 1918 aged just 21.

Close to the entrance to the park a sign explains that here is where "lie the remains of about 3000 men, formerly pensioners of the Royal Hospital, removed from the infirmary burial ground in 1875. They served their country in the war which established the naval supremacy of England and died, the honoured recipients of her gratitude".

The remains were transferred from the old site to the present one, which had already been open since 1857, due to the construction of the Maze Hill railway tunnel. The East Greenwich Pleasaunce is also the first sign that we're about to enter Maritime Greenwich.

Back on the marathon course, Woolwich

Road gives way to Trafalgar Road and the scenery changes to one dominated by restaurants and shops. Chimneys from the Greenwich power station dominate the sky to the right.

As Trafalgar Road becomes Romney Road, your surroundings become regal, for you're entering Royal Greenwich. If you wish to walk in the footsteps of literary royalty, take a right turn and make the short trip to the riverside to find the Trafalgar Tavern. Charles Dickens was a frequent visitor to the pub in its early years and often wrote of the merry nights he had here, something which is proudly highlighted in a leaflet on its history the barman handed us with our drinks.

Now, the wood panelling on the walls are gone and the ballroom upstairs has seen its activity downgraded to mere functions, but the Trafalgar is well worth seeking out especially, as I've done in winter with its burning log fire. Emerging after dark it's easy to see how this location would have fired up the imagination of Dickens. The waves of the Thames at high tide crash onto the wall beneath the footpath. The river may appear to be busy, but the traffic is mostly tourist and police boats. As Charles walked home from the pub he'd have done so alongside one of the busiest trade routes in the world. Lights would have burned brightly across the water, the wind carrying the sounds of busy docks, blending in with the waves.

Lights still burn brightly, but they're a reminder of what the docklands have become, a corporate powerhouse, the home of many of the world's leading banks, and a number of media organisations. So much has changed on the opposite bank, and the Trafalgar Tavern, tucked away from the main road into Greenwich has watched it all.

On a warm afternoon in May we sat outside and, whilst enjoying our round of drinks which cost nearly as much as lunch for two in the Millennium Café, we discovered from the leaflet about the pub's long held connection to high class dining and entertainment, its speciality being whitebait dinners. Whitebait are small fish which are dusted in flower and deep fried, which sounds like posh scampi to me.

The Trafalgar hosts the Saints and Sinners Club, founded in 1947 by the band leader and impresario Jack Hylton together with Fleet Street journalist Percy Hoskins.

"Membership is limited to just one hundred and is made up of larger than life characters from all walks of life - the self professed Saints wear white carnations and the Sinners red. The Club has arranged whitebait suppers since 1973."

During the 19th century politicians would turn up en masse to mark the end of the annual sitting of Parliament by tucking into whitebait dinners.

The Ship, a rival pub close by, also served whitebait and it became tradition that the opposition would come here whilst the government of the day would dine at the Trafalgar. Whilst the Tavern still stands, the Ship took a direct hit from a German bomb in 1940. It's now a dry dock, home of the Cutty Sark, and is where I'm heading next.

Chapter 6: 'It's About Time' - Greenwich

Many of the clipper ships that sailed the China Seas in the second half of the 19th century were wrecked or lost in their first few years. Few of them lasted more than twenty years and only seven saw the twentieth century. By the mid-1920s, only one was still afloat. That ship was Cutty Sark.

Launched in 1869, Cutty Sark had been built for seasoned sailing master John 'Jock' Willis, with one aim in mind, to become the fastest at sea in the competitive tea trade. Her longevity is not as a result of an unusually quiet life; masts were lost in storms, and rudders were ripped off by violent waves. The harshness of life at sea meant men were washed overboard; one killing took place on deck and a captain committed suicide.

In her latter years as a working vessel she was owned by the Portuguese, but by the 1920s there was real danger of her falling apart through neglect. She was retired and returned to the UK, spending time in Cornwall and Kent. In 1957 the Queen opened Cutty Sark, which was by then in her final Greenwich Dock resting place, as a memorial to the Great Days of Sail and to all who served in the merchant service.

Now she's one of London's leading tourist attractions, part of Royal Museums Greenwich and, after the London Marathon start, the first truly atmospheric point on the course. Whilst there is much to explore and enjoy in Greenwich, from the London Marathon point of view, Cutty Sark is certainly the headline act. This chapter will focus on her and what else there is to like about SE10.

London has four locations listed by UNESCO (United Nations Educational, Scientific and Cultural Organisation) as World Heritage Sites. The London Marathon course passes through, or by, three of them. As well as Maritime Greenwich there's the Tower of London, and the Palace of Westminster (including Westminster Abbey and St Margaret's Westminster). The fourth is the Royal Botanic Gardens in Kew.

"Maritime Greenwich was added to the list of World Heritage Sites in 1997 for the concentration and quality of buildings of historic and architectural interest in the area. These can be divided into: the group of buildings along the riverfront, Greenwich Park, and the Georgian and Victorian town centre." (Visit London website)

As runners head along Romney Road, they pass the Royal Naval College on the right hand side. Originally the Palace of Placentia, built in the 15th century, both Henry VIII and Elizabeth I were born here. The English Civil War saw the building fall into disrepair. It was rebuilt, first to house the Royal Naval Hospital, before becoming the Naval College. The military were trained here until 1998; thereafter the Greenwich Foundation took over ownership.

One of the College's most significant graduates was Sir Robert Falcon Scott. Scott led the Terra Nova expedition, the aim of which was to become the first men to reach the South Pole.

After having already been camped in Antarctica for ten months, Scott's team set out for the pole on November 11th 1911. Battling through blizzards and enduring temperatures as low as minus 23, they reached their target on January 16th 1912 to be greeted by a Norwegian flag and a note from the explorer Amundsen stating that his party had beaten them to it by over a month. The Norwegians had achieved their goal on December 14th 1911.

Morale and body both shattered, the team set out on the 800 mile return journey. Initially progress was good despite the bad weather; however Scott and his companions soon began to suffer from the cold and exhaustion, plus their food supplies were running dangerously low. They spent their final days stranded in their tent, unable to continue the journey due to severe blizzards.

Scott's last words in his journal read: "We shall stick it out to the end, but we are getting weaker, of course, and the end cannot be far. It seems a pity, but I do not think I can write more".

The date of that diary entry was March 29th 1912. Nothing noteworthy about that you might think, other than, coincidentally, seventy nine years later it was the day 7,000 runners passed through Maritime Greenwich for the first London Marathon.

The teaching which takes place at the Royal Naval College now is for students at Greenwich University, and at the Trinity Laban Conservatoire of Music and Dance. The latter also has a site a mile or so further along the marathon route, across the borough boundary in Lewisham.

Perhaps the most important contemporary name attached to the former Naval College site is that of Stephen Lawrence. Stephen was murdered by a racist gang whilst waiting for a bus in nearby Eltham in 1993. Over the following two decades a series of investigations, trials and legal challenges circled around a small group of suspects, meanwhile the Met Police were branded as professionally incompetent and institutionally racist (Macpherson report - 1999). In 2005, the government scrapped the double jeopardy legal principal which prevented suspects from being tried twice for the same crime, but it was not until January 2012 that two of the suspects arrested in 1993 were convicted of Stephen's murder.

The gallery in Stephen's name at the Greenwich University campus, in the former Naval College on Romney Road, houses a number of exhibitions a year with the aim of promoting diversity via visual arts produced by young artists. Stephen's mother Doreen Lawrence was a student at Greenwich University at the time of her son's death.

There's a break in the college buildings on the river side of Romney Road, allowing for a clear view from Queen's House, on the left, down to the water.

The Queen's House was commissioned by Anne of Denmark, wife of James I. It's said that James gave Anne the manor of Greenwich by way of apology for swearing at her in public after she shot one of his favourite dogs during a hunt in 1614. Certainly a better peace offering than a bunch of flowers from the petrol station on the way home from work.

This was to be a private retreat and place for hospitality. Anne never got to enjoy the house since she fell ill in 1618, at which point work was halted. Anne died the following year.

The project was only completed when Anne's son Charles I gave Greenwich to his other half, Henrietta Maria. People of Greenwich, ever get the feeling you weren't wanted by these 17th century kings? As far as we know, no animals were harmed during the making of this part of the story.

Up on the hill in Greenwich Park stands the Royal Observatory. A red Time Ball, positioned on the roof of Flamsteed House, is one of the world's earliest public time signals and is visible from Romney Road. The ball drops every day at 1 pm so that any ships anchored in the Thames could accurately set to Greenwich Mean Time.

A right turn from Romney Road into King William Walk, and Cutty Sark is in view, as are thousands of people lining the route. With live music pumping out, it's often said this section of the course is as much like Notting Hill Carnival as a sports event. Perhaps when I ran the marathon I expected more because of the hype, for the noise didn't hit me in quite the way I thought it might. This would lead to a touch of atmosphere complacency later on, but more on that, like I say, later.

The route which runners follow to take in the Cutty Sark sees them run around three sides of the Greenwich Market. On one of my research visits I walked through the middle, a covered area surrounded by buildings, with stalls and shops specializing in works of art, crafts, vintage clothes and intriguing objects from all over the world. My friend Ellie, who accompanied me for my Greenwich research, spotted a bowl identical to one she'd bought in Turkey a few weeks earlier.

The market is dominated by the smell of food, which fills the air, as there are a number of stalls throughout this 19th century courtyard serving different kinds of foods; Indian, Japanese, Chinese, Vietnamese - I had to think at least twice before walking away from the Dutch waffle stall.

The market in its present form dates from 1827; however, Greenwich has been a market town since the 1400s. In 1700 a charter from Lord Romney was assigned to the commissioners of Greenwich Hospital, for the next 1000 years, to run a market on Wednesdays and Saturdays. The hospital is no more; the market is now one of London's most popular, open six days a week.

When I set out to research areas the London Marathon passed through, Cutty Sark was one of those I was most looking forward to discovering more about. My awareness of the ship has entirely come through the London Marathon. For years I knew the ship only as a popular viewing point during the race and one which caught fire in a spectacular way, but I knew very little about the clipper itself. As I learnt more, a story I especially liked surrounds her name.

As the Cutty Sark guide book explains, "almost all Jock Willis' ships were named after rivers or villages in the area of the Scottish

Borders that he came from – such as The Tweed, Whiteadder and St. Abbs. But the name 'cutty sark' is more obscure. It comes from Robert Burns' narrative poem 'Tam o' Shanter', published in 1791. The poem tells of how Tam gets drunk every market day in Ayr and what happens on one such occasion when, in the evening, he rides his faithful horse Maggie home.

"Tam rides the few miles to Alloway but is suddenly surprised to see lights in the church. Curious, he urges Maggie forward for a closer look. Peering through a window he sees that the church altar has been desecrated and the building is full of warlocks and witches dancing to a tune played on the bagpipes by the Devil himself.

"The witches are all repulsive old hags, except one, Nannie, a young beauty cavorting in a 'cutty sark' - a short shirt.

"Ae winsome wench and waulie
Her cutty sark, o' Paisley harn
That while a lassie she had worn,
In longitude tho' sorely scanty,
It was her best, and she was vauntie

"Tam, overwhelmed by the sight of Nannie in her revealing outfit cannot help but cry out *'Weel done, Cutty-sark!'*

"The witches and warlocks now spot Tam and a wild chase begins. Tam urges Maggie to race for the Alloway Bridge because he knows witches cannot cross water. Just as they reach the keystone of the bridge, Nannie grabs Maggie's tail, but horse and rider press on and escape, leaving Maggie's tail in Nannie's hand."

The guide book concludes that "it is not surprising that Scotsman John Willis should take a name for his ship from the writings of his country's greatest poet. But why he chose to name the vessel after the undergarment of a witch, a creature unable to cross running water, remains a mystery!

"The ship's figurehead is Nannie, dressed in a 'cutty sark' with her arm outstretched. One of the duties of the ship's apprentices, whenever she was in port, was to place a wad of unpicked rope in her hand to represent poor Maggie's tail."

Jock Willis's dream of bringing tea back from China quicker than any other ship was never realised; the closest the crew got to success came in 1872. Spotting another vessel bound for Britain loading in the same port, the Cutty Sark was able to build a 400 mile lead early on its return journey. A large storm in the Indian Ocean meant significant damage to the rudder which had to be repaired at sea. Their advantage wiped out, the Cutty Sark eventually arrived home one week after their rival.

Cutty Sark was competing against the clock almost immediately after she launched, both at sea and technologically. The Suez Canal opened in November of the same year she took to the waves, and it was inevitable that the much shorter journey, and the new waterways' unsuitable conditions for sailing ships in favour of steam, meant that by the 1880s Cutty Sark was carrying wool back from Australia instead. Here she did triumph, setting new speed records year after year; however it is tea that she is most celebrated for, something which is in evidence the moment you exit the ticket office and find yourself walking through the hull of this famous old boat. Images of tea packages are everywhere, including under your feet, giving some indication of what the clipper would have looked like during the voyages of the 1870s.

Being a man who can't start the day without a brew, a tea timeline display drew my attention. After an especially tough training run when preparing for a marathon, it's not energy drink or gel that picks me up, but a decent strong cup of tea, black as the night sky of course - none of this spoiling it by adding milk you understand! The timeline told me that in 1658, the first newspaper advert for tea appeared in London. Two years later, Samuel Pepys wrote about his first experience of a cup of tea. In 1669, the East India Company brought its first cargo of tea to England from China, but it wasn't until 1706 that a Mr Thomas Twining opened London's first tea room. Tea was a luxury few could afford for much of the 18th century; however the reliably liberal-minded Dutch came to the rescue, smuggling tea into the UK meaning it became widely available. In 1784 action was taken to clamp down on the murky world of the underground tea trade, with taxes slashed from 119 percent to 12.5. Henceforth, the nation's mornings got off to a far better start.

By now, all this reading about, and being surrounded by images of tea was making me ready for one, but there was plenty more ship to explore first.

As you wander through the inside of the ship, you're able to see the wrought iron frame which holds the wooden planks of the hull together. There's a replica model of this too, with an accompanying sign informing visually impaired people, such as me, that "if you touch this model, you can feel all the components that lie behind the ship's wooden planking". I did, and it put me in mind of Meccano.

Some steep stairs negotiated, which can't have been much fun in a storm, and visitors arrive at a section mostly filled with kids-minded interactive stuff that did little for me - especially since there were plenty of kids running around.

A series of multiple choice questions were scattered around the display, that wouldn't have looked out of place in the early stages of 'Who Wants to be a Millionaire?'.

"Copper was used to cover the inside of the hull, why?" crowds of school children are no doubt asked.

"Was it: A. it looked pretty, B. it made the ship go faster, or C. it protected the ship?"

"What's that Johnny, you think its B and C? Well done. Try this one."

"The ship's rib cage was made from iron, was this because: A. it was cheaper, B. it took up less space, or C. it was strong?

"No Johnny, you've already answered one, let someone else have a go."

"Was it cheaper miss?"

"No, it's actually B and C again."

"I was going to say that miss," whines Johnny, who proceeds to sulk for the rest of the trip.

A more difficult question posed was:

"Can you guess how many bolts are used throughout the ship?"

Or it would be more difficult if it had been phrased differently, as the obvious answer is, no. I can't guess, what do I win? The answer by the way was 19,460, although the sign was slightly unsure on this saying "about 19,460", so really, your guess is as good as mine.

More stairs and a gust of wind in the face welcomed me on deck.

A typical crew for the Cutty Sark during her tea years was 30. Fewer men were needed for the transportation of wool; in 1890 the ship left London with just nineteen men on board. Most who sailed with Cutty Sark did so only once; they would be paid off on return to London and would have to find a new ship. Of the 682 who sailed on Cutty Sark, only five were lost at sea. The majority of crew who never returned saw work on the clipper as a free passage to Australia - the outward journey to China would make a stop there. In 1876 for example, 12 of the 15 able seaman deserted, meaning they had to be replaced by more expensive Australians.

This may seem an obvious thing to say, but it's only when you stand on the deck of an ancient ship such as this, that you realise how little space there would have been for thirty people to spend up to ten months together, and how exposed they were. There's little comfort in the cabins, the bunks looked like it would be a squeeze for me to lie down in, and I'm not the tallest at five foot seven!

A sign on deck marks the spot where the murder took place, a brawl between two men with fatal consequences. We spotted Nannie, rope in hand. Maybe Portugal wasn't such a bad experience for her as she looks to be reaching out to a branch of Nandos.

The deck of the Cutty Sark is a good place to look at the tall buildings which dominate London's skyline, Canary Wharf, The Shard and so on. It's perhaps more important to admire what's around and beneath you though, since so much of it could have been lost forever. Early in the morning of May 21st 2007, a serious fire significantly damaged the Cutty Sark. However with a restoration project already well underway, large parts of the ship, including the three 100-foot masts, many of her wooden planks and Nannie the figurehead, had been removed. As the Guardian reported at the time "Much of the damage was to a temporary wooden roof installed to provide cover for the sixty-five carpenters, shipwrights, fabricators and other conservationists working on the project".

Looking back at media coverage of the event, initial suspicion was that the fire might have been started deliberately. Subsequent belief is that a vacuum cleaner left switched on overnight was the cause of what became a £50m recovery exercise.

Whilst Cutty Sark lives on in Greenwich, one London landmark that can no longer be seen here is the Gipsy Moth.

Sir Francis Chichester commissioned Gipsy Moth with the aim of beating Cutty Sark's record-setting journey time carrying wool back from Australia in the 19th century. Clippers would take an average of 123 days to cover the distance; Chichester hoped to do so in 100.

On August 27th 1966, with the 64 year old Chichester at the helm, Gipsy Moth set sail. Significant damage to the ship's steering on the outward journey, and near death and further damage to the ship around Cape Horn on the way home, meant that the challenge was close to failure on three occasions; however Chichester eventually returned to Plymouth, breaking numerous records. These included the fastest voyage around the world by any small vessel and more than twice the distance covered by a single handed sailor.

After Chichester's death in 1972, Gipsy Moth was given a spot to soak up the glory, alongside the ship she was built to take records from. Too many tourists wandering across the yacht's deck contributed to a steady decline in her condition, with eventual closure to visitors. After a campaign led by the editor of Yachting Monthly, Paul Gelder, Gipsy Moth was restored and returned to the sea to mark 40 years since Chichester's historic voyage. Now she is based at Cowes on the Isle of Wight, but she did return to London for the Queen's Diamond Jubilee celebration in 2012, spending time moored at St Katharine Docks in the Avenue of Sail exhibition, upstream of Greenwich on the north bank of the Thames.

You can still visit the Gipsy Moth in Greenwich, but only for a pint at one of the many nautically-named drinking establishments in the area.

On leaving Cutty Sark you walk underneath the hull. Unsurprisingly lots of finger marks can be seen, where people have jumped up to touch it. Sadly, my already-mentioned height meant I was a couple of inches too short. The opportunity to see the ship from this angle is new; she was raised eleven feet onto steel supports as part of the restoration project following the fire. As Richard Doughty, director of the Cutty Sark Trust told the press as the reopening day approached: "The view under the hull is really the highlight of the ship. When you see this magnificent shining gold-coloured hull, it makes you catch your breath. It looks absolutely stunning".

Whilst the café was extremely tempting (I was craving tea, remember) as were both the Gipsy Moth and Spanish Galleon pubs across the road, there was another duty to attend to whilst visiting Greenwich. One question I've always wanted to know the answer to is, why the Greenwich bit of Greenwich Mean Time? I mean, why didn't they draw the line somewhere else? I've always assumed the short answer is because that's where the Observatory is, but hoped there was a bit more to it than that.

The answer lay somewhere under the big red time ball.

When buying our tickets at the Cutty Sark, which give you entry into all the Maritime Greenwich attractions, we'd enquired as to the best way of getting to the Observatory. My first research visit coincided with the downtime between the Olympic and Paralympic Games so the stadium for the 'horse sports' was still dominating Greenwich Park. Whether we hadn't been given clear information or we didn't pay attention, I can't remember, but off we went, back along Romney Road, taking a somewhat longer route into Greenwich Park than was necessary.

Once in the Park it wasn't immediately obvious which paths were shut and which weren't. We sought the help of an oldish-looking couple who seemed as if they knew the area. As we explained to them, "the signs here aren't particularly clear".

Mistake!

80

"I know," came the reply. "They've not been very good at living up to their promises over access to the Park."

It seemed we'd had the misfortune to pick a man who was taking on the role of local spokesperson for the 'grumbling about the Olympics association' and was doing it rather well, clearly keen for those of us who weren't locals to be left in no doubt as to how damned inconvenient the Olympics were.

Eventually he pointed us in the right direction, but in that infuriating way of telling you what you can't do before giving you the answer you want.

"You see that path there, you normally could cut through there, but you can't at the moment as it's blocked off. If you walk across here, over to where those trees are…"

Why he didn't just cut to the chase and tell us about the trees, I've no idea. Presumably he wanted to make sure we'd understood that "these closures are a right nuisance."

And did he think we could get back down the hill the most direct way when we'd finished?

"Oh yeah, my mate said to me the other day he said, you can't get up that hill because of all the tourists, but I know you can…"

"Are you sure?" his wife interjected.

"Oh yeah, we walked up there this morning remember?"

"No, we came through here…"

"No, we definitely walked up the hill, we came through here yesterday."

Spotting they were now talking amongst themselves, and that this was a conversation that was likely to run for some time, we thanked them, and fled for the safety of "those trees", hoping by the time our friends had reached an agreement on which of the few paths still available for the public to walk on they'd actually used earlier in the day we'd be far enough away for them not to try and talk to us anymore.

If you get the chance, its well worth walking up that hill, for this is perhaps the most important view on the marathon route. Virtually the whole panorama of the event is laid out in front and around you. With the start somewhere over your right shoulder across Greenwich Park, the early miles wind round out of sight to your right, heading in the direction of the O2 Arena, before turning left and running across down below, past the Naval College, the Queen's House and Cutty Sark. Tower Bridge is clearly visible in the distance away to the left, but most striking of all is the second half, for Canary Wharf stands dominant in your eye-line, the magnitude of the Isle of Dogs loop stares right back at you from the north bank of the Thames, and there's still the last quarter to run!

I tried to imagine what sort of view of Marathon day this spot would actually give. Soon, though, my mind wandered through some of the sights this hill would have looked down upon throughout London's history. Medieval armies advancing up the Thames, the even more terrifying sight of fire raging through the streets of the city in 1666. The evolution of the docks to become a world trade powerhouse, a blur of cargo boats, first sailing masts, then funnels for steam ships giving way to a skyline dominated by smog, cranes and ultimately, decline and desolation as the Docklands died. In recent years, standing on this hill, one could watch the East End transformation from industrial ghost town to vibrant business district, Canary Wharf being the most obvious trophy of this; the London headquarters of HSBC is one of the many other impressive buildings. I once walked the Thames path from Charlton to Tower Bridge, and with the loop in the river around the Isle of Dogs, it seems as if you're walking past the HSBC offices for several miles. Then there's the newest addition to the view laid out below. Anyone who lingers here will be drawn eastwards to see the Olympic Stadium standing proud. What a fantastic sight the fireworks in the night sky must have been, as Sir Chris Hoy carried the British flag in the opening ceremony, or when Coldplay took to the stage as the Paralympic flame was extinguished at the end of the most memorable summer of sport this city has ever seen. This hill was the backdrop as British Olympic history was made as Charlotte Dujardin joined Dame Kelly Holmes, Rebecca Adlington and Laura Trott as one of four British women to win two gold medals in the same Olympics. Her Dressage gold, along with fellow Brit Laura Bechtolsheimer's bronze, were Britain's first ever in the individual version of the dancing horses event.

I can't lie, the horse sports do little for me. I don't doubt the difficulty in getting a horse to shake its thing to 'Live and Let Die', but I've always considered running to be the Olympic event which is easiest for someone to take up, and therefore most likely to turn legacy talk into action. All you need is some kit and somewhere

83

to run. The fact so many people want to attempt the London Marathon at least once is testimony to this.

If you've already run this, or any other marathon and want to admire your achievement in completing 26.2 miles, Greenwich Park on a sunny day, with London spread out beneath you is a pretty good place to do so. If you've not done the distance, but are struck by this view, and you know a friend, relative or work colleague that has done, I suggest you get them a drink next time you and they are near a bar. Mine's a pint of Pilsner, courtesy of the local Meantime Brewing Company if you're asking: cheers!

And on the subject of Mean Time, whilst it's easy to stand for hours in Greenwich Park, the Observatory doesn't stay open all night.

"Come and have your photo taken standing on the Meridian Line", the Observatory website encourages, and boy, do people come!

Information boards tell those who aren't too busy posing that this is zero degrees longitude and here marks the line between the eastern and western hemispheres. Nothing specifically about why this location was chosen to be the home of time though.

Deciding not to join the queue of people waiting to have their photo taken by a line on the concrete, our attention was grabbed instead by what remains of William Herschel's forty foot telescope. The thing which especially interested me was what a waste of money it appears to have been!

Built between 1785 and 1789 and located in the grounds of Observatory House in Slough, where Herschel lived, it was the world's largest telescope, and was funded by a £4,000 grant from George III.

Whilst Herschel discovered the sixth and seventh moon of Saturn (Enceladus and Mima), it appears uncertain whether this was achieved with the forty foot telescope, or one of the others he also used at the time. The new toy was not a significant improvement on existing telescopes, as bad weather often restricted its use, it was unwieldy and the mirrors used for looking at the sky proved problematic.

After its final observation in 1815, the telescope stood unused for more than twenty years. William's son John had the frame dismantled in 1839 as it was feared the rotting structure might collapse, posing a risk to John's young children. Mrs Herschel was no doubt relieved to see her father-in-law's old heap out of the way.

As if things hadn't gone badly enough, the tube, which lay on the ground resting on stone blocks, was crushed by a falling tree. The ten foot section of tube that remains is what's on display in Greenwich.

Interestingly, part of the terms of the funding deal for the telescope was that William's wife Caroline was granted a pension of £50 per year, working as his assistant, thus making her the first woman in Britain to be a professional astronomer.

Flamsteed House, that's the one with the big red ball on the roof, is the oldest building on site. The original observatory is one of Sir Christopher Wren's creations; he pops up quite a bit around the marathon route. A look round is as much about seeing where those who worked here lived - a bedroom, dining room and study set up to represent the layout of the time.

There's a vast Time Gallery, with an equally large selection of time measuring devices from throughout the history of the Observatory. Walking around, I found myself wondering what impact the evolving ability to accurately measure the time had on the people of the day. What percentage of folk grumbled about how they "don't like change" and that "we've managed perfectly well up to now". And what are the great legacies of this world changing research that took place in Greenwich? Football managers ranting at referees because they think too much, or too little injury time has been played, and commuters getting much more stressed than is necessary because if they don't run for the tube they'll have to wait all of three minutes for the next one!

Yet another display reminded anyone, who still wasn't sure, that "longitude separates east and west in the same way the Equator does north and south".

Having not looked on a map of the world for some time, I couldn't list the countries that zero degrees passes through. This would make a good pub quiz question, the answer being: Great Britain, France, Spain, Algeria, Mali, Burkina Faso, Togo, Ghana and Antarctica.

The display went on to tell that, until the 19th century, many different mediums were used on maps and charts around the world, but in 1884 international agreement was reached to measure longitude eastwards and westwards of Greenwich. Zero degrees longitude was measured through the eye of the telescope in the room where I was standing.

86

This wasn't the only meridian line to have been used at Greenwich. British maps featured a meridian line set in 1750 which was 20 feet to the west, and many early satellite navigation systems went with a different line some 335 feet to the east. All of which does suggest a 'pin the tail on the donkey' approach to finding your way home.

I've combined the information in the exhibition with that which can be read on the Royal Museums Greenwich website to give what would seem to be the best available answer as to why time is measured from Greenwich.

"Since the late 19th century, the Prime Meridian at Greenwich has served as the co-ordinate base for the calculation of Greenwich Mean Time. Before this, almost every town in the world kept its own local time. There were no national or international conventions to set how time should be measured, or when the day would begin and end, or what the length of an hour might be. However, with the vast expansion of the railway and communications networks during the 1850s and 1860s, the worldwide need for an international time standard became imperative."

Incidentally, London's first railway line ran from Greenwich into Central London. I pay it a visit in the next chapter.

The Museums' website continues: "The Greenwich Meridian was chosen to be the Prime Meridian of the World in 1884. Delegates from 25 nations met in Washington DC for the International Meridian Conference. By the end of the conference, Greenwich had won the prize of Longitude 0° by a vote of 22 in favour to 1 against (San Domingo), with two abstentions (France and Brazil). There were two main

87

reasons for the victory: the USA had already chosen Greenwich as the basis for its own national time-zone system and, at the time, 72% of the world's commerce depended on sea-charts which used Greenwich as the Prime Meridian.

"The decision, essentially, was based on the argument that by naming Greenwich as Longitude 0°, it would inconvenience the least number of people."

So the answer to: Why there? appears to be: Because it was there. My question should have been: why did Charles II decide Greenwich would be a good spot to found an observatory?

The most likely answer to this is: With Greenwich being a long-standing location for one of many royal homes, a convenient hill and closeness to the river made it a logical choice.

With time ironically against us at the home of the stuff, we headed out through the gift shop, where you're inevitably directed at the end of your visit. The French had wanted Paris to be the home of time, presumably they abstained their vote in protest at missing out on the lucrative tea towel, shortbread and postcard industry. We left the Observatory down Croom's Hill, the most direct way which had been available all along.

The draw of the excellently-named, and, in my experience, equally fine in character, drinking establishments of Greenwich was too much to resist. We chose The Spanish Galleon, one of many pubs listed in the London Marathon guide as a good place to go to view the race. On this occasion we were joined by a man in a pink tutu and brightly coloured tights, a costume I've seen on Marathon day, although the endurance event he was taking part in this evening was his own stag night. His group of mates were already lining up the tequilas at 6.30 pm!

On leaving the pub a couple of hours later, we were greeted by a sight that must strike fear into the hearts of locals, and those who have invested thousands of hours and millions of pounds into the Cutty Sark's restoration, for a fire engine was parked alongside her. Luckily though, on this occasion, they had been called to investigate a mysterious smell in the nearby Greenwich Foot Tunnel which provides a crossing under the Thames to the Isle of Dogs. Seven pedestrians were taken ill, with BBC News later reporting fire, police and ambulance spokespeople all stating that no hospital treatment had been required, and the cause of the smell to be "unknown".

Runners catch sight of the entrance to the Tunnel, a large glass dome alongside Cutty Sark which covers the area where pedestrians can take either the stairs or a lift down to the tiled walkway which runs under the Thames. The Tunnel was opened in 1902 replacing a ferry service regarded as expensive and sometimes unreliable, and it provided a crossing for workers in the docks who lived south of the river. It is part of the UK's National Cycle Route 1, linking Dover with Shetland - and you thought a marathon sounded like a long way!

Once past Cutty Sark, runners turn left into Greenwich Church Street, before a right turn onto Creek Road and then the run towards Deptford. Soon on the left, next to the Up The Creek Comedy Club is the Lord Hood pub, notable for being named after the man Admiral

Lord Nelson described as "the greatest sea officer I ever knew". A mentor to Nelson, Hood led ships in the Seven Years War, the War of American Independence and the French Revolution. A busy chap, when not at sea, he found time to become a Tory Member of Parliament. The clothes worn by Nelson during the Battle of Trafalgar are on show in the Maritime Museum at Greenwich. His bullet-punctured jacket, bloodied waistcoat and even blood-stained socks paint a grim and vivid picture of the reality of war at sea.

The church which gives its name to Greenwich Church Street can be seen a short distance from the junction with Creek Road. St Alfege takes its name from the 29th Archbishop of Canterbury, who was bludgeoned to death by a bunch of marauding Danish pirates in 1012. The Danes invaded Kent, kidnapped Alfege and took him around the coast and up the Thames, holding him prisoner at Greenwich. Knowing that his people could not afford the £3,000 ransom being demanded, Alfege refused to let them pay. At a feast on Easter Sunday the pirates set about killing Alfege with ox bones and the hafts of their axes, before someone realised their dinner was getting cold, and finished the job off with a single blow to the head.

Records don't show the exact date at which the first church was built, but a shrine to Alfege would have been erected as soon as the Danes had cleared off home.

With the Royal Palace being down the road, many key servants were buried here. As Greenwich is the birth place of Henry VIII, he was baptised at St Alfege.

Disaster struck the church on November 29th 1710. A violent storm hit, causing the roof to fall in. Damage was estimated to cost around £6,000.

Following the Great Fire of 1666 a tax was put on coal with the aim of raising money to repair the significant damage caused to St Paul's Cathedral. Yet by the time of the storm of 1710 the work on St Paul's was close to completion and the duties on coal for that project had several years to run so would raise considerably more than would be needed. The people of Greenwich campaigned to Parliament for a share; this led to the creation of the Commission for Building Fifty New Churches, of which the restored St Alfege was to be the first. We find evidence of this initiative further along the marathon course as St Paul's Deptford and St Anne's Limehouse were both built around this time.

The replacement church in Greenwich was a creation of Nicholas Hawksmoor, a pupil of Sir Christopher Wren. St Alfege's would not escape the Second World War unscathed, taking a direct hit in 1945. As the church website explains:

"The incendiaries lodged in the roof of the church causing a mass of blazing timbers and molten lead to collapse into the nave. Fortunately the walls, the tower and the organ dating from 1552 survived."

Professor Albert Richardson who would go on to become president of the Royal Academy led the restoration, but it was another costly affair.

Chapter 7: 'Fun City, SE8' - Deptford

At the start of 2013, Time Out published their A to Z of London Cool. Under 'D' they offered up, the whole of Deptford, Dancing solo (this partner thing was apparently so 2012), and the rather odd suggestion of South London Dog shows, where they pose the question "who doesn't like seeing a Labrador in a dinosaur outfit?" I'd have thought the obvious answer to that is the Labrador, but apparently it's not consulted on the matter! This strange ritual of making your pet look like a Natural History Museum exhibit was new to me, as was the existence of the Bermondsey Street Festival where, every September, the Labrasaurus can be found walking the streets near Tower Bridge.

On Deptford, the A to Z of London Cool enthused:

"SE8 has enjoyed an Olympics Effect boost to its already rising star: the galleries are moving in, followed by the chic eateries, followed by that bellwether of hipness, the postironic tattooist."

I confess the concept of post irony has passed me by. Perhaps I'll try and figure it out during a future marathon; I may well need three and a half hours to get my head round the idea.

Look beyond the bewildering wordplay, the point being made is Deptford's a pretty decent part of town many Londoners are yet to explore, and is where it's at if you like interesting, community focused, non-commercialised art and places to eat owned by seventies disco acts: what, you mean I've misunderstood the reference to

'Chic' as well?

As the runners leave Greenwich and the atmospheric surrounds of Cutty Sark, they enter one of the, relatively-speaking, quieter stretches of the course. Many people may experience an adrenalin surge at popular viewing points such as Blackheath, Cutty Sark, Canary Wharf and Tower Bridge, so the chance to concentrate on the rhythm of running and refocus the mind is extremely welcome. As we're not into double figures for miles covered yet, self control is key to achieving the goal of completing the distance.

The final two weeks of a marathon training programme is the bit we refer to as tapering, where the usual routine of long runs at the weekend and squeezing in as many miles as possible after work during the week, is replaced by shorter, easier runs. This is so that there is no fatigue in the legs on the big day, and any lingering injury niggles have the chance to recover. On race day, the sensible marathoner will run the opening miles at a pace that feels so relaxed it seems they're merely jogging. As you might imagine, this is all about conserving energy for the latter stages, postponing the pain for as long as possible, and to allow for soaking up the atmosphere and enjoying the moment. Everyone who stands on the start line of a marathon has worked damn hard to get there, so it is crucial to enjoy the race while you still can. It's very easy to get caught up in the event, to look at your watch and see you're a couple of minutes ahead of schedule, believing this to be time in the bank and then, be driven on by a crowd such as London offers, and keep going at too fast a pace which will be regretted in two hours' time. Those that join running clubs or visit online running forums won't have to look too hard to find a horror story of where marathons have gone wrong through ill-judged pacing.

The course follows Creek Road into Deptford, crossing the bridge over Deptford Creek, a tidal stretch of water that links the River Ravensbourne with the Thames. This is one of numerous sections of the London Marathon route where dockyards dominate the historical narrative. Founded in 1513 by Henry VIII, Deptford was the first of the Royal Navy Dockyards, and one of three large yards in the UK, alongside Woolwich and Belfast. Among its claims to fame is that it was the location for the knighting of Sir Francis Drake, and for building the many ships that sailed under Admiral Nelson's command.

Creek Road has undergone significant regeneration with the demolition of the Deptford Power Station, the construction of many new homes as well as a student village serving Greenwich University, the Trinity Laban Conservatoire, and Goldsmith's College. At approximately the seven mile mark on the right hand side, is a pub called The Duke, which has a page on their website encouraging locals to view the race from their terrace.

Meanwhile on the left is Creek Side, the first of two turnings leading deeper into Deptford. It is a street that hosts a mixture of converted warehouses and residential property, and is home to a number of art spaces that have helped contribute to Deptford being branded as 'the new Shoreditch', a tag I personally wouldn't be too comfortable with. I've nothing against

Shoreditch necessarily, but I don't get why something or somewhere has to be branded as 'the new' or 'the next' anything.

Further along Creek Road, just past a Methodist Church, is Deptford High Street, which hosts one of South London's busiest markets.

Whilst certainly not an unpleasant stretch, after the landmarks and crowd excitement of Greenwich, it's easy to see how this section would be considered rather uninspiring. It's also one of the areas the runners pass through where, unless they have some connection with SE8, they may well know very little about what goes on here. Truth be told, when I made my initial list of things to write about in this book, I included Greenwich and Bermondsey, but completely overlooked Deptford. By way of showing it's not just me being unintentionally dismissive of this part of South London, Andrew, one of my regular guide runners who has ten London Marathons to his name, agreed it's easy to keep your eyes on the road at this point, caring more about the quarter distance mark being reached, than wondering what might lie down a side street. As I boarded a train at London Bridge station one showery summer Saturday afternoon, it was those side streets I was heading to explore. Perhaps this section of my journey is as much for those looking for a different viewing point as for runners.

Built on a viaduct four miles long, known locally as 500 arches, the London Bridge to Greenwich line was the first railway in the capital, opened in 1836. Now numerous galleries

95

and artist studios can be found sheltering beneath the arches in Deptford. Another interesting first came in 1852 when a bookstall appeared at London Bridge station run by a Mr. W. H. Smith.

Train enthusiasts would doubtless be saddened to find that Deptford, the reputedly oldest passenger-only railway station in the UK to be still standing on its original site, doesn't have a single member of staff working on a Saturday afternoon. In addition to the noticeable lack of humanity, something I did think was slightly odd, as Saturday is one of the days of the Deptford Market, is that there's an equal absence of evidence of Deptford station's historical claim to fame. Only the brickwork in the subway looked to be showing its age, which did lead me to wonder what the graffiti artists of 1836 might choose to scrawl on their shiny new local train station walls?

If indignant at the staffing neglect of such an important location on the UK railway history trail, the train enthusiast's mood would be lifted no end by a right turn out of the station, a short walk along the High Street to a café in The Deptford Project, housed in a converted railway carriage. I too found this place to be an excellent start to my afternoon - as a food enthusiast I can highly recommend the cheese and bacon quiche.

The thirty-five tonne South Eastern Trains carriage became an addition to the local scenery on Valentine's Day 2008, as what the owners described as their "gift of love to Deptford High Street". If a level of affection is judged on effort alone, it certainly beats a bunch of flowers that will be dead within a week!

Posters cover the walls advertising local art shows and each stool has a name or slogan inscribed onto the seat: the Love Stool, the Naughty Stool, Window Seat or the inviting Sit on Me! Mine simply read 'I'm free' which did suggest I could take it home with me. My friend Abi, whose local knowledge saw her join me for the afternoon, appeared to be sitting on a stool specifically for the winner of 'Rear of the Year'.

On this occasion the café wasn't busy, but I got the impression that even had it been packed, this isn't the sort of place where customers rush. The Deptford Project also offers outdoor film screenings, and has an adjacent garden which comes complete with that indigenous South London plant, the palm tree.

Our locally-produced lunch consumed, we retraced our steps past the train station to seek out what thousands of runners don't have time to look for on a Sunday morning in April.

Deptford High Street, with its arts spaces (including one showing works by recent Goldsmiths' graduates), its market and numerous shops catering for multinational culinary needs, put me in mind of Brick Lane or Kingsland Road in Dalston. Whilst it's misleading to compare the three, they do all have one thing in common; that you exit the train station or turn off the main road, and, instantly, know you're in a pocket of London like no other.

There was a children's TV series which I used to watch as a student called Mopatop's Shop. Mopatop was a big green muppet, who, together with a red duck/dog hybrid called Puppyduck, ran a shop where "you could buy anything you could think or dream of". I realise

97

that, if you've never heard of this programme, you might think it's a weird dream I had, but it does exist - Google it, you might like it. You'll also learn that co-production credits go to the Jim Henson Company, hence the appearance of a muppet.

Heading back along Deptford High Street towards Creek Road and the London Marathon course, we passed plenty of 'we sell everything' shops where you can go to buy your plastic bin, mop, knitting kit, hula hoop (the toy, not the crisps) and SpongeBob SquarePants lunchbox. I half expected that, were I to enter one of the shops, I'd be greeted by a big green muppet, or find a red duck/dog manning a stall in the market. The range of products on sale outside was just as eclectic.

A short distance past the railway bridge, the market comes to an end. There are more art spaces, including the closed looking SE8 Gallery, opposite which is one of the area's major landmarks, St Paul's Church. Designed by architect Thomas Archer, a pupil of Sir Christopher Wren, it was built between 1712 and 1730. Like St Alfege's in Greenwich, this was also part of the Commission for Building Fifty New Churches with the hope of instilling pride in Britain and encouraging people to stay in London, rather than emigrate to the New World. The church was acclaimed by the Royal Commission on the Historical Monuments of England, who merged with English Heritage in 1999, as one of the finest Baroque churches in the country. Such is its striking nature that poet John Betjeman is attributed to describing it as "a pearl at the heart of Deptford".

Had the sun been shining, the rose garden could have proved a good spot to people-watch from, but it wasn't, and we had a pub to find.

If I ever secure another place in the London Marathon - given the roughly one in four chance of my name being drawn from a future ballot I could be waiting some time - I'm not certain if my knowledge of what The Duke offers will be a help or hindrance. We've entered the world of the gastropub, something I don't always embrace. Too often their main features appear to be pretty wall paper and an expensive menu where the creativity far outweighs stomach satisfaction. Having just had lunch, and with a pudding venue already in mind, we didn't investigate The Duke's menu, apart from the discovery that their nibbles list included popcorn.

The pub was empty when we arrived. As we retreated to a leather sofa in the window which was surrounded by book shelves offering reading material including The Model Railway Manual and The All Colour Guide to Toy Trains, it felt as if we'd dropped by for a beer in the barman's front room. I really could have stayed all day. I suspect that if you want to bag yourself a spot on a sofa for a Saturday evening, turning up in the afternoon would be a good idea, for this fine drinking establishment is close to student accommodation, and offers live music at the weekend.

It was this musical connection, as well as the location, that brought The Duke to my attention, for the pub was an integral part of the music scene in Deptford in the late seventies. The local council had a policy of only letting property in the nearby Crossfield Estate to young single people or couples with no children, due to a dual carriageway running through the middle. This allowed for a creatively minded community to grow, with The Duke becoming a focal point. Bands to emerge from this period include Squeeze, Dire Straits and Alternative TV, the latter the musical vehicle for Mark Perry, the man behind legendary punk fanzine Sniffin' Glue, which also featured Danny Baker as a regular contributor.

An article on The Duke's website quotes local musician Bobby Valentino, formerly of the band The Bluebirds, recalling the Crossfield's Free Festival, a late seventies one day music event where the line up was almost entirely made up of bands from the area "performing on a makeshift stage on a perfect Sunday afternoon, with long extension leads coming from Mark Knopfler's ground floor flat powering a makeshift PA".

Presumably the dual carriageway in question is the now far less dangerous Creek Road, as, on leaving The Duke, we crossed over into Creek Side and soon spotted a sign for the Crossfield Estate. Whilst I enjoyed The Duke very much, there was a part of me that wondered what it would have been like when Knopfler, Valentino, Perry, Tilbrook and co. might have called it their 'local'. Dire Straits' first demo tape, recorded in 1977, included a version of future hit 'Sultans of Swing', so we can assume they'd have played it down The Duke. At the height of punk I wonder how that would have been received? Reviewing their self-titled debut album, Rolling Stone magazine's Ken Tucker wrote that the band plays "mixtures of rock, folk and country music with a serene spirit and witty irony. It's almost as if they were aware that their forte has nothing to do with what's currently happening in the industry, but couldn't care less". Their laid-back, roots rock style, especially in songs like 'Down to the Water Line' certainly would have sounded great on the "perfect Sunday afternoon", Valentino described.

If the Deptford area was notable for its musicians thirty years ago, the creative flame still burns strongly in SE8 today. Creek Side appears to serve two purposes: to be an artist playground and a rat run for people that want to get from Greenwich to Deptford in a hurry.

One of the first things those drivers will fly past is an impressive brick building housing the dance facilities for Trinity Laban Conservatoire of Music and Dance. Marathon runners may notice this too, if looking in the right direction. With one of the largest teams of specialist dance teachers in the world, Trinity Laban is acknowledged internationally as a leader in the contemporary arts. It also boasts one of the UK's largest pilates studios. Being someone with no coordination on a dancefloor, and who has always thought pilates sounds far more tiring than it's given credit for, I'll stick to running, and don't stop for a second look.

The Trinity Laban website promotes their location as being "part of south east London's thriving arts community", and we find evidence of that on the wall of Cockpit Arts, in the form of a community cohesion mural featuring pictures of sign language, a cartoon of St Paul's Church and some people in wheelchairs playing hockey.

Under another railway arch and the Creekside Discovery Centre is advertising "wild events for city families. Discover wildlife history and habitat along and around Lewisham's waterways".

It looked shut, so we can't. Evidently the wildlife of Lewisham was in no mood for being discovered today.

Further along, the Art and Perpetuity Trust (APT)'s gallery doors were open encouraging passers-by to wander in to view their latest exhibition, with work on show selected from their annual open call for artist submissions. The exhibition title, Delineation, meant that each of the thirty four chosen artists were allocated equal space in the gallery, with the order in which they were displayed being determined by names drawn from a hat. This randomness would, so they hoped, allow for viewers of the work to do so with an open mind, without relating a piece to the one shown next to it.

Among the works to catch our suitably open-minded eyes were a painting showing the ripples sound waves make on water, and a picture of a man holding a net, which had been displayed in an actual net. In one corner of the exhibition a load of fluffy chicks, such as you might find on the top of an Easter cake, had been squeezed into a plastic tube and were, not unreasonably, looking rather claustrophobic. A few did appear to be making a break for freedom. If I were a fluffy chick I'd certainly prefer to be sitting on top of a nest made from Shredded Wheat guarding a couple of Cadbury's

Mini Eggs.

Outside, and unrelated to the APT exhibition, several hundred door shapes made of wood, each identical in size at no more than two inches tall, had been stuck onto a wall. Across the road a wine cash and carry was conveniently placed; no exhibition private view is complete without vast quantities of alcohol. Having worked at a few such events, I'm sure half those that turn up do so mostly for the free booze.

The thing which really struck me about Deptford was that, wherever you looked there were examples of how, with a bit of imagination, something which might initially appear ready for the scrap heap had been transformed into a place of real character. Perhaps the best known example of this is the Big Red.

Readers of Time Out are likely to be familiar with this place, for no guide to the things to do in London, quirky places to visit or the Capital's best eating establishments is complete without this pizza restaurant and bar which is next to The Bird's Nest pub on the corner of Creek Side and Deptford Church Street. In their words:

"Quite how a No. 30 double decker ended up in Deptford is anyone's guess - Toto, we're not in Hackney anymore - but it seems to be having fun in its new location and new role as a pizzeria. Under the long concrete curve of an elevated section of the DLR, and with an unlovable portion of Deptford Creek tucked mercifully out of sight, it's a surprisingly convivial spot."

As well as being a little harsh on the location, they go on to critique the food and drink on offer, and give quite a detailed description of the range of plants decorating the covered seating area alongside the converted route master. The kitchen is built onto the back, giving the impression that a driver of the number 30 was so frustrated at being this far south, he attempted an ill-judged three point turn, and crashed into the side of The Birds Nest.

We didn't get to board the bus ourselves, for a kids party had beaten us to it and already had the look of descending into chaos. It's no wonder the excitement level was running high. A classic London bus is a fantastic place to stimulate a child's imagination and certainly beats upstairs in McDonalds, no matter how many Happy Meal toys and colour-in pictures of Ronald McDonald are handed round.

Instead we sat in the garden, fortunately in the covered bit as the heavens opened just as the cheesecake arrived. I highly recommend it, in case a Time Out food critic ever reads this, and more than made up for my first choice not being available: I bet those pesky kids did a run on the chocolate fudge cake.

You know those mornings when you slowly wake up, remembering the dream you had, and thinking how cool it would be to experience it in reality, no matter how random it might seem in your already fading memory. The owner of Big Red might well have had one of those moments, where, in the dead of night, his subconscious took him to a quirky, part pop-up, part installation, bus-based dining venue. There's a lorry parked nearby, that offers live music and film screenings, and with a late licence and mojitos on the drinks list, the Big Red is far from just one man's dream.

Things were hotting up at the kids party. They seemed to have lost interest in simply running up and down the stairs, and were now flying back and forth between bus and garden. As we were paying our bill, one mini human went hurtling past, only to return moments later at a similarly high speed, crying their eyes out after falling over. There's always one that means a party ends in tears.

Chapter 8: 'Let's Go Down to the Water Line' - Deptford to Rotherhithe

I spent just over a year researching this book and, because I'd never been to Deptford other than running through it on London Marathon day, this was the first place I wanted to visit. A year later, with much of my research completed, Abi and I were back to see what lay beyond The Duke.

The station still has no staff on a Saturday; quite what South Eastern Trains expect a visually impaired passenger not familiar with the local area to do when they arrive is anyone's guess.

The market was as chaotically brilliant as I remembered, the SE8 Gallery still looked shut - I can only assume one must view by appointment, but not everything was the same as it had been on my last visit.

Feeling hungry and needing to load up ahead of an afternoon's exploring, we headed straight for the train carriage, only to be greeted by a sign telling us that The Deptford Project was temporarily closed and would, they hoped, be finding a new location soon. I hope that by the time you're reading this book the people of Deptford are able to enjoy one of its finest eating places once again.

On reaching Creek Road it was very tempting to turn right and be lured into The Duke, but on the off-chance we might find it not to be as we remembered it either, and not feeling able to handle double disappointment before midday, we went left instead, and began the walk

106

towards Surrey Quays.

Immediately Creek Road became Evelyn Street, named after a man who brought a touch of creative flair to Deptford centuries before punk rock, community art and post ironic tattooists.

Seventeenth century diarist John Evelyn was a contemporary of, and regular correspondent with, Samuel Pepys, although the latter's work has gone on to be the more famous of the two.

Evelyn provided commentary on London life, politics, the arts, architecture, environmental issues and major events of the time, including both the Great Plague and the Great Fire of London in the 1660s. He was a founder member of the Royal Society and was commissioned to write by Charles II, but never found the company of the Restoration Court to his liking, describing their conversation as "fruitless, vicious and empty".

Evelyn lived in Deptford from 1652 at Sayes Court, a house owned by his wife's family. The house became famous for the garden which John Evelyn designed and landscaped.

On the Evelyn Archive, the British Library says: "The collection is enormously rich and varied, consisting of 605 numbered manuscripts and approximately a hundred further volumes, boxes and bundles of letters and papers. As well as the original manuscript of the Diary, the archive contains Evelyn's extensive correspondence including letters from some of the most notable figures of his day, Samuel Pepys, Sir Thomas Browne, Grinling Gibbons, Robert Boyle and Sir Christopher Wren to name only a few."

On Evelyn the man they add: "Hitherto John Evelyn has principally been known from his Diary. The Archive allows him to be seen in his true milieu, that of the community of seventeenth century intellectuals who aimed to establish a major programme of scientific and technological development, linked with social and economic progress. He emerges as this community's most long-lived and versatile member: scholar, connoisseur, bibliophile and horticulturalist, as well as a writer and thinker of sometimes startlingly current relevance."

In 1884 a descendant of John Evelyn approached the social reformer Octavia Hill with a wish to see land from the Sayes Court estate given over for public use and the house to be made available as a museum. At the time no such body existed to support such an offer. It took ten years for one to be formed by which time the opportunity for Sayes Court to come under their ownership had passed, but Deptford can lay claim to being involved in the foundation of the National Trust, for that is the organisation that was formed.

Modern day Sayes Court appears to be mostly council housing; we took a quick look down a side street but found nothing of any real excitement.

At first there seemed to be nothing memorable, or even noteworthy about Evelyn Street either, but the great thing about walking the streets of London in an open-minded way, looking for things to catch your attention, is that soon you'll be rewarded, no matter how small your discovery might be.

The residential landscape was given a splash of colour by the sign for a children's centre. A fairly boring looking brick building was made unmissable by huge, brightly-coloured tubes stuck onto the fence, spelling out the name Clyde in purple, yellow, red, green and orange.

Colours aside, Clyde was unremarkable on its own; it was the first of a row of buildings each of which appeared to be from an era unrelated to its neighbour.

Next door to Clyde stands a Georgian town house, home to a boutique spa and café, and alongside that St Luke's Church, built in 1870, more recently than we'd thought, which was hiding behind scaffolding.

The quartet was completed by a traditional fire station, hopefully still with pole inside.

The contrast between the four, and the relatively new appearance of the children's centre made me wonder whether this is evidence of World War II bomb damage, perhaps a second Georgian house took a direct hit?

As we considered this question Abi told me of a work colleague, now in his fifties, who grew up in South London and who tells stories of playing in post war rubble as a child. It's amazing to think how much these areas have improved in the lifetime of people we mix with during our daily lives.

As St Luke's church was clearly out of action a board was pointing anyone looking for an alternative worshiping spot to head for the nearby St Nicholas' - not on the marathon course. For more information we were encouraged to visit Deptfordchurch.org. When I

109

did, I found the following story explaining the believed origin of the skull and crossbones symbol.

"The famous flag of piracy sent shivers down the spine of unfortunate mariners whenever they came across it, but where did the flag originate? Legend has it that the flag was based on the skulls which still stand on the gate posts of St Nicholas'."

The website explains how an economic and maritime war was fought at sea for centuries over trade routes between Europe and the Americas, Africa and the Indian sub-continent. This battle for supremacy was largely contested by Britain, France, Spain and Holland, often by private ships outside the control of the Royal Navy.

British ships not wishing to display their nationality needed a new flag, one which would also strike fear into the heart of those they were approaching. As many of these ships would depart from Deptford it is believed they took inspiration from the symbol outside their local church. Given the importance religion played in British life it seems reasonable to assume those displaying what became known as the Jolly Roger believed a link to St Nicholas' gained them protection from God.

On the opposite side of Evelyn street The Black Horse pub looked an acquired taste, with Millwall FC flags in the window and a poster advertising their 'gentleman's evening' where exotic dancers are brought in to entertain the locals. I wonder how the chaps would respond if one of these ladies reveals, along with everything else, that she supports West Ham?!

A surprise was waiting for us at number 35. We discovered several pieces of street art, graffiti and murals during this stretch of the marathon course, with one of the best examples being an excellently-detailed picture of John Lennon, looking a little out of place, close to a business centre.

As Evelyn Street gives way to Lower Road, the trophy of regeneration and resurgence in this part of London looms ahead of us in the shape of the Surrey Quays shopping centre. We didn't go in; it's probably no better or worse a way of spending the afternoon than Brent Cross or Westfield.

Look on a map and this area's international diversity throughout the centuries stares back at you in the form of dock, street, park and church names. Quebec Way, Canada Water, Greenland Dock, Russia Dock Woods; as we went further into Rotherhithe we discovered a strong Scandinavian presence, noticing places of worship for the Norwegians and Finns.

Turning into Redriff Road, we stumbled across a relic of the dock era, in the form of a dockers shelter.

The men who worked in the shipyards had no contracts, and would arrive early each morning to discover whether they had employment that day. They would gather in shelters such as the one we were standing by, which looks like a large brick bus shelter and must have provided little comfort or protection from the elements in winter. Men would huddle together each morning, probably in the dark, desperately hoping for good news that they'd been chosen for a long, body-breaking shift. The alternative, whilst less exhausting, meant no pay.

Of all the historical locations I found around the marathon course, this was one of the simplest yet most evocative. What would the atmosphere have been like each morning? Would there have been communal comradeship? Each man knowing what his fellow workers were going through, the tough day which potentially lay ahead, and the even tougher prospect if there would be no work this time. Or, did the competitive desire to be the chosen one over-ride any mutual appreciation of he who waited alongside? Was there a pecking order for jobs? Did the mob rule, as it does in 'On the Waterfront', the 1950s film starring Marlon Brando depicting union violence and corruption in the docks of New York?

Inside the shelter is a mural in tribute to the lives of those who stood here, day in, day out. Old copies of the South London Press, pictures of dockers going to work, national identity cards, and school tickets which gave a child's name, the name of the school they attended and their pupil registration number.

You can learn a lot from a well-curated exhibition, but although this shelter was directly opposite a giant retail complex with South London traffic as a backdrop, I felt it gave as good an impression of dock life as anything you'll find in a clean, air-conditioned museum. I was really pleased the shelter was still there and hadn't been knocked down. Sadly, but unsurprisingly it smelt of urine - nice to know the locals show it the respect it deserves!

A Docklands Heritage Trail sign directed us to take a walk down to the edge of the dock, which we did, passing another relic: an enormous lump of metal which, on closer inspection, turned out to be a winch.

The Greenland Dock, originally the Howland Great Wet Dock, was built between 1695 and 1699 on land owned by the Duke of Bedford. Greenland whalers used the dock from the 1720s, which led to the eventual renaming as Greenland Dock. A number of blubber boiling houses, which sound lovely, were built to produce oil.

By the end of the 18th century the whaling trade had declined, with timber becoming the main cargo brought into Greenland Dock. In 1807 it was taken over by the Commercial Dock Company, merging with Surrey Dock in the 1860s to form the Surrey Commercial Docks.

Greenland was the oldest of the Surrey Docks, which existed in various forms between the 1690s and 1960s. At their peak there were nine docks, six timber ponds and one canal, covering an area roughly 85 percent of the Rotherhithe peninsula.

Firstly bomb damage from World War II, and then the rise in container shipping which required larger docks, brought an end to centuries of shipyards in this part of London - both north and south of the Thames.

The Surrey Docks area lay largely derelict through the 1970s, which must have made this a pretty grim part of town. The first few years of the London Marathon will have experienced the end of this period, as the London Docklands Development Corporation was formed in 1981. The shopping centre, one of the major parts in this regeneration, opened in 1988.

As the marathon has grown, so too has the stock of the Surrey Docks, now known as Surrey Quays. Runners do a loop around the shopping centre and leisure complex, cinema, bowling alley, Mecca Bingo - our Saturday afternoon was sorted. However we had other ideas, our map showed us the intriguing prospect of an inner London woodland which presented a more tempting prospect than spending the rest of the day in the company of South London OAPs and/or hen parties crossing out numbers on a piece of card.

How have I never heard about Russia Dock Woods?

Turning off the road to the left we followed a path into a park and were soon surrounded by willow, oak and silver birch trees.

A wooden footbridge crossed a stream, with a metal arch decorated with birds and a squirrel, and the name Alfred Salter written on it. The bridge is named as a memorial to Dr Salter, who set up a medical practice in Bermondsey at the end of the 19th century, offering healthcare for free to anyone who couldn't afford to pay for it. The area was predominantly working class and with a high level of poverty, bad sanitation and poor air quality. Dr Salter had been a Labour MP between 1923 and 1945 and his work was a forerunner to the formation of the National Health Service under the post war Labour government.

For brief moments, between the sound of aeroplanes, sirens and a helicopter, the only noise was that of the wind in the trees. You could easily lose yourself and any sense of time, in here and pretend you're in the countryside as the woods had a real secluded feel to them. That is until another plane rumbles over head.

Continuing through the trees we reached a clearing, wherein we found a large metal mooring chain fixed to the ground by concrete. The path changed from a dirt track to a granite strip, which we later found out was left over from the time when it had been the side of a canal. When the docks closed in the 1970s, the water was drained away from the Grand Surrey Inner Dock and the space was filled in. Nature ponds were created and the woodlands planted either side of the old quayside, across an area of 34.5 acres.

In the next clearing we discovered a circle of sculptures made from sections of trees. It looked a bit like the kind of place the Rotherhithe druid society might hang out, if there is such a group; and in the centre, was the most amazing school project I think I've ever seen. Welcome to the Stave Hill Ecological Park.

Children from St John's School had drawn pictures of birds, hedgehogs and butterflies, and a nature treasure map marking where different types of wildlife can be seen.

We learnt that the large pond, which we passed on our walk through the wood, has rushes and reeds and is popular with the local heron who likes to visit to find small fish and frogspawn to eat. The pond has water in it all year round and is kept clean by chalk around its edge. Primrose Bank is a popular sunbathing spot for foxes, whilst hedgehogs live in the hedge which surrounds the clearing.

The map also marked a story teller's chair and where rhubarb could be found growing in a vegetable garden. I was particularly taken by the idea of Goblin Wood, where the children had made goblins to live in the trees out of drink bottles and plastic bags, so part science project, part storybook fantasyland. Could there be anything not to like about this place?

Via the medium of art and getting out of the classroom, kids had been taught about nature and biology, and that rubbish they'd normally chuck away can be used creatively. No doubt teamwork, and the satisfaction of producing something this impressive, were also important life skills to learn, even if subtly disguised among everything else.

As someone who had a hit or miss relationship with teachers at school, I either got them and their subjects or I didn't; I loved the work of St John's school. Had my school used art to teach science they may well have had me at 'hello', but as it was, I found it all rather dull and uninspiring. Geography - an interest in the world around me - being the only subject that wasn't the arts or sport which I had any interest in.

Walking away from the ecological park en route back to the reality of roads and traffic, Abi suddenly stopped in her tracks.

"Hear that running water? There's a pond, and next to it a rather lovely small trickley waterfall, and some stepping stones, which we've now got to try and negotiate without getting our feet wet. This could go badly wrong for both of us."

Who'd have thought we'd find stepping stones in an inner London park? We could have been in the New Forest, Yorkshire Dales or the Lake District rather than the London Borough of Southwark!

On leaving the park, feet successfully dry - well done us - we found a large compass on the ground highlighting the directions and distances that certain cargo had arrived from, timber of various forms from Finland, Russia, North Africa and Canada, tea, cotton and spices from India, and dairy products from the US. With the creation of the woodland in 1980, imports were still coming to the former docks, this time fast-growing plants from places as far apart as Sumatra and Norway.

Before industrialisation took hold of the banks of the Thames, this area was covered in marshland used for grazing cattle. One thought as to the origin of the name Rotherhithe is from an Anglo-Saxon word 'hryder' meaning cattle, and 'hyd', meaning land or haven.

And we were about to see some actual cows for ourselves, as signposts on Salter Road direct visitors to Surrey Docks Farm, one of a number to be found in inner city London.

Surrey Docks Farm is right on the riverside. Whilst not very large it's home to every animal you'd expect: cows, chickens, goats, children being given donkey rides, even a turkey! We saw nature's amusing juxtaposition between the residents of the farm and London's pigeon population who'd long since figured out there was easy feeding to be found here.

Someone who seemed to be having a harder time finding their lunch was a pig. So certain was he that a plastic tub contained food, he'd up-ended it with his snout and was now frantically pushing it around the pen. His grunts and the sound of the tub thudding and scraping on the floor could be heard from anywhere on the farm. A notice on the fence sternly warned anyone who might want to stroke this aggressive looking beast that sticking a hand into the pen was not a good plan. I certainly wasn't tempted; it looked like this fella could have your arm off at the first opportunity.

The run around the Rotherhithe peninsular takes in roads with names inspired by local history. Redriff was an alternative name for the area, especially the waterfront until the 19th century.

In 'Gulliver's Travels', or 'Travels into Several Remote Nations of the World. In Four Parts, by Lemuel Gulliver, First a surgeon, and then a Captain of several Ships' to give it its full, wonderful original title, Lemuel sets out on his adventures meeting the little people of Lilliput and the seventy foot tall giants of Broddingnag, from the port of Redriff.

As well as Dr Alfred, Ada Salter, his wife, is also an important local historical figure, becoming London's first female mayor in 1922 when elected to lead the council in Bermondsey.

We're back on Salter Road now, a largely residential street which is the definition of suburban London. We got a little disorientated by the number of roads that appear to connect Salter Road with Rotherhithe Street, where the farm is, but which mostly led into dead ends, when we eventually did make it back onto the marathon course we were further confused by the appearance of Russia Dock Woods on our right hand side. For a moment we wondered if we'd totally lost our bearings and were heading back towards Deptford, but then we spotted the underpass connecting the main wood, which we'd been exploring earlier, with a smaller extra bit on the opposite side of the street.

For a road which wasn't that busy, there were a lot of subways which, coupled with the 1980s houses on either side, led Abi to comment that it "looked a bit like Milton Keynes, only bendier".

Salter Road appears to be a perfectly nice, relatively quiet place to live. Someone was playing a saxophone in one of the gardens, with the smell of a barbecue drifting across the road. We discovered the Lavender Pond Nature Reserve, where the nature seemed very reserved given that it was hiding behind a fence. We soon found a viewing platform, although ducks and reeds were about all that was on show today. As we were considering the question of whether different coloured ducks meant different breeds, a heron majestically flew in, in such a way that suggested he'd been waiting for an audience before joining the nature party. Could this be the same heron who likes to go hunting for small fish and frogs born in Russia Dock Woods?

More houses, flats, trees and occasional water soon led us to an intriguing, three storey high round brick tower on the left hand side of the road which, on closer inspection, turned out to be the Rotherhithe Tunnel airshaft. Not the most glamorous of finds, but worth telling you about, if for no other reason than it was constructed by an engineer called Maurice Fitzmaurice - I do love names like that! It was built between 1904 and 1908 and is now a listed structure.

Suddenly we were faced with a variety of historically-named pubs to satisfy our well-earned thirst. Lord Nelson may well have had some connection with Rotherhithe, I'm not so convinced Adam and Eve are noted south Londoners though, so we decided on one round the back of the Brunel Museum whose local claim to fame cannot be disputed.

Built in the 17th century, The Mayflower has been a favoured drinking spot for many illustrious adventurers, including Christopher Jones who set sail in the Mayflower in the 1620s in search of the new world.

And so it was that two well-travelled, highly-experienced and hungry explorers began their own journey of discovery, through the door to the bar in search of the advertised lamb madras and 'fine selection of traditional ales'.

Chapter 9: 'Caliban's Dream' - Rotherhithe to Tower Bridge

"Be not afeard; the isle is full of noises, sounds and sweet airs, that give delight, and hurt not.

"Sometimes a thousand twangling instruments will hum about mine ears; and sometimes voices that, if I then had wak'd after long sleep, will make me sleep again; and then, in dreaming, the clouds methought would open and show riches ready to drop upon me; that, when I wak'd, I cried to dream again."

A speech by Caliban in Shakespeare's The Tempest, delivered by Kenneth Branagh from on top of the Glastonbury Tor in the middle of the Olympic Stadium. Branagh was in character as Isambard Kingdom Brunel during the Green and Pleasant Land segment of the London Olympic opening ceremony, demonstrating the dawning of a new industrial era in Britain which I.K. Brunel was very much a pioneering figure within.

Brunel's work played a major part in an opening ceremony which was universally acclaimed as a triumph. Personally I've never liked opening ceremonies. When I had the opportunity to go to the Manchester Commonwealth Games opener in 2002 I watched it on TV from London. At the time people said I'd regret doing that; I still don't.

Danny Boyle managed to achieve the seemingly impossible, to show Britain to the world in a way that touched every emotion, appealed to all tastes, and said pride in a genuine, non awkwardly British, over the top, stage-managed sort of way. I, along with many I know started to watch, as much in hope that it wouldn't be dreadful. Boyle had me at the appearance of Frank Turner performing during the prologue, and by the time Paul McCartney was on stage four hours later, Great Britain knew these Olympics were actually going to be alright, and I wanted to watch it all again. That said, I was slightly disappointed that Isles wasn't spelt aisles and we weren't treated to the stadium show version of Dale's Supermarket Sweep.

The musical soundtrack was perfect, from the choice of Underworld as main composers to the performers on stage, supported by clips of British music which always worked. We all laughed at Mr Bean playing 'Chariots of Fire' and nobody sneered at the inclusion of 'My Boy Lollipop'.

Our first sight of Brunel's work came during the countdown film via historical shots of the Thames Tunnel, before the worldwide audience was taken through the Rotherhithe Tunnel back to the Olympic Stadium, accompanied by the fantastic Muse song 'Map of the Problematique'.

And it's Brunel's Rotherhithe where we are now.

Having been trapped by the Mayflower - Abi to enjoy its views and prime riverside location and me it's catering - we returned to Rotherhithe a few weeks later in order to fill in the final section of the London Marathon course before Tower Bridge.

Our day began closer to the marathon finish line at Embankment tube station, meeting point for one of the Brunel Museum's regular tours. It's a very relaxed affair, same time, Saturday morning at 10:45, same place, riverside exit of Embankment station, no booking required, just show up. You're taken by Thames Clipper on a journey which includes several of the Brunel family's most famous works, as well as many of London's iconic sights. For me it's a nice reminder of what London Marathon runners pass in the closing miles.

This week there are around thirty of us. Our guide introduced himself as an actor and musician and no doubt impressed many in our party with the revelation that he appeared in 'Four Weddings and a Funeral', but this was nothing compared to the discovery that we were about to spend the morning in the company of Tim Thomas, who not only co-wrote, but sang the Rainbow theme tune!

I'd have quite happily got off the boat right then, how could Thomas tell me anything more exciting? As by then we were in the middle of the Thames and speeding downstream I stayed where I was. As we left Waterloo behind us Abi pointed out that she thought the busker we passed on the way over Hungerford Bridge might have been playing the Rainbow tune on the steel drum; should we tell Tim he had some royalties to claim?

On a sunny morning there can't be many better ways to see the sights of London than from a boat. I hope someone taking the Thames Clipper for the first time doesn't think there will always be a man pointing out famous landmarks, but it was certainly a bit of unexpected value for money for the Saturday morning traveller fortunate enough to be in earshot.

Three generations of Brunels have their work on show along the Thames. French engineer Marc, his son Isambard Kingdom and grandson Henry Marc.

Isambard Kingdom Brunel is perhaps most famous for designing Bristol's Clifton Suspension Bridge; at the time its span of over 700 feet made it the longest suspension bridge in the world. Delays to the project due to riots in the Clifton area driving investors away meant I.K. Brunel never saw the bridge completed. Among those brought in to finish the project were John Hawkshaw, engineer for the railway line which ran through the Brunel Tunnel from Wapping to Rotherhithe, and William Barlow whose plaque in Charlton is passed by runners on the London Marathon red route.

I.K. Brunel designed many bridges across the Thames including railway crossings at Windsor and Maidenhead, plus Hungerford - the foot bridge close to Waterloo and Charing Cross stations. When a railway crossing replaced it in 1859 the suspension chains were used in the completion of the Clifton Bridge. Whilst we can't see Brunel's foot bridge in London anymore, the original supports still stand in the river today.

Another bridge which no longer stands is the original railway crossing at Blackfriars. Now only the columns remain from the bridge which was built in 1864, but it's the current Blackfriars Railway Bridge which has the Brunel Legacy. Opened in 1886 and co-designed by Henry Marc, it was named St Paul's Bridge until the station it served changed to Blackfriars in 1937.

The modern day structure sees the

124

station platforms run out across the river - you wait for your Thameslink train with the water flowing beneath you. The 1864 piers partially support the extended platforms.

What is less well known is the Brunel connection to Tower Bridge. Henry Marc formed a partnership with John Wolfe-Barry in 1878, and the pair designed Blackfriars Railway Bridge together. Wolfe-Barry was the chief engineer for Tower Bridge.

All the while Tim was building up to the moment where he could highlight the exact point at which we crossed the Brunel tunnel. As his big moment arrived he was interrupted by an automated female voice reminding us to read the safety leaflet provided.

We leave the boat on the north bank opposite Greenwich and are shown the spot where the Great Eastern was launched. Completed in 1858 she was the largest ship in the world at the time, with the capacity to carry 4,000 passengers non-stop around the globe without refuelling. Later in this book we pass a plaque on the wall of Burrell's Wharf on Westferry Road which marks the location, but it's more impressive from the riverside. A u-shaped landscaped patch of grass faces the river, surrounded by the obligatory new build. A fenced-off area has parts of the wooden structure used to launch the ship. Being too long to go in bow or stern first, the ship had to enter the river sideways. As Tim was explaining this, a couple of women standing behind me let out horrified gasps at the thought of the ship hitting the opposite bank - all very over the top.

A great example of how ahead of his time

I.K. Brunel was, the Great Eastern was designed with a double hull. Now all ships are built this way. Had the Titanic had a double hull as it set sail in 1912, over 50 years after the Great Eastern, the iceberg probably wouldn't have struck a fatal blow.

By this time I was beginning to wonder how we were getting back to Rotherhithe, imagining an epic walking tour taking us through the Greenwich Foot Tunnel and along the riverside, but on reaching Island Gardens we headed for the Docklands Light Railway to take the quicker and more logical route back.

Once on London Overground, which at Shadwell is reached by descending several flights of stairs below ground, we headed for the finale of the tour. We must have made a confusing sight for our fellow passengers, arriving en masse and alighting after just one stop at Wapping, gathering in a large group on the platform. Tim was giving the next stage of the tour the big build up, explaining that we were about to enter the world's oldest tunnel to run under a navigable river. I'd love to tell you what else he said, but he was drowned out by the arrival of a train to Highbury and Islington on the opposite platform.

Back on the train, this one going to the well known tourist attraction of West Croydon, we hurtled through the historic underwater crossing in a matter of minutes. I really think Transport for London should have a special announcement before you leave Wapping or Rotherhithe stations, as, to the average traveller, this must look like any other stretch of tunnel. It was a grandad Brunel project, the 16 year old

Isambard joined the team fresh out of school a year after the first workman had gone underground.

Writing in a foreword in 'The Brunel Tunnel', a book produced by the museum which I bought at the end of our tour, Michael Palin says of its construction:

"The story of Brunel's tunnel under the Thames is a fine combination of drama, farce, ingenuity, showmanship and sheer engineering chutzpah, the like of which we shall probably never see again. In a modern world of cost-overruns and wringing of hands when any great national building is delivered a few months late, it's worth remembering that this pioneering tunnel under the Thames took over fifteen years, or almost five hundred percent longer to complete than had originally been estimated."

The accompanying timeline reads as a list of floodings, strikes against unhealthy working conditions, financial uncertainty and attempts to convince the general public and, more importantly the money men, that this was a project which could and would work. The very fact that no tunnel had ever been built under a river the size of the Thames before, it's no surprise that as it often filled with water, convincing those who mattered that this was a worthwhile exercise must have often seemed a thankless task. The Brunels' way of doing this was to invite anyone and everyone who had cash and might invest, to a sit-down banquet in the half-built tunnel. The event was immortalised in a painting by George Jones, but what I'd love to know is what the invitations said?

Back above ground, it's raining now.

There's a mural on the wall of a train with drawings of animals and fish peering through the windows. On the side of the road next to the Brunel Museum is a hatch which, when opened, reveals a hole into which we're to descend for the final part of the tour. First we must negotiate a series of metal ledges fastened to the wall which act as foot and hand supports. Next it's a crawl of a few metres through a tunnel no taller than to allow for the average sized human to crouch down, and for us to proceed in single file. This is not the tour to be carrying a large bag with you. Even as proper grown ups there's nothing quite like the thrill of climbing on or crawling through things.

The adventure is completed by some exciting scaffolding stairs which brought us down into a large, circular space, perhaps two floors tall and twenty metres long. We're triumphantly welcomed into the 8th wonder of the world - a label given to the tunnel by the never understated Victorians.

When the crossing was first opened, the floor, which our chairs were lined up on, didn't exist and pedestrians would have continued down to the level at which the trains were currently rumbling beneath our feet.

The first Londoners crossed their city under its river in 1843. We shouldn't underestimate what an extraordinary, and probably rather terrifying, idea the Brunel Tunnel was to the average person. As Michael Palin explains:

"Brunel knew that everything had to be done to coax the public down into this strange, somewhat threatening subterranean world, so they built a shopping arcade under the Thames, and in 1852 an underwater fair, where by the light of Boggett's patent Prismatic Reflectors visitors could enjoy watching Mr Green the celebrated Bottle Pantomimic Equilibrist or dancing to music of the Montreal Minstrels in a Ballroom 150 feet long."

Just as in the caves under Blackheath, and at the Charlton Horn Fair, excesses ran away with themselves with the party-pooping authorities stepping in to curb hedonistic enthusiasm.

When the railways arrived in the 1860s, crossing by train was considered a more attractive proposition than on foot, but the entry shaft remained for a century and a half. The room we'd clambered into was created during the redevelopment of the East London Line as part of the London Overground network during the early part of the 21st century. Now the museum has a programme of music events in the former entrance hall; this is certainly one of London's most interesting and atmospheric performance spaces. There's a bar set up down here; given the unusual way of entering, it must be an interesting challenge getting out again after an evening on the wine. The Friends of Brunel Museum are hoping to raise £100,000 to build a more conventional way in including a lift. Those with health and safety forms to fill in will sleep more easily at night when this happens. If you're feeling generous, this is a project well worth supporting.

Climbing back out of the hole in the ground I imagined for a few seconds that I was a Teenage Mutant Ninja Turtle. As it had been hours since breakfast time, and we'd done a considerable amount of exploring, this was not the time for invoking the motto "evil moves fast but good moves faster", nor relying on our Turtle Power on an empty stomach, so we went in search of lunch instead. Where's a Pizza Hut when you need one?

We looked in at the Adam and Eve, but there was a lot of quiet, attentive watching of football going on and, since, as everyone knows the Football League is better than the Premier League, we headed back to familiar ground of The Mayflower - for pie and mash this time. We're joined by two friends Jodie and Graeme, who point out that they can see their new flat on the opposite bank from the pub terrace. As the crow flies this is probably their 'local', but it involves a swim, a train ride, or significant detour by road, in order to nip out for a quick pint! We discuss whether it's possible to walk through the Rotherhithe Tunnel. We're not sure but don't think it would be pleasant if you can, and, as to walk home from here you'd need to go via Tower Bridge which is where Abi and I are heading, so Jodie and Graeme decide to join us for the rest of the afternoon.

As marathon runners approach the Brunel Museum, Salter Road becomes Brunel Road - they like naming their streets after significant locals round here. The Brunel Museum and The Mayflower are on the right but, instead of rejoining the course runners would take, as I'm interested in finding evidence of Scandinavian immigration for which this area is known, we take Albion Street, which soon bends round to run parallel with Brunel Road.

A flag pole, with a Finnish flag flying from it, tells us we're looking in the right place, and behind it is the Finnish Seaman's Mission, the newest built Scandinavian church in London, dating from 1958.

To cater for the large numbers of their seamen in foreign ports, each Scandinavian country founded an international seaman's mission. As most seamen arriving in London entered the Surrey Commercial Docks with the timber trade, Rotherhithe became the location for their churches.

The first two of these churches built in London were north of the river in Wapping: first a Danish church in Wellclose Square in 1696, thanks to a donation from the then King of Denmark, followed by a Swedish church in 1723. The latter church closed in the early 20th century with the opening of another in Rotherhithe in the 1890s.

The first church for Norwegian seaman didn't arrive until the 1870s with the building of the Ebenezer Church close to the Commercial Dock Pier. In 1927 worshipers moved to a much larger church, St Olav's on Albion Street.

The drizzle had evolved into proper rain. As our new companions were not suitably attired for a walk in the wet, having only really popped out for a quick trip to Surrey Quays Shopping Centre, there was the desire for an impulsive umbrella purchase. The Albion Street Community Shop across the road from the Finnish church looked a likely target and, after some searching, the lady behind the counter produced an enormous brolly which could keep all four of us dry if necessary. The girls emerged having bought shoes and a picture frame - you can buy what you like as long as you don't expect me to carry it - and on we went. A flier we picked up told us that the shop exists to "provide long term community benefit through a niche but quality attraction". Once the overheads are paid, any money left over is divided between four local churches: the Finnish and Norwegian ones on Albion Street, plus the nearby St Mary's and St Peter's.

The Finnish and Norwegian churches, along with Southwark council and community groups, organise a large Christmas market on Albion Street which draws a reported 20,000 people.

During the Second World War many governments exiled from their own countries sought headquarters in London. The Norwegians came to Rotherhithe using St Olav's Church. It can be seen from the roundabout where Brunel, Lower and Jamaica Roads and the entrance to the Rotherhithe Tunnel meet. A plaque on the wall tells us that "Crown Prince Harald of Norway named this St Olav's Square on November 25th 1990". Should you need a starting point to learn some Norwegian the same words appear in that language too. Perhaps unsurprisingly, the weather vane on the church's roof is in the shape of a ship.

Interesting though the church was, we were all more excited to discover a dog-grooming shop called Mucky Pups on the other side of the roundabout. We were also drawn to a metal sculpture in the middle, depicting a man on a racing bike. As looking for an inscription would involve taking our lives in our hands, and playing

132

chicken with the traffic, I know nothing more about it.

For a short distance Jamaica Road has park on either side: Southwark Park, complete with a bandstand built in 1884 on the left, and King's Stairs Gardens on the right. There's a rose garden in Southwark Park, named in memory of Ada Salter who was elected as Labour's mayor of Bermondsey in 1922 making her the first female mayor in London. Among her other noteworthy achievements were to be part of the British delegation to the 'Women's International League for Peace and Freedom' conventions in Zurich and Vienna after the First World War, and, as a member of the London County Council, she was chair of the Parks Committee in the 1930s, working to introduce a Green Belt around the capital.

Today, wedding photos are taking place in Southwark Park. I feel they have us to thank for the rain stopping in time for their big moment; the charity shop umbrella never performed any task other than to be carried. Could the wedding have been responsible for the deflated pink balloon one of our party spotted, now looking rather sad in a tree?

Having three pairs of eyes with me instead of the usual one meant I received a mixture of information which was interesting, amusing, and at times completely useless, like for example a critique of the fashionableness, or not, of the ladies in the wedding party. In addition to the random spot of the balloon, I can tell you that there were mushrooms growing on the roundabout, there was bunting hanging on what we thought was a nursery – kids party alert – and that the hill in King's Stairs Gardens looked good for rolling down.

King's Stairs Gardens is an extension to Southwark Park opened in 1982. At the time of writing this book the park is under threat, with Thames Water having identified the area as a possible location for digging a large shaft, 100 feet wide and 250 deep, as part of the proposals to create a 30 mile super sewer - the Thames Tideway Tunnel, to give it its official name. Whilst the company says this is not their preferred location, a cloud still hangs over the future of the park as it remains on their 'shortlist'.

The 'Save King's Stairs Gardens Action Group' website paints a picture of an area of land surrounded by residential property, providing much-needed open space for those living in the area.

"The park has been designated as a Site of Importance for Nature Conservation. It contributes to an unbroken green corridor from Surrey Quays to the Thames. King's Stairs Gardens has many mature trees and provides an important mix of habitats which is important to local wildlife."

On a damp Saturday it's deserted, but is no doubt extremely popular when the sun comes out. I guess Thames Water has got to dig their sewage shaft somewhere, but I hope they don't pick here!

Jamaica Road's main purpose appears to be to get you from one end of it to the other with minimal fuss, for a not especially noteworthy collection of residential and retail properties are to be found on either side. Those who reside on the Rotherhithe/Bermondsey border are well catered for if they need their nails done and don't want to spoil them by cooking their tea, for nail shops mingle with takeaways.

Bermondsey tube station is one of the places I'd recommend, if you ever want to watch the London Marathon from several places. The year I ran, my Dad came here before catching the Jubilee Line to Canary Wharf and, having spotted me for the second time, was back on the tube, getting off at Waterloo and using the Brunel family legacy to cross the river via Hungerford Bridge to Embankment.

During the Brunel's London river walk, Tim Thomas highlighted comparisons between Isambard Kingdom Brunel and Charles Dickens - two British icons revered worldwide. Both revolutionary thinkers in their field, whose influence and legacies were felt long after their deaths, both men died at the age of 53 leaving behind them a body of work which was ahead of their time. And it is the work of Dickens we come to next. As Jamaica Road runs through Bermondsey, it takes us to the location of the climax of Oliver Twist.

At the beginning of chapter 50, 'The Pursuit and Escape', Dickens writes:

"Near to the part of the Thames on which the church at Rotherhithe abuts, where the buildings on the banks are dirtiest and the vessels on the river are blackest with the dust of colliers and the smoke of close-built low-roofed houses, there exists the filthiest, the strangest, the most extraordinary of the many localities that are hidden in London, wholly unknown, even by name, to the great mass of its inhabitants.

"To reach this place, the visitor has to penetrate through a maze of close, narrow and muddy streets, thronged by the roughest and poorest of waterside people, and devoted to the traffic they may be supposed to occasion. The cheapest and least delicate provisions are heaped in the shops; the coarsest and commonest articles of wearing apparel dangle at the salesman's door; and stream from the house-parapet and windows. Jostling with unemployed labourers of the lowest class, ballast-heavers, coal-whippers, brazen women, ragged children and the raff and refuse of the river, he makes his way with difficulty along, assailed by offensive sights and smells from the narrow alleys which branch off on the right and left and deafened by the clash of ponderous wagons that bear great piles of merchandise from the stacks of warehouses that rise from every corner. Arriving at length, in streets remoter and less frequented than those through which he has passed, he walks beneath tottering house fronts projecting over the pavement, dismantled walls that seem to totter as he passes, chimneys half crushed half hesitating to fall, windows guarded by rusty iron bars the time and dirt have almost eaten away, every imaginable sign of desolation and neglect.

"In such a neighbourhood, beyond Dockhead in the borough of Southwark, stands Jacob's Island, surrounded by a muddy ditch six or eight feet deep and fifteen or twenty wide when the tide is in, once called Mill Pond, but known in the days of this story as Folly Ditch."

A graphic description in great detail of the notorious slum Jacob's Island where Dickens sent the robber Bill Sykes to meet his end in the mud of Folly Ditch. Dickens is thought to have visited the area with the river police, access which allowed him to paint such a vivid picture of a part of London many knew nothing of, and those who did would avoid if at all possible. Some politicians even tried to deny its existence due to the extreme poverty which could be found there.

"In Jacob's Island," Dickens wrote, "the warehouses are roofless and empty; the walls are crumbling down; the windows are windows no more; the doors are falling into the streets; the chimneys are blackened but they yield no smoke. Thirty or forty years ago before losses and chancery suits came upon it, it was a thriving place; but now it is a desolate island indeed. The houses have no owners; they are broken open and entered upon by those who have the courage; and there they live, and there they die. They must have powerful motives for a secret residence, or be reduced to a destitute condition indeed, who seek a refuge in Jacob's Island."

Today he or she, or in our case he and she, who venture to the part of the Thames, close to where the many churches of Rotherhithe stand, and who chooses to penetrate the streets alongside the bank of the Thames will find them to be dominated by posh flats, a mixture of redeveloped warehouses and expensive new builds. A look through an estate agent's window told us that a one or two bedroom flat would sell for one to two million pounds. One four-bed apartment was going for ten million!

A plaque marks the spot where Folly's Ditch used to divide Jacob's Island from the rest of this run-down part of London. It incorrectly

137

suggests that Fagin's den was located here; anyone who has read Oliver Twist knows this is not the case, for 'the Jew', as he was often referred to, mostly resided in an area closer to Clerkenwell.

The only relic of times gone by are bridges which cross some of the narrow streets and would, at one time, have linked warehouses allowing workers' rolling barrels to cross without coming to ground level. Now they're mostly balconies or small gardens for the owners of expensive flats.

The cobbled street called Shad Thames has given the wider area tucked in between the river and Tooley Street its current name. It's also referred to as Butler's Wharf, after the largest of the warehouse conversions. The Design Museum can be found here, as can plenty of expensive restaurants, owned by the likes of Terence Conran. To me 'Shad Thames' is the name of a fantastic instrumental track by St Etienne, who do seem to have named pieces of music after most areas of London.

Chapter 10: 'Watching the River Flow' - Tooley Street to East Smithfield

As the runners head towards the half way mark, they take a right turn, leaving Tooley Street to join the A100. Continuing for roughly 250 metres, that landmark they've had in mind since Blackheath has almost been reached. Just another road, a noticeable incline although nothing significant. London's a largely flat course, remember; then the small matter of a river crossing, another right, and there it is, 13.1 miles completed - simple. Do the same again and you're a successful marathon runner. No matter how many marathons I've run, reaching the halfway point remains a significant moment.

It would be simple, were the A100 just another road. You might know it by its other name, Tower Bridge.

Having been slightly underwhelmed by the atmosphere at Cutty Sark, and with previous experience of competing in front of a large crowd at the City of Manchester Stadium in 2002, I was more interested in reaching that half way point and being able to tick the next target off the list than what might be in store above the Thames. Yet, as I made that right turn and began the ascent up Tower Bridge Road I quickly realised this was different.

Football crowds are often described as being able to metaphorically suck a ball into the net. As you run up the slope to cross this iconic London landmark it's as if the thousands lining the road are reaching towards you, tucking their

139

arm through yours, lifting the weight from your feet and propelling you that next step on your way. You hear the noise of the crowd getting louder with each stride; I can imagine the lift this must give to those who are already struggling with the enormity of the challenge they've taken on.

Most people can only experience the atmosphere of a major sporting arena from the terraces or stands. Tower Bridge is the everyday runner's equivalent of walking out at Wembley or Twickenham, being an England cricketer during a home Ashes series or a boxer making their ring walk in front of their own fans; it's the opportunity to live the adrenalin rush of being hit by a wall of noise then carried by it on the quest for glory.

Even though there's nothing stopping the sound from escaping into the London air, and with the crowd packed in on both sides of the road, you feel as if you're running through a tunnel of noise. As I crossed Tower Bridge, even though in reality I'd probably slowed down, it felt as if I was working extra hard. Not because the support didn't lift me, but because it caught me by surprise. I actually felt a tightening across the chest - I can say for certain that the atmosphere at that point is literally breath-taking. Some people I know who have many more London marathons to their name than me say that, even though they know what's coming, it can still get them. Nothing comes close to matching this atmosphere anywhere I have run before or since not even the 2002 Commonwealth Games, the closing mile of the Berlin Marathon along the iconic stretch up to and through the

Brandenburg Gate, or the Embankment, a couple of hours after crossing Tower Bridge during 'London'.

Having been in the crowd as Bradley Wiggins was roared to victory in front of Hampton Court Palace in the Olympic cycling time trial, and experienced David Weir receiving similar support as he won gold in the wheelchair 5000m final in the Olympic Stadium during London 2012, I knew that I too have benefited from British sports fans' unrivalled ability to bellow at the top of their voices, whether they're familiar with who or what is in front of them or not.

Throughout the last thirteen miles I've been arguing there's more to the London Marathon than meets the eye. It's ironic that the point where we can all agree the route is as visually striking as any other big city marathon, the view is overshadowed by the atmosphere, and the impact of this famous river crossing isn't as strong as it might be. Many runners won't fully appreciate the views, either because they're swept along by the wave of noise - the crowd is so emotive there isn't enough time or opportunity to look around - or because Tower Bridge is such a significant target in the overall plan for getting from Blackheath to Buck House that they don't really care about scenery at this point.

Cross Tower Bridge on any other day of the year and you won't walk far before colliding with a camera-brandishing tourist in search of that city-defining photo opportunity. Take the lift to the high level walkway 110 feet above the road, and even the born and bred Londoner will be playing 'spot the famous building', then taking a picture on their phone because they live here and didn't think to bring a camera.

It was a crisp, cold, clear sunny Saturday in February - perfect running conditions in fact - but today I too have come to be a tourist. The Tower Bridge Exhibition offers visitors the chance to cross the river 139 feet above the water (that figure is the mean average high tide point), before descending to the Victorian engine room to see how the bridge would originally have been operated by steam.

After the Bridge's opening in 1894, the then uncovered high level walkways between the towers were only accessible by stairs, and with a perfectly adequate pedestrian crossing at road level, the walkways were seldom used by the public, developing a reputation as a haunt for prostitutes and pickpockets. They were closed in 1910, reopening in 1982 as part of the Tower Bridge Exhibition. As they are enclosed from the elements, which on a cold windy day as it was when I visited is probably a good thing, I couldn't help thinking the experience was lacking something by not providing the opportunity to be knocked about by whatever the weather feels like throwing at you.

We go up in the lift with an attendant whose job appears to be to go up and down all day telling people what they're about to see, reminding them that there's a gift shop to be trapped by, and hoping they enjoy their visit.

On reaching the top the first attraction is a rather odd film. The story of Tower Bridge's creation is told in what is described as an "entertaining and light-hearted way which will appeal to all ages". The film attempts to reconstruct a meeting held between Queen Victoria (who does the standard impression people adopt when trying to represent our current queen), Sir John Wolfe-Barry, the designer of Tower Bridge (who delivers his idea with Brian Blessed-like gusto), and bridge architect Sir Horace Jones.

The good news is that 'Vicky' seems to like their plan for the new river crossing and we're free to continue our visit - £6 is quite a lot simply to spend a few minutes in the company of a lift attendant! In fact £6 is actually extremely good value, especially when you consider that you pay four times that for a higher vantage point from the top of the Shard.

On this particular Saturday the East Walkway, giving views of Canary Wharf and South East London, is closed for maintenance work. Visitors are directed to the West Walkway which is on the side of the bridge that offers a greater number of recognisable land marks to look at.

A river crossing has stood on, or near, the site of London Bridge since AD50. By the 1860s the demand for further crossings had seen the building of bridges at both Westminster and Blackfriars. No new bridge was built east of London Bridge as the area immediately downstream had developed into a major port.

A tunnel was built in 1869 which connected Tower Hill and the wonderfully named Pickle Herring Stairs near Vine Lane (off Tooley Street), and for its first year people were ferried across in a wooden carriage. After just a few months the operating company went bankrupt and the crossing was converted into a pedestrian toll tunnel. In his Dictionary of London, Charles Dickens Jr commented on the smallness of the tunnel. "There is not much headroom left and it is not advisable for any but the briefest of Her Majesty's lieges to attempt the passage in high heeled boots or with a hat to which he attaches any particular value."

With traffic journey times over existing crossings lasting up to several hours, in 1876 the City of London Corporation requested design submissions for a new bridge. Fifty were received, but none met the varied list of criteria that would allow for tall mast ships to pass underneath, whilst at the same time not significantly impacting on road traffic.

It wasn't until Sir Horace and Sir John got their heads together to produce a design in 1884, that the 'Special Bridge or Subway Committee' was satisfied.

And their plan? Steam-powered bascules would lift as and when tall ships needed to pass underneath. The machinery which powered Tower Bridge was designed to operate as quickly as possible so as not to significantly interrupt traffic flow. Bascule is the French word for seesaw; the bridge concept evolved from the idea of a drawbridge.

Construction of Tower Bridge took eight years. Sir Horace Jones never saw the project completed as he died in 1887. This shiny new bridge meant the end for the nearby tunnel; Londoners took the not unreasonable view of: why pay the halfpenny toll to use a tunnel when you could cross a bridge for free? The tunnel now carries water mains.

The Tower Bridge Exhibition guidebook

gives this account from The Times of the Bridge's Royal opening:

"On Saturday 30 June 1894, there was only one place to be - as near to Tower Bridge as possible. For this was the day of its spectacular Royal opening, when it seemed all of London had turned out to raise a cheer.

"All over the bridge and round about, there were flags and bunting, flowers and crimson cloth as far as the eye could see. The river too was awash with vessels big and small - barges, sailing boats and steamships - many booked weeks in advance by those keen to catch the best view.

"All eyes were on the carriage carrying the Prince and Princess of Wales as they drove from Buckingham Palace to Tower Bridge, past the crowds in Pall Mall, along The Strand, down Fleet Street and past St Paul's Cathedral to Mansion House. Here they were joined by the Lord Mayor, the Sheriffs and a colourful escort of Life Guards.

"When the royal couple arrived at Tower Bridge it was to the sound of stirring music, courtesy of the Band of the Royal Artillery. But this was soon drowned by the roars of the crowd as the carriage crossed and re-crossed the bridge.

"They finally halted before the Royal Pavilion extravagantly draped in pink and green and covered in pale pink roses. Here the Prince of Wales, on behalf of his mother Queen Victoria, solemnly turned a special silver cup that was mounted on a pedestal and linked to the hydraulic equipment and declared Tower Bridge open.

"Up rose the bascules, silently and with

such majesty that the noisy crowd for a moment became hushed…until a great cheer erupted, all but drowning out the guns of the Tower of London and the Bishop of London's blessing.

"Their duty over, the royals returned to Westminster in the Palm, a steamboat owned by the Victoria Steamboat Association. But if they were on their way home, the crowd were most certainly not. And the happiest party must have been that taking place on the south shore of the Thames, where all those involved in the building of the bridge, together with their wives and children, were being treated to the day out of their lives."

It's easy to imagine how this magnificent structure was greeted with an outpouring of public celebration. Those in attendance would have talked about that day for the rest of their lives. The guidebook goes on to mention a lady named Beatrice Quick who had crossed Tower Bridge on that first day. Still with us in 1982, she was invited to attend the opening of the Bridge as a tourist attraction, following a £2.5 million facelift. We can only imagine what would have gone through her mind, given the transformation our city has seen in her lifetime.

Once again the public were able to cross the river from on high, an opportunity that provides one of the best vantage points to admire what London has to offer. On a clear day the Wembley Stadium arch can be seen standing proudly in the distance. In the foreground is a panorama of some of London's most famous landmarks. A helpful sign tells you what each of them is, especially useful as some are quite tricky to spot if you're not sure where to look.

146

On the south side, closest to the bridge is City Hall, home of the Greater London Authority. Next in line is Guy's Hospital, dwarfed by its new neighbour The Shard, which divides opinion between a masterpiece of contemporary architecture and a building that looks like it's not quite finished. Either way, visitors are welcome to spend the best part of 25 quid to look at London from the top.

Peeping out in the background is the London Eye. Even though it only arrived for the Millennium, the idea of a London skyline without it seems hard to imagine now.

An ever-present landmark I knew virtually nothing about is HMS Belfast. The warship is moored on the south bank of the Thames and is clearly visible from Tower Bridge. It wasn't until I read up on it for researching this book that I realised you could look round it - I've no idea what I thought it did all day.

Across the water, working from west to east the Tower Bridge building-spotter can observe the BT Tower, St Paul's Cathedral and the Old Billingsgate Market. Now a City of London events and hospitality venue, this building was once home to the world's largest fish market. Built in 1875, like Tower Bridge, this was another of Sir Horace's creations.

I cover the north bank locations in more detail later, as the marathon course passes by, or close to, many of them including my first visit to the Tower of London since schooldays, and climbing the Monument.

Look to your right from the Tower Bridge Walkway and it's like the crazy funsters in the City have organised a novelty building competition. There's The Gherkin - for those who don't know it's a large office block which looks a little like the bit no one wants to eat in a Big Mac. Then at 20 Fenchurch Street is the Walkie-Talkie, the building which can actually melt cars. In early September 2013 the owner of a Jaguar returned to his vehicle to find that part of it had melted due to intense heat generated by the sun reflecting from the 37 floor skyscraper.

The office block landscape is completed by Tower 42, which has a posh bar at the top, and Heron Tower that my friend Geraldine, who visited the Tower Bridge exhibition with me, said has an impressive fish tank in its reception area.

On the left hand side of the Tower Bridge West Walkway is a display entitled Great Bridges of the World. It's worth coming up here for this alone in order to marvel at some of the eccentric, extravagant, awe-inspiring, or just plain weird constructions people have built in order to get from one side of a big gap to the other. The Brooklyn, Golden Gate, and Sydney Harbour Bridges all feature, but two other bridges, in particular, caught my attention.

As I fancy running the Prague Marathon one day, I was reminded that those taking part in this event run across Charles Bridge, its official name being Karlův Most. This bridge gains its iconic status from the thirty statues that line the crossing and depict saints and patron saints that were venerated around the turn of the 18th Century. I hope they cheer loudly like the folk on Tower Bridge do.

Perhaps the most intriguing of all bridges is one which neither you nor I are likely to ever get close to. The Hangul Bridge, located in the

148

joint security area between North and South Korea, nicknamed the Bridge of No Return as it was used for prisoner exchanges at the end of the Korean War in 1953. Prisoners of war captured by the US army would be brought here and given the choice of staying in the country where they were being held, or crossing the border. If they opted for the latter, they could never go back.

Further along the Walkway is a section on significant events to happen on Tower Bridge; the London Marathon is summed up by one short statement: "the world's largest fundraising event". That does make a race that attracts the greatest runners in the world, which witnessed Paula Radcliffe set the women's world record in one of our country's finest sporting moments and has played a major role in boosting mass participation running in Britain, sound like a giant raffle.

The bridges' display also referred to a celebration event for Sir Francis Chichester; you'll remember from the Greenwich chapter that he was the one who built Gipsy Moth with the aim of beating the round the world sailing record set by Cutty Sark.

There's also a mention for American illusionist, endurance artist and all-round fruitcake David Blaine, who spent forty four days living in a transparent box suspended nine metres in the air, in a stunt titled 'Above the Below'. Blaine survived on just 4.5 litres of water a day; the box measured 3 feet by 7 feet by 7 feet and housed a webcam so viewers could tune in to see how he was getting on. Why people might want to watch a bloke sitting in a plastic box high above the Thames doing nothing at all is anyone's guess, but strangely enough they did, and the media covered it to saturation point. A decade on and I've still no idea what the point of it all was. Until the moment of reading about him at the Tower Bridge Exhibition I'd forgotten all about David Blaine. The best part about the stunt were the pranks which attempted to put him off, my favourite being flying a burger up to his box on a remote controlled helicopter.

One person not to be featured in the display is Australian daredevil motorbike rider Robbie Maddison. You may know him as Daniel Craig's motorbike stunt double in 'Skyfall'. On 13 July 2009, Maddison completed a bike jump over an open Tower Bridge, clearing it by 25 feet, and throwing in a cheeky mid-air back flip.

Maddo's motto "face your fears - live your dreams" is a pretty good mantra for life and would make a perfect inspirational banner to display on Tower Bridge on London Marathon day. The debutant runner's darkest moments are still to come as they leave the bridge and head for their circuit of the Isle of Dogs.

Having crossed the Walkway to the south side of the river, it's back down in the lift. Exiting via the shop, because who doesn't want the opportunity to buy a money box shaped like a post box, phone box or soldier, we follow a blue line with the rather cute addition of paw prints to the engine room part of the exhibition. Was Tower Bridge really powered by dogs?

I've always been fascinated by the idea of things being run by steam. It may well be a legacy of childhood - Thomas the Tank Engine, the bit in The Wind in the Willows where Toad escapes from prison dressed as a washerwoman and blags his way onto a steam train; maybe it's my appreciation of characters like Sherlock Holmes who existed in the era of coal, fire and water powered railway journeys.

As you walk round the engine room exhibition you're shown each piece of equipment that took lumps of coal and turned them into enough power to open and close Tower Bridge 655 times in its first month. In 1894 the bridge operated 24 hours a day. Nowadays a vessel has to give a minimum of 24 hours' notice if it needs the bridge to open, which only happens approximately 15 times a week. The relative infrequency of opening times is no surprise. For me what was surprising is that Tower Bridge was still operated by steam as recently as 1976.

There's a child-friendly display that encourages you to turn a handle and make a model of Tower Bridge lift. This did make me wonder whether the bridge might have been built a few centuries earlier if they'd have used prisoners from the nearby Tower of London. Nothing like a back-breaking few hours, heaving a bridge open and closed, to make you wonder if committing treason was such a good idea after all.

The marathon runners pass the old engine room on their left just before crossing the river; however, as mentioned at the start of this chapter, they're more likely to be riding the crest of the atmosphere wave than taking much notice of it. Tower Bridge is far quieter today. With dusk falling and the temperature plummeting, the warmth of a nearby pub is called for.

The website viewlondon.com offers potential spectators a list of pubs that provide excellent viewing points for the marathon. I figured it was only fair that I should use this book as an opportunity to find out for myself whether these are reliable recommendations. Among the suggestions for the first half of the course that I'm prepared to second are The Spanish Galleon in Greenwich and The Duke in Deptford. One of the final alcoholic beverage retailing establishments before the half-way point is on the right hand side of Tower Bridge Road, a short distance before the bridge. Whilst The Draft House may not be the most memorable pub I've ever set foot in, that's not to say it's not a perfectly fine place for a pint, and it does have two standout features worth noting.

It sells one of my favourites, a beer from Belgium called Kwak which is 'fruity, deep amber in colour, with a malty aroma and hints of herbs and caramelised banana'. I'm always hearing how bananas are good for running, so clearly this is the beer of choice for the athletically minded. With an alcohol content of 8.4 percent, if you decide to dive into one or two of those when watching the tide of runners on marathon day, by the time the fancy dress clad runners are streaming past, it's quite possible you'll wonder whether that really was the Eiffel Tower in a pair of running shoes, or if you did just see a green hippo lumbering alongside Bagpuss and a giant chicken?

When the time comes to use the facilities, on descending the stairs you'll notice that this pub has Ghostbusters wallpaper. Once again, you won't be imagining things.

As runners leave the bridge on the north side, the Tower of London marks the point on their left where, later that day, they'll pass with just a few miles still to run. It's important not to be distracted by that thought, so neither will I. Instead, let's focus on the road, and the next to come is East Smithfield; not the Smithfield where the famous meat market happens, sadly no steak or bacon-sampling for me in the name of research.

To the east of Tower Bridge is St Katharine Docks. The origin of the name dates from the 1100s as it was the site for the Hospital of St Katharine, founded by Matilda, wife of Stephen of England (king between 1135 and 1141). The Black Death of the 1340s led to two cemeteries being opened in East Smithfield where, at the height of the epidemic, around 500 bodies were buried each day.

As foreign ships were not permitted to use the wharves within the city of London, St Katharine Docks became a major arrival point for non-British boats, thus beginning the influx of immigrants which characterised the East End, in particular Jews fleeing persecution in Eastern Europe.

The area of East Smithfield was the location of the Abbey of the Minoresses of St Clare, which is the origin of the word Minories, which is both the name of a parish, and a street running from Tower Hill to Aldgate. It's also the name of the pub which I've gone to after watching the London Marathon each year. Perhaps not a thought I'll enjoy when I do get another entry place as I'll be passing by twice, the second time with still at least four miles to go.

Chapter 11: 'The Middle' - Sporting Greatness runs amongst us

I'm often asked what I think about when I run; a question people are curious about given that visual stimulation is not an option for me. As my circumstances mean I always have company, long training runs provide plenty of time for talking as well as thinking. What you're about to read in this chapter is the result of many conversations during marathon training about a sporting issue which has long bugged me: why does the British public not seem to fully appreciate the achievements of Paula Radcliffe as a marathon runner?

There's a reason for writing about this now. When you're running in a big city marathon like London, it's easy to forget that you're in the same field as some of the best distance runners in the world. For many this is a good thing, better to focus on your own race than get sidetracked by wondering how fast the winning time might be. It can be soul destroying when you realise the leaders are warming down as you reach the toughest point on the course. The half-way mark in the London Marathon presents an interesting psychological challenge. The thrill of knowing you've reached 13.1 miles can give you a real lift; however running along The Highway just after crossing Tower Bridge, you see faster runners heading for the finish having already completed 20 miles. I consider myself fortunate as I had the elite runners passing me in the other direction. I didn't feel there was anything off-putting about being on the same stretch of road as those guys, as to me they appear untouchable. I have since wondered what it must be like for those who get round in 5 hours or more, who throw a glance across the road to see people that look just like them, who aren't professional runners, yet are still so much further ahead. I've also wondered how it must feel to be back on The Highway, look left to the halfway point and see nobody. At least for me I could gain a lift from the thought that, although I was shattered, I'd done that loop round the Isle of Dogs, and at least I wasn't dressed as a hippo, bouncing a ball or playing the guitar.

For me the knowledge that certain runners were trying to break the world record in an event that I was taking part in was exhilarating. I actually hoped one of them would achieve it. Imagine being able to say you ran the year Paula Radcliffe lit up London with her spectacular world record. A decade on, no woman has come close to beating it!

That said, as an athletics fan, I'm glad I was able to fully enjoy sporting history by watching, on TV in 2003, over a period of 2 hours 15 minutes and 25 seconds, one of the greatest British sporting performances of all time.

In world championships on the track Paula Radcliffe's best performance came in 1999: silver in the 10,000m. She made her marathon debut in London in 2002, winning in a time of 2:18:56. Later that year she would break the women's marathon world record in Chicago clocking 2:17:18, before smashing her own record the following April in London with a time of 2:15:25. The size of the improvement was extremely significant for female marathon running as, for the first and only time, it saw the women's world record come within ten minutes of the men's - 2:05:38.

More than ten years after that great day in London, the closest any woman had come to beating Paula's time was Paula herself, 2:17:44 set in the 2005 London Marathon. The closest any other woman had come to Radcliffe's world record was #Liliya Shobukhova of Russia, running 2:18:20 in Chicago in October 2011. In 2003 Paula was averaging 5 minutes 9 seconds per mile. It's a striking thought that had the two athletes run their best times in the same race, Shobukhova would have finished at least half a mile behind.

Distance running is a sport dominated by Africans. In his book 'Running with the Kenyans' journalist Adharanand Finn states:

"The fact that someone like Paula Radcliffe can come through a field so skewed against her, to shatter the world record in the women's marathon is, in some respects, a minor miracle".

The field he cites is one dominated by athletes from Kenya, where running is considered the golden ticket to a better life. The combination of running presenting opportunities which nothing else can, up-bringing, a simple diet, living and training at altitude, an enormous talent pool, and countless role models for young runners to aspire to, are just some of the things Finn covers in what is a fascinating insight into one of the most successful global sporting powerhouses. He argues that a European runner can stand on the start line of a major distance race and be psyched out by the mere presence of Kenyans. Europeans like Shobukhova do break through (she too is a London Marathon winner) but none with quite the impact of Paula Radcliffe by setting a women's running standard that even the production line inside Kenyan training camps was unable to challenge in the decade following that famous Sunday in London.

Yet, in the mind of many a general or casual British sports fan, Paula Radcliffe is an underachiever, or even worse, a failure.

Why?

The 'O' word.

Following the announcement that Radcliffe would not make the start line for her home Olympic marathon, Charles van Commenée, UK Athletics head coach for London 2012, said: "It is important that we don't look at Paula's career in Olympic cycles. She is undoubtedly one of the greatest female distance runners of all time".

That Olympic cycle saw Radcliffe compete at four games; the closest she came to a medal was finishing fourth in Sydney in the 10,000m.

A year after the London Games, ahead of the ten year anniversary of her world-record breaking run in London, Radcliffe gave an interview to BBC sport admitting a worry that she may never be able to run competitively again and detailing the foot injury that has plagued her career.

"I had a collapsed arch which led to a stress fracture in 1994, which took nine months to diagnose. The foot was basically knackered. I'd been running on a non-union stress fracture (a broken bone which fails to heal) for about 18 years and has been causing damage. That's now repaired and healthy."

Within minutes of the article appearing on the BBC website, the flood gates opened with pages of posts calling her a choker, a failure and accusing her of only being interested in earning appearance money and always making excuses when she was unsuccessful on a major stage, not to mention the many comments which had been removed, presumably due to their offensive content. One self-appointed expert announced "I don't think she's finished a proper race in 10 years". Their analysis excluded the World Championship marathon which she won, the London Marathon (the course she broke the world record on twice), the New York and Berlin marathons, so essentially anything that wasn't the Olympics.

Whilst we shouldn't take seriously the ill-informed opinions of those who mouth off on message boards, behind the safety of a computer screen and protected by the anonymity of user names, unfortunately this example does show us that her career and legacy will always come with question marks. As well as not starting the 2012 Olympic marathon she didn't finish in 2004 in Athens. The one time she did cross the finish line, it was limping and outside the top 20.

The fact that the Olympics are considered the pinnacle of athletics, means that greater achievements, away from the shadow of the five rings, are often portrayed in the media as less significant, and simply as stepping stones on the way to the next Olympiad. As a result, the public holds that view too.

This is with some good reason. Qualifying standards are set higher for an Olympic or Paralympic Games than any other competition. For many sports the Olympics is the one time every four years when the world is watching. In the case of the Paralympics this can be said for every sport, so the pressure to succeed is that much greater. For sports like basketball, football and tennis, there are bigger deals in global terms than the Olympics: the NBA (National Basketball Association), the World Cup, the Premier League, and Grand Slams are what young hopefuls dream of competing in. Even though athletics has world championships, big city marathons and the Diamond League, the Olympics are still considered to be the ultimate prize.

On the track, high profile rivals avoid one another as they don't want to risk losing, and as a result hand a psychological advantage to their rival before a major championship. With fields weaker and with the vast number of Diamond League meets saturating the schedule, an Olympics is without question the ultimate show down.

But marathons are different. As it's physiologically impossible to achieve peak performance in more than a couple of races a year, there isn't the same over-exposure to a small group of athletes. Plus, with three runners from one country being the limit in major championships, it can be argued that the Olympic marathon is by no means a sign of who is the best in the world, given the strength in depth of distance running in countries like Kenya.

The men's Olympic record of 2:06:32 is a long way down the all-time best marathons list. Whilst undoubtedly one of the world's most significant races, a championship marathon is a different type of test, and doesn't necessarily tell us who the best runner over that distance might be. Championship races over long distances tend to be tactical, with competitors watching one another, rather than the clock. It doesn't matter how long it takes to win, just make sure you get that medal.

Then there are the running conditions to consider. When stadiums are built for Olympic Games, the running track is designed to produce fast times. At London 2012 the swimming pool was the most technologically-advanced hole in the ground, filled with water, you could imagine, with the aim of producing world records. The Olympic marathon course was designed with, amongst other things, spectator convenience and London looking good on TV in mind. Seeing the fastest race of all time did not appear to be the objective. After the test event on a course made up of Central London laps, rather than the London Marathon route I'm writing about, participants said they didn't believe it would provide a world record as there was a greater chance of it being windy, plus cobbles near St Paul's Cathedral would slow runners down. The men's race was won in a time over 4 minutes outside the world record; the women's race, despite being an Olympic record, was 7 minutes 42 seconds slower, or over a mile in distance behind, Paula's 2003 performance on different streets in the same city. If Paula's lack of Olympic success makes her a failure, then surely the same should be said for the many other female athletes who have dared to run faster, making the Olympic record time appear outside the top 120 performances of all time.

So if the Olympic marathon is not the ideal environment to show is who the best marathon runner in the world, why should the fact that the fastest female marathon runner of all time, by some distance, never succeeded on that particular stage cast a shadow over her career? Her critics point to the fact that city marathons have pacemakers (something not allowed in Olympic or World Championship marathons) but Paula Radcliffe proved she's a championship marathon performer by winning a world title in 2005 in a time which remains a championship record nearly ten years on.

Roger Bannister is considered a sporting hero in this country for being the first to break the four minute mile. So much so that he was a popular public choice in media discussions about who should light the Olympic flame at London 2012. The closest Bannister came to an Olympic medal was in Helsinki in 1952, but his British record performance in the 1500m failed to secure him a spot on the podium. So if his place as an iconic British runner is assured for achievements away from the Olympics, why isn't it the same for Paula Radcliffe?

The London Marathon is as much an opportunity to see world class sport for free as it is one of the world's great fundraising events. I wonder if the images of celebrities and people in fancy dress mean that Paula Radcliffe's achievements on this course aren't taken as seriously because the London Marathon is best known for its mass participation appeal, carnival atmosphere and fundraising potential? Do people under-estimate Radcliffe because a colleague at work may also have run the race making the event seem less valid from an elite sport point of view?

The Highway, just after the half way point, is an ideal spot for watching and tracking the progress of those going for glory at the front, for runners pass this point twice, before and after their loop of the Isle of Dogs. Even though the next stage of the marathon takes runners east, away from the finish line, the psychological hurdle of half way has been jumped. Every step of the way now is closer to the end than the start, yet this is also where things get tougher. If this is your first marathon, as London was for me, your own personal desire to succeed is tested in a way you're unlikely to have experienced before. In short, this is where the challenge really begins.

#In April 2014, after the publication of this book, Liliya Shobukhova was given a two year competitive ban by the Russian Athletics federation for doping, following the discovery of abnormalities in her biological passport.

Her results were annulled back to October 9th 2009, these include those referenced in this chapter - her three victories in the Chicargo Marathon (2009, 2010 and 2011) and her win in London in 2010.

Chapter 12: 'Highway to Hell' - Tower Hill to Limehouse along The Highway

2005 saw a small alteration to the course, which led to one of the biggest changes to the route runners take during the second half of the race. There is a stretch of cobbles in front of the Tower of London which participants had to run across. In 2005 the Isle of Dogs loop was reversed in order to cut that section out. Runners now take in Narrow Street in Limehouse, Canary Wharf and Poplar first. Before I explore those areas, there's more to The Highway than meets the eye.

When Bill Bryson visited The Highway on a trip down professional memory lane he described the area, swamped as it was by new development, as "looking like an ugly building competition". I've no idea if this area has changed much since the mid nineties when Bryson was writing 'Notes from a Small Island', so perhaps I'm going to need to work extra hard to show a more interesting side to this stretch of road. Certainly the further east you go the more varied the surroundings become: church spires, a small park, and a mixture of commercial and residential buildings, but the real interest is not necessarily found via the eye of the beholder.

What I can offer you are murders, protests and, for nearly thirty years, one of the most powerful media organisations in the world. So, not just a bunch of architectural monstrosities.

If I mention the words East London and notorious murders, doubtless the name Jack the

163

Ripper would come to the mind of most readers. The Ripper's shadow does indeed hang over this part of London, not least as his identity was never discovered; yet his legacy has evolved from a serial killer whose actions terrorised the East End into that of a mysterious fictional bad guy, such as Sherlock Holmes might have been sent to track down. Public appetite for the telling of the Ripper's story has spawned countless books, films and caricatures. Those drawn to morbid tourism are able to join Jack the Ripper walks through the narrow side streets of Whitechapel. However, as his story, such as we know of it, has been told countless times, and his hunting ground is not directly on the London Marathon route, as far as we know, I'm ignoring Jack.

As we leave Tower Bridge and head along The Highway, deep into the heart of Tower Hamlets, there's another 19th century tale of murder to be told, one which also saw fear and panic sweep through the overcrowded streets of the East End and which, like the Ripper story, is still shrouded in mystery. Two gruesome murders with seven victims, the first taking place on The Highway, then known as the Ratcliff Highway, meaning the name of this busy road into the Docklands will forever have a dark association.

Late in the evening of December 7th 1811, Margaret Jewell, a serving girl at the draper's shop at 29 Ratcliff Highway, was sent out to run a couple of errands for Timothy Marr the shop's owner. She was away longer than expected, something which saved her life for, within the hour, Marr, his wife, their baby son and the shop's apprentice boy were all dead.

164

When Jewell returned she was unable to enter the building, neither could the passing parish night watchman. A neighbour, who said he'd heard some unusual noises through the wall an hour earlier, went to the back of the shop and found the door open. On entering, he was greeted by the horrific murder scene.

On the night, a police search found a heavy shipwright's hammer, called a maul, with the head covered in blood. The only other discovery of note was around £150 in cash; had the motive of the suspects been burglary they'd have left empty-handed. A further piece of evidence was found: two sets of blood-stained foot marks leading away from the back of the building.

In the days that followed leaflets were distributed widely offering rewards for information which might lead the police to find whoever had committed this grisly crime. Given the overcrowded nature of the area and the relative lack of security to the buildings people lived in, we can only imagine the fear that descended on Wapping, Shadwell and beyond. Arrests were made; suspects were questioned and released without charge, and a fortnight passed with little progress.

Extraordinarily, it took those with the murder weapon in their possession two weeks to discover the initials JP engraved on it. A fresh appeal for information was circulated, informing the public of this latest discovery. That same night, December 19th, Wapping was plunged into terror once more. Were these events linked? Had the initials on the maul been discovered sooner, would the events of this night have been prevented? Did the murderers act by way of reaction to the new piece of evidence emerging, or were those responsible always intending to lie low for a while, waiting for the fear to subside before striking again?

Whatever the answers, who knows? What cannot be speculated is that, by the morning of December 20th 1811, three more people were dead, taking the total victims of the Ratcliff Highway murders to seven.

A watchman on patrol discovered a man escaping from an upstairs window of The Kings Arms on New Gravel Street (now Garnet Street) shouting that murder was taking place in the building. What must have added to the shock were the similarities between these murders and those of the Marr family two weeks earlier.

A local seaman, John Williams, was arrested two days later. He had been seen drinking at The Kings Arms a short time before the murders took place. However the one witness, the man who had raised the alarm, gave a description of a man which didn't match that of Williams. That mattered not, with Williams held in custody over Christmas 1811.

By now the identity of JP, the initials on the weapon used to murder the Marr family, had been discovered - a seaman named John Peterson. The revelation came via the landlord of the Pear Tree tavern, himself behind bars for debt. It gave those keen to charge John Williams more evidence to support their case, for Williams was a lodger at the Pear Tree and could theoretically have used one of Peterson's tools.

The day after Boxing Day, a packed courtroom awaited the prisoner's arrival;

however it was a prison officer who entered the room, breaking the news that Williams had been found hanging in his cell.

Despite this latest twist, proceedings continued and by the end of the day, the magistrates had heard the rest of the evidence. Even though the facts did not appear conclusive, it was decided that Williams had alone conducted all seven murders. To show the residents of the area the killer was dead, his body was paraded through the streets on New Year's Eve.

With Williams buried, questions still remained as to whether he was the murderer; had he acted alone and what was the motive?

The historical account of the case from the Thames Police Museum which I have used to support this chapter, references research and analysis from, amongst others, a book titled 'Maul and the Pear Tree' by P.D. James and T.A. Critchley. The account points to the desire, on the part of the prosecutors, for speed over accuracy when resolving the case as one reason why we can never be certain that some of those involved in the killings didn't still walk the streets once Williams had been put in the ground. The murder motive appears unclear, although it is suggested that a score may have been left unsettled from the time Williams and Marr were at sea together. Another name, William 'Long Billy' Ablass also seems to have question marks attached to it. He too was at sea with Marr and Williams and had been drinking with Williams in The Kings Arms on the night of the second murders. Not only that, but he also matched the description given by the Kings Arms lodger more closely. Then there is the evidence gathered from

167

29 Ratcliff Highway. You'll remember that two sets of footprints were found leading away from the building - who might the other pair have belonged to?

One more question is left unanswered. It might seem logical that, were Williams the killer, he may have decided to take his own life rather than face public execution. Alternatively, fearing he would be convicted for a crime he did not commit, or that others committed alongside him, suicide is also understandable. But how easy would that have been in a prison cell, especially since it is believed he was manacled at the time? Bob Jeffries, author of the Thames Police Museum account, concludes by wondering, as an attempt to silence Williams and protect other gang members, might Williams have been the eighth victim of the Ratcliff Highway murders?

An interesting aside to both the Ratcliff Highway and Jack the Ripper stories is how the public would have learnt of both cases and any developments in the hunt for the killers. Certainly, by the time the Ripper walked the streets, a burgeoning newspaper industry was emerging. In reporting the search for the Ripper, journalists were often frustrated by the lack of information and went to print with material which met deadlines and the desire for news, rather than waiting for reliable facts issued by the police, as these were often too slow in coming for the journos' liking. Fast forward to the 21st century and the newspaper industry finds itself under great scrutiny for its relationship with the police, although this time it's for appearing to be too close, rather than impatient publishers.

The cops of course haven't come out of

things squeaky-clean either. What with Hillsborough and the notorious Sun headline 'The Truth', Plebgate, phone-hacking and revelations given to Lord Justice Leveson, the relationship between the police and the press is very much under the spotlight, and public perception of what is produced in our daily newspapers is far from rosy. The finger of blame is pointing, in particular, in the direction of a large converted warehouse close to The Highway - the home for nearly three decades of Rupert Murdoch's UK newspaper operation. Formerly News International it was rebranded as News UK in June 2013 as an attempt to, as their press release announcing the change put it, "address the problems of the recent past".

It's likely that the news tellers haven't been 'the news' with quite such regularity in the history of the British press as has been seen in recent years. However, there was a moment at the beginning of 1986 when the glare of the spotlight was directed fully in the face of those usually angling it towards others. The relocation of Rupert Murdoch-owned titles to Wapping led to industrial disputes that are as synonymous with the name Wapping, as the Ratcliff Highway murders are to the street which runs through the area.

In 'Notes from a Small Island' Bill Bryson, who was a journalist at The Times between 1981 and 1986, recalls the moment when a simple office move turned ugly. When Bryson joined the paper it was, to use his words, a place where "overmanning and slack output were prodigious to say the least". A working environment that was always to prove

169

unsustainable as the technological age was showing the glimmers of pre-dawn glow. When Murdoch bought The Times, as Bryson describes: "Within days, the building was full of mysterious tanned Australians in white short-sleeved shirts, who lurked in the background with clip boards and looked like they were measuring people for coffins".

Whichever account of the events which unfolded over a weekend at the end of January 1986, you care to read, they all seem to show that the move to purpose-designed new editorial offices on Wapping wasteland was sudden, with no warning, and greeted with dismay. Hardly surprising; imagine if your boss announced on Friday night that come Monday morning you'd be working in a new building, several miles away and with equipment and resources you were totally unfamiliar with. Your boss then offers you the alternative of finding another employer if you're not willing to join the new regime.

An interesting insight into the confusion the move caused comes from a Guardian article published the following Tuesday (January 28th 1986) by Alan Rusbridger, now the Guardian's editor.

"What a world awaited them," he wrote. "When they had left work on Friday night they had left behind them a slightly seedy office – paper-strewn, dog-eared desks with ageing typewriters and half-drunk cups of coffee. And there on Monday morning was a gleaming dust-free open-plan room. A clinic more than an office. The whole of it was bathed in soothing computer-compatible light. For there in front of them stood row upon row of gleaming dust-free computers."

It must have been chaos as bemused, hardened hacks, used to typewriters and shorthand, were confronted with technology they couldn't use, in an environment which was alien to them. Not half as chaotic as scenes that would dominate the surrounding streets in the months which followed.

On the evening of January 24th 1986, nearly 6,000 members of the National Union of Journalists (NUJ) went on strike, in protest at the relocation of four titles: The Times, Sunday Times, The Sun and News of the World to Wapping and, in particular, at a legally binding agreement that saw flexible hours, a no-strike clause and the adoption of new technology. Every striker was instantly sacked. With military precision members of the Electrical, Electronics, Telecommunications and Plumbing Union (EETPU) were brought in as replacements, and not a day of production was lost.

Months of protests took place, many gathering on The Highway before marching to the gates of News International.

With the support of the Thatcher government, sufficient journalists and staff to keep the four titles operating, and police protection to enable workers and lorries carrying papers to arrive and leave the Wapping site, News International was content to ride out the strike as it was not hitting them where it hurt. After just over a year, in February 1987, the strike collapsed.

It should be noted that, whilst the methods were aggressive, the timing hasty, and the execution of the plan calculated, the legacy of the Wapping dispute appears to have been to

171

kick-start a technological shift which probably needed to happen anyway. The newspaper industry seems to have been dragged kicking and screaming into the modern era, and in many cases, to the Docklands. By 1988 the majority of newspapers had abandoned their traditional Fleet Street roots.

When the Murdoch titles were bundled into the East End, employees were given a weekend to get used to the idea. In 2013, the company announced it was moving out of Wapping, this time with a year's notice. It's likely that relocation to their new home next to the Shard was greeted with more enthusiasm.

As runners take the south side of The Highway towards Canary Wharf, and the north side on their return, I did likewise and set off, past the entrance to St Katharine Docks, to take a look at the area believed to be where the infamous number 29 stood, the shop where the Marr family was murdered. Two hundred years of redevelopment and regeneration means it's a difficult task to pin down a precise location, although a number of bloggers attempted to do so around the time of the 200th anniversary in 2011. One, Ian Visits, speculated that the exact spot is on the site of the Wapping printing press. The Londonist blog puts the location as somewhere between a BMW showroom and the BP garage on the south side of the road, the latter being where the bacon roll mentioned at the beginning of this book was bought. I've watched the marathon from this spot a couple of times, and one year saw a runner look longingly at the McDonalds and announce to anyone who might have been listening that she "could really do with some chips right now" - she still had half a marathon to run.

Having chosen the hottest day in London for seven years for exploring The Highway and its surroundings, Shadwell Basin, tucked away behind the buildings on the river side of the road with its nominal breeze coming from the Thames, provided a merciful break from the relentless thunder of traffic.

The Basin is flanked by new build apartments, brightly painted in red and blue, and, I should imagine, vastly expensive to live in, such is their quiet, appealing location. A short distance from their front door is the Thames Path, giving an easy walk or cycle to Canary Wharf or the City.

Across the water from the wall we were sitting on, a spire peeps out from behind the trees and yet again, it's a view where Canary Wharf strikes a pose in the background.

Shadwell Basin is an oasis of fitness enthusiasm, even on a sweltering Monday morning. Runners and cyclists complete circuits of the water, passing sailing boats awaiting their next opportunity to flex their mast and rigging. A voice boomed from the centre of the inlet, giving instructions to two double canoes loaded with school children.

"And remember, Rebecca, this is a race!"

There's always one not feeling the competitive spirit who gets chastised in front of the rest of the class.

Sensing some sporting action was about to break out, we took up a position on the edge of the bank. Final instructions given, which may or may not have been understood, the two boats, one orange, the other blue, launched themselves towards the opposite end of Shadwell Basin with great enthusiasm and a not inconsiderable amount of splashing.

As both teams waited on the start line, it was difficult to predict a winner. Orange had more children, but they were younger. Plus, numbers did not necessarily guarantee speed - too many oars thrashing about could slow the boat down and allow blue to take victory.

As it happened orange took an early lead and, despite heading perilously close to the bank, never looked in any real danger of being beaten, even with the added weight of an adult at the back who seemed to be unbalancing the boat quite considerably.

With orange now a clear boat length ahead, and, disappointingly just about managing not to capsize or crash, we did the equivalent of leaving when your team's three nil up with ten minutes to go.

Walking away from the basin back towards The Highway, we found ourselves in Pear Tree Lane, so-named because the Pear Tree tavern, where the second Ratcliff Highway murders happened, once stood in this narrow street.

Back on The Highway, close to the entrance to a large block of flats, we spotted a blue plaque, courtesy of the Stepney Historical Trust, to Captain James Cook.

"The ablest and most renowned Navigator this or any country hath produced, lived in a house a few yards from this spot, 126 Upper Shadwell, from 1763 to 1765".

Three years later Cook set sail on the first

of his three voyages to explore the Pacific Ocean. During the debut journey he made a complete map of the New Zealand coastline. His crew were the first Europeans to reach the eastern coast of Australia.

His second voyage saw him charged with discovering the mythical continent Terra Australis. Instead he sailed around the southern Pacific and Atlantic, discovering islands and claiming them as British, which must have thrilled anyone he met along the way. Among his discoveries on this trip were the wonderfully-named South Sandwich Islands.

Chapter 13: 'Limehouse Blues' - Narrow Street to Canary Wharf

One of my favourite episodes of 'Thunderbirds' titled 'Brink of Disaster', features a dodgy investor proposing to build a cross country driverless monorail. Jeff Tracy, Brains and Tin-Tin go to check it out and, along with the crook behind the scheme, become trapped on a train, which can't be stopped as it hurtles towards a collapsed section of the track. One of those classic race-against-time scenarios, when you know it will all work out in the end because it always does, and which has no shortage of drama along the way.

Trains on the DLR have no driver, although there is a human on each train doing some sort of work, but I remember that episode whenever I board one of their brightly-coloured trains. Maybe it was partly Gerry Anderson's doing, perhaps it's because I rarely use the DLR, or that it twists and turns around areas of London I know little about, but I've always found there's something quite exciting about catching London's sleepiest rollercoaster. The lack of a driver, and that many of the stations are high above the ground on what appear to me to be nothing more than steel structures, give the impression of a theme park ride. Then there are the evocative sounding stations, Gallions Reach, Pudding Mill Lane, Pontoon Dock, Mudchute. Intriguingly there's one called Abbey Road; I hope bewildered music pilgrims come here by mistake.

Every boy, even me when I was losing

my sight, at some point in their childhood wants to be a train driver. Little did we know that Transport for London could provide the next best thing, for the front seats of DLR trains, like the top deck of the bus, allow you to look out of the front window as if you were in control. The front seat on the DLR is highly sought-after, and only likely to be secured if you get on at Bank, Tower Gateway, Lewisham or another station at the beginning of one of the lines.

I realise that if this is your daily commute you probably think I'm getting over-excited about something which has the ability to regularly do your head in; I completely get that the novelty would wear off fast when you're waiting for a delayed train in the middle of winter, but securing that sought-after front seat is always something to aspire to. Sadly, as I embark on this part of my marathon exploration, a family of four had beaten me to it. It's summer holiday time and the teenage kids sound like they're being dragged somewhere unwillingly; they're at the age when hanging out with Mum and Dad is far from cool.

"We're not having a picnic, I'm not 4 years old!" one of the ungrateful buggers can be heard whining as the train rumbles towards Limehouse (which, as DLR stops go, is not the most exciting of names), the starting point for today's adventure. As my teenage years are a distant memory, my Mum has come too.

There's an exhibit in the Museum of London Docklands where a street has been recreated to attempt to give us some idea of what the East End might have looked like when the docks were at their busiest. Tiny shops squashed together either side of a narrow, cobbled street, the most interesting of which offers a letter-writing service emphasising the high level of illiteracy in communities such as this. On the corner of the street is a pub. Walking in you are greeted by the sound of conversation and laughter with traditional Irish music playing in the background. Irish workers flooded into the docks looking for work, especially following the potato famine of 1845 to 1852, when young adults were faced with no option but to leave in search of work and money. Many would never return home. In 'Our Man in Hibernia', the journalist Charlie Connelly gives a fascinating, detailed account of one such Irishman, his ancestor John, who arrived in the East End under exactly those circumstances.

The exhibit could be a recreation of any one of many streets which cris-crossed this vast industrial landscape, but as Narrow Street in Limehouse, where runners head after The Highway, is both that by name and nature, it's not unreasonable to try and imagine this to have been what the museum designers had in mind. Such was the level of poverty along Narrow Street in the 19th century that social reformers and political activists campaigned hard for better working conditions in this and surrounding areas, leading to the foundation of London's first trade unions.

There's a familiar tale to be told about Narrow Street; a traditionally working class area with the harshest of living conditions, it was bombed to pieces during the second world war and left to rot as the docks around it closed one by one. As the Canary Wharf development rose

178

from the rubble so too did the reputation of Narrow Street. Once a no-go area, it's now a desirable place to live. There was a time when you lived by the river in this part of London because you couldn't afford to go anywhere else; now a river view adds several noughts to the value of a property.

Walking along Narrow Street on a warm summer's day the past seems more than a couple of generations ago. The older buildings on the right, backing onto the river, have been converted into apartments. On the left hand side are mainly new build, a mixture of residential, shops and offices.

After a few minutes walking, we reached a swing bridge, the first of many we'd cross today; this one carrying traffic over the entrance to the Limehouse Basin, the home for numerous expensive-looking leisure boats. With the tide low, there's a drop of about 20 feet to the water. The booming voice of a guide from a tourist boat reaches us on the wind from the Thames, but aside from that, all is quiet.

The Limehouse Basin connects the Thames to the Limehouse Cut, a stretch of canal which runs between here and the Lea Navigation. The Cut was opened in 1869 to provide a quick route, both in distance and travelling time, from the River Lea to the Thames - for until then boats had to wait for favourable tides before circling the Isle of Dogs.

This is the route David Beckham and his speedboat took, when carrying the Olympic torch to the Stadium during the 2012 opening ceremony, through Limehouse Basin and the Limehouse Cut - one of countless inspired ideas

179

for the Games.

Before the bridge, on the right, is one of the signs that Limehouse is now a classy part of town. The Narrow pub provides a perfect location to watch the river, and the world go by, with a sun trap terrace and shelter from the breeze. It's also owned by Gordon Ramsey, so I'd been keen to sample its menu, but at 11.30am we were too early by half an hour. Online reviews, which should never be taken as gospel, are mixed; some say it's amazing, others suggest it's the opposite.

As hanging around waiting for the pub to open doesn't appear to be a very Narrow Street thing to do, we continue our walk, past quaint-sounding house and street names, Sail Master's House, Papermill Wharf and my personal favourite, Shoulder of Mutton Alley.

Narrow Street becomes Limehouse Causeway, where a century ago a small Chinese community gained much literary notoriety through the writing of Sax Rohmer and his character Fu Manchu, an evil Chinese genius plotting world domination from his Limehouse lair.

Agatha Christie was another to use the Chinese and Limehouse for a tale of good versus evil. In 'The Big Four' Hercule Poirot takes on another Chinese villain plotting to bring the world to its knees and at one point Poirot's assistant, Captain Hastings, is taken prisoner in a Limehouse opium den. Sherlock Holmes could also be found mingling in the drug-taking circles of Limehouse.

Meanwhile Thomas Burke, author of 'Limehouse Nights', was mixing fiction and journalism in a series of short stories and newspaper articles, feeding the reading appetite of suburban Britain with stories of working class Londoners and their Chinese neighbours, whose lives were played out in the mysterious East End and featured that winning, dangerous combination of crime, sex, drugs and violence.

In 'Limehouse Blues: Looking for Chinatown in the London Docks 1900-40', Dr. John Seed of Roehampton University explores how this area came to gain such a reputation. This next section has been written with reference to Dr. Seed's research and analysis and an interview I conducted with him.

"Few parts of London attracted as much attention as did Limehouse between the Great War and the 1930s. Limehouse and its ghostly double 'Chinatown' figured as a dangerous and exotic place in novels, films, magazines, even popular songs."

Describing the area itself, Seed writes:

"By the beginning of the twentieth century Limehouse and the whole riverside district of East London, stretching along the Thames from the Tower to Limehouse and inland up to the Commercial Road was a notorious slum area. Its streets of little terraced houses were squeezed among canals and railway line, timber yards and sawmills, lead works and coal yards, dry docks, ship repair yards, factories and workshops. There was overcrowding along with low, irregular wages, foul air and bad sanitation, among the highest levels of child mortality and poverty in London. What made Limehouse and its riverside neighbours distinctive were their maritime connections. This was the most cosmopolitan district of the most cosmopolitan city in Britain."

So clearly, not the kind of place you'd choose to live in if you could help it, although not something to be said for just Limehouse, south of the river had similarly challenging locations. What is interesting about the idea of Chinatown is how the reputation and the reality of this area appear to differ. So why was it that the image of Chinatown and its inhabitants was recycled numerous times for the entertainment of those who never set foot in the neighbourhood?

Dr. Seed told me about the number of issues which made up this story. Britain was a country used to having power and influence over others around the world, but since China was not part of our empire it was perceived as somewhere very different - a far away land many knew little about. There was a strong fascination with all things oriental, often viewed as mysterious or magical. As the first Chinese people arrived in the London Docks in the late 19th century, they would have stood out due to their unfamiliar appearance. In Victorian London 'different' often meant 'suspicious'.

They also brought opium with them. Up until the 20th century the drug was easy to get hold of in London, but around the time of the First World War the British government made opium illegal. The Chinese sailors continued to arrive with their own supply and the drug would not have been difficult to find should a Londoner have wanted it and been prepared to venture down the narrow alleys of Limehouse.

When Sherlock Homes and the Oscar

Wilde character Dorian Grey were dabbling with opium, so too would have been many readers. With the rise of the Limehouse den came a shift in public attitude towards the drug. Dr. Seed quotes a 1907 newspaper article headlined 'Opium Smoking and East End Dens' that cried out about how "the opium victim intent on satisfying his desire " (crucially they're regarded as 'victims' now) "rubs shoulders with criminals and desperadoes of the worst type". No longer a playground for the English gentleman, or an adventure of youthful experimentation, now this has become something much more sinister. We should assume there was trade between the Chinese and Londoners wishing to smoke opium, but nothing of the scale that was represented in the media and popular fiction.

Already the picture is forming: immigrants, who were at best unfamiliar, at worst feared, and a drug-taking culture which the press were covering with hysterical enthusiasm. Wouldn't it be convenient if there were significant numbers involved?

Dr. Seed's research provides census data which shows a noticeable rise in the Chinese population in Limehouse post World War I, but never was it exclusively a Chinese area. He points out that the figures should only be considered as a representation, reminding us that the Chinese themselves would have been reluctant to share information with the British authorities. He highlights census figures for 1931 that puts London's Chinese population at 1194, and compares this with "25,000 Poles, 18,000 Russians, 11,000 Italians and over 9,000 French and Germans". He notes that by this time the population shift was already in motion with a drop of almost half for those living in Limehouse since 1921, with West and Central London areas of Kensington and Westminster in particular seeing a significant rise. However by the 1930s the literary and journalistic damage had already been done.

The immediate post-war timing is important. London had numerous social challenges, the docks especially so. Whilst when we think of bomb damage our minds turn to the Blitz of the 1940s, Britain, and London in particular, also came under attack from the air during the First World War.

With Britain at war, a huge work force gap was left at home. The arriving Chinese were ready and willing to take jobs left vacant by the British fighting in the trenches of Europe. Even before the war, trade unions were particularly unhappy about the increased number of Chinese immigrants. There was some trouble in London, with significant rioting in Liverpool and Cardiff. During the war there were rumours that Chinese seaman on British ships were spying for the Germans. The Chinese looked different, they spoke differently and their numbers were increasing; the jumpy, paranoid British public would have been happy to go along with this idea, true or not.

The Chinese did play a valuable supporting role during the First World War. With so many men required to fight on the front line, almost 100,000 Chinese were brought in by both the French and British, building, repairing, and digging. This work didn't earn them the right to stay post-war, and they were repatriated in the years after.

With the public hungry for stories showing the oriental immigrants in a bad light, the press were more than happy to oblige. Dr. Seed refers to articles which, post-war, swarmed around the idea that whilst our brave boys had been away fighting for king and country, the Chinese had taken their jobs. Whilst there would have been an element of truth to this, it wasn't to the extent reported. Sax Rohmer was a journalist, as well as a novelist, and would spend time hanging around Limehouse, sent by his newspaper to find a story to write. It is thought he got the idea of Fu Manchu when observing a well-dressed Chinese man arrive in an expensive car, accompanied by a pretty local girl. A big part of the mystique was the potential for impressionable young British women to be sucked into a dirty, dangerous world, an idea which could easily take over the public imagination – lock up your daughters, one of those evil oriental types is prowling the streets!

The 1907 article had warned its readers that society women were also being tempted into Limehouse dens. The press went into overdrive post-war when Billie Carleton was found dead in her hotel room the morning after the victory concert at the Royal Albert Hall. The inquest found her to have taken cocaine which, unsurprisingly, was linked to Limehouse.

John Seed quotes two newspaper articles which appeared in the same week in 1920. The Daily Express ran a headline 'Yellow Peril in London' where it described a drug, sex and gambling syndicate run by a mysterious master which lured women who were "without exception young and pretty". The Evening News went further by telling of how children were caught up in this terrifying world hidden down alleyways in London's foggy docks, their story accompanied by the headline "English Girls' Moral Suicide".

So societal issues such as immigration, unemployment, a housing shortage, a bit of drug smuggling, fear of what might happen to the daughter of the house if she ran into the wrong kind of foreigner, and a portion of racism, put together with the desire for a good story with a bit of danger, and the excitement of the exotic, plus a small group of Chinese settlers and a steady stream of sailors found themselves under a spotlight prompted largely by hysteria.

Whilst Sax Rohmer did have some experience of Limehouse, Thomas Burke did not. Dr. Seed quotes from Burke's autobiography:

"At the time I did them (Limehouse Nights) I had no knowledge of the Chinese people, and all I knew of Limehouse was what I had automatically observed without aim or purpose during my unguided wanderings in remote London. I had thus been able to write those stories with the peculiar assurance a man has who knows nothing of what he is writing about".

There is very little evidence as to how the Chinese felt about all this. When I spoke to Dr. Seed about his work investigating this topic, he told me about talking to a man who was born in Limehouse in the 1920s – half English, half Chinese. He remembered that, in the 1930s, Limehouse had become something of an exotic tourist attraction, with coaches bringing people in to drive around the area and stare, to the bemusement of the locals who couldn't work out what all the fuss was about.

It was around this time that the Chinese population of Limehouse was diminishing. Partly as the number of sailors coming through the docks was lower, but also as the bright lights of the West End provided new employment opportunities. Laundrettes and food were the two things the Chinese were most able to earn money from, and with the emergence of a desire to eat Chinese food, the westward migration began.

And with that, I continue eastwards. Leaving Limehouse Causeway, runners join Westferry Road before beginning their circuit of the Isle of Dogs. A sign directs people leaving the nearby Westferry DLR station to the Museum of London Docklands - yet another riverside warehouse which has been given a second life. A few months before the day I spent exploring the docklands, I visited this museum, something I highly recommend.

As well as the street exhibit already mentioned at the start of this chapter, which may or may not have been Narrow Street, another one to catch my attention was a 21st century East End Monopoly board. Designed by local youth group, Tolerance in Diversity, it gave an interesting and amusing snapshot of the lives of kids growing up in inner city London.

Liverpool Street is the only square to remain from the original board, described as a place where you can go anywhere from. I imagined kids looking starry eyed at the departure board - there's a world out there: Southend, Colchester, Norwich!

The other three stations are Tower Hill, marking the edge of Tower Hamlets, Stratford "for the Olympics and Westfield", and Canning Town.

Other locations which replace the old favourites of Old Kent Road, Bond Street, Mayfair and the Waterworks - is it just me, or were the utility companies the rubbish ones to land on? - include:

Spice-Hut - there are two on the board; "you can buy fried chicken here, one is better than the other"; Mile End Park - the locals appear to have nicknamed it Teletubby Land, due to it having a couple of small hills; and Cider Park - this is an alternative name for Stepney Green, although this can be said for yours and my local park too; the fun you can have with a bottle of White Lightning.

There's no crossword competition winning going on in this game's collection of Chance cards. Instead the potential offered by landing on one of those squares includes:

"Go to your home; move directly to your home; do not pass go; do not collect job seekers allowance."

"Hey mate, you won a bet at the bookmakers. Jackpot baby! Collect £100!"

"Electronic tag removed; no longer confined at home."

"Local riots lead to street repairs: £40 per house; £150 per hotel."

Canary Wharf, the face of regeneration in this part of London, is the location of a shopping centre that was a popular after-school hangout.

The riverside is described as expensive; however the bend in the river is highlighted as an East End icon. The Isle of Dogs, the next section which runners head to, is apparently famous for "the Asda supermarket, driving, shopping, but little else". They don't appear bothered whether it was Edward III or Henry VIII who kept their hunting dogs here, one of many suggested reasons for the Isle's name.

In 2012, a map published by the Campaign to End Child Poverty showed that Tower Hamlets had the highest rate of child poverty in the UK. Fifty-two percent of children are considered to be living below the poverty line, compared to the national average of 20%. Of the top five local authorities only one, Manchester, was outside London, with Islington, Hackney and Westminster being the other three.

Children were classed as living in poverty if their household's annual income fell below 60% of the national average of £25,000, a situation which makes affording the basics of food, clothes and heating extremely difficult. London's dominance of statistical analysis, such as this, is partly explained by the higher cost of living in the capital compared to other parts of the UK; but even with this in mind, these figures paint a far different picture of our city than what many from other parts of the UK believe to be the case.

One of the issues with 21st century poverty in the UK is that it's often behind closed doors. The likes of Blackwall and Poplar, in the shadow of Canary Wharf where many earn far above the national average income, are amongst London's most challenged areas.

By way of highlighting the contrast, in the Docklands Museum's café I picked up a copy of the Docklands & City Magazine, a glossy lifestyle publication targeting those who work in the financial districts of both areas. This issue was providing its aspirational readers with a guide to the best places to go for afternoon tea, as well as articles on locations for weekend city breaks.

A wander through the Museum gives you a sense of the rise, fall and resurrection of the Docklands. Colonial expansion during the 1700s brought a huge increase in the level of maritime trade to London. Cargo handling facilities, however, did not increase to meet the demand. Long delays in unloading, rising costs of warehouses and insurance, damage to commodities and significant losses due to theft were all serious issues as the undeveloped ports creaked under the weight of booming industry. By the end of the 18th century it was estimated that £500,000 worth of cargo was being nicked every year. In 1800 a senior magistrate published a report stating that around 10,850 people were involved in theft on the river in what he described as "a system of matured delinquency which is perhaps unparalleled in the criminal history of any other country".

He concluded that this showed "a very unpleasant picture of the state of morals among the labouring classes".

London's merchant community, in particular the West India Committee, put pressure on the government to take action. They responded by setting up four separate Select Committees between 1796 and 1801 to address the situation leading to the formation of a number of off-river docks including: the West India, East India, Royal and Millwall Docks.

Investors were keen to become involved as certain docks were given a twenty-one year monopoly on specific products. At their peak the London Docks were the largest and busiest in the world.

In an attempt to cripple the UK economy the Docklands suffered extensive damage during World War II. A favourite German tactic saw countless incendiary bombs being dropped on London's ports, designed to catch fire wherever they landed, causing docks, buildings and valuable cargo to go up in flames. One of the Docklands Museum exhibits is a metal dome with a small entrance and a couple of seats inside. These portable shelters were given to those who had to work outdoors in locations which were likely to be targeted. Whilst they might protect against flying shrapnel, I couldn't see what good it would do you if a building close by was transformed into a raging fireball.

A museum display board showed how quickly chaos could take over, illustrated by the story of September 8th 1940. A blaze at St Katharine Docks soon raged out of control, flames leaping from warehouses across to barges loaded with copra and paraffin wax. Burning oil swept across the surface of the water and soon the whole basin was engulfed in flames.

The same night the Rum Quay at Canary Wharf caught fire. Blazing spirits poured from barrels and barges broke loose from their moorings.

It's little wonder there was anything of the docks left after that; however, Stanley Keath,

191

an administrator at West India Docks recalls that not everything went to waste once the fires had been put out.

"We had tens of thousands of tons of sugar which went up in flames. One offshoot of the burning sugar and the firemen's efforts with their hoses was a very nice thick layer of toffee. Since there were hardly any sweets in those days, the labourers would come in and chip lumps of toffee off the road and take it home. I often remonstrated with them about that, saying it was unhealthy but two or three of them told me it's alright, we washed it when we got home."

The 1950s saw a brief resurgence in the fortune of the Docks, but by the 1970s they were a sad shadow of their former selves. At the beginning of the 1980s, trade and industry had all but left.

A number of my friends ran the London Marathon in its early years and say this was a bleak, tough section of the course, a deserted stretch of decline and desolation, with little crowd support to give you that lift you need with one quarter of the distance still to go. It's worth noting that the first London Marathon pre-dates the formation of the London Docklands Development Corporation, a government quango which began work in 1981. During its existence between 1981 and 1998, large sections of Tower Hamlets, Southwark and Newham saw significant investment, with the building of Surrey Quays Shopping Centre, where we've already been, the DLR, which I've already travelled on, and Canary Wharf, where I'm heading next. A new airport, London City, was built, as was the ExCeL Exhibition Centre where the London Marathon exhibition is held each April in the week before the race.

Chapter 14: 'I Am the Resurrection' - Canary Wharf and the Isle of Dogs

Having arrived half an hour too early for lunch at Gordon's gaff in Limehouse, we were hungry by the time we'd negotiated the head-spinning road network of Westferry Circus. It's very easy to get confused and find yourself walking through a tunnel where you're lucky not to be gassed by lorry fumes. As we stood trying to figure out which of the unsigned roads to take (in the era of satnav and Google Maps who needs one of those boring, old fashioned road signs?) we watched a confused driver concede he was lost and turn round. Deciding to follow the bus route we head over a bridge and the landscape changes once again.

On Blackheath, in Charlton and Greenwich, when crossing Tower Bridge and at Shadwell Basin, Canary Wharf was always there, lurking in the background or peering over buildings. Now the One Canada Square tower is right beside us, as is a rather odd-looking zig-zag sculpture on a patch of grass.

We stop at a café selling convenience food for the suited and booted, people who feel more comfortable ordering a sandwich if it comes in ciabatta bread, and with the pointless addition of rocket or coriander, but is no better than food I've eaten on a train. The kind of clientele who don't raise an eyebrow at being charged 50p for a tiny tub of marmalade to go with their croissant - eat it dry or pay extra. Paddington Bear would not be amused.

Food consumed, we take a detour away

from Westferry Road and wander through Canary Wharf at lunch hour. Outside the café we stopped at is an area of grass with trees, benches and a great view of the London sky line. Standing at the top of the steps leading down to the Thames Cruises Pier we got a real sense of where London Marathon runners would have come from. Columbia Wharf in Rotherhithe stares back at us from across the wide stretch of river, and, away in the distance to the right, are the icons of the City - the Cheese Grater, Walkie Talkie and the Gherkin - every new tower seems to need a novelty name these days. Once, One Canada Square was Britain's tallest building, but that crown was taken as The Shard rose from a Southwark building site and now stands proudly above everything else - you can pay nearly £25 to experience the view from amongst the clouds. Bars, restaurants, offices and flats will fill most of the floors, Al Jazeera TV is one famous name moving in. However the first resident managed to live up the top rent free for two weeks.

In February 2011 a fox, named Romeo by those who discovered him, managed to find his way to the 72nd floor via the stairwell and survive for a fortnight on food scraps left by builders. Whilst catching him and clearing up his poo must have been frustrating, it has given The Shard a golden opportunity to make money from tourists as you can now buy your Romeo the Fox toy, clad in hard hat and high vis jacket, from the shop at the top of the building.

I felt as if I should have brought a name badge for walking around Heron Quays - the stretch of water close to the Canary Wharf office blocks - as people hurry in all directions too busy to take theirs off. It could have been fun to cheerfully greet them by name; had I been smartly dressed rather than wearing my Berlin Marathon T shirt I might have done so:

"David Hi, good to see you again. Looking forward to receiving that report you said you'd forward to me when we met on Thursday".

Then watch as David looks blankly back at you trying to remember at which post-conference networking drinks event you and he had pretended to be interested in one another.

Once this area would have been busy with dock workers; now small groups stand around outside Café Rouge and All Bar One, suit jackets removed as they're released from the air-conditioned office.

As many of the buildings surrounding the water are glass, they reflect off one another in the summer sunshine. A large news ticker screen shows a continuous loop of FTSE100 share prices; it makes surprisingly addictive viewing. Marks & Spencer down 89p, Tesco down 71p, Sainsbury's down 69p and Morrisons dropping only a mere 9p. What is it about Morrisons that means it's performing better, or less worse than the others today? RBS looked to be doing well with a rise of just over a pound; the Prudential, meanwhile, was having a very good Monday, up £2.45. Well done everyone, off you all go for a mozzarella and rocket toasty.

Returning to Westferry Road we pass a very grand-looking block of flats, conveniently placed for folk to make the short walk from their luxury home to their plush office, dining out at one of the many eating places on the waterfront each night. Bog roll and teabags must be about all they sell in the Tesco Express next door.

As we walked, we almost missed a plaque on the pavement which highlighted something I was keen to find, but that we were finding difficult to spot due to the lack of numbers on any buildings. It read:

"Millwall Rovers football club was founded on this site by workers at the Morton's jam factory in 1885."

You might think that to specialise your factory in jam production might be a bit niche, and you'd be correct. John Thomas Morton began trading in Aberdeen in 1849 in the business of food provision for lengthy sea voyages. His firm expanded to the Isle of Dogs in the early 1870s, taking over the site of the former Price's Oil Works. It was from here that food was supplied to Sir Robert Scott for his polar expedition of 1910-1912. It was workers at this canned and other preserved foods company who, over a decade after it opened, were involved in the foundation of Millwall Rovers. Whilst J. T. Morton's produced jam as one of their many products, perhaps there's an element of evolution in the telling over the years, from preserved food, to preserves, to jam, that has led to the commonly-held belief that rough and tough Millwall have their roots in something we'd now associate with little old ladies at village fêtes.

So why did Millwall, by then having dropped the Rovers from their name, relocate from their birthplace on the Isle of Dogs to their present home near New Cross in South London?

The Club had four different homes on the Isle of Dogs during their early years. This included converting land, which was little more than a swamp, into a football ground and using another patch of grass which, at the time of identification as a potential playing area, had cows grazing and potatoes growing on it. A combination of being moved on too many times, including once by the Millwall Dock Company who wanted to build a timber yard, and attendances which were lower than the Club hoped for (usually less than 10,000), saw Millwall looking south. They arrived in Bermondsey in 1910 and attracted a crowd of 25,000 to The Den for their first match against Brighton.

Whether the story that Mudchute was chosen for the name of the DLR station instead of Millwall Dock on the Isle of Dogs to avoid the risk of marauding football fans showing up, is true or an urban myth I don't know, but what can't be disputed is that the name Millwall does, despite the best efforts of the Football Club, still trigger negative thoughts in the minds of football and non-football fans alike. For every community-focused act, such as high-profile support for the Save Lewisham Hospital campaign, there are incidents like the significant trouble in the Millwall end during their 2013 FA Cup semi-final against Wigan Athletic - hardly the positive boost the Club's reputation would have liked in front of a worldwide TV audience.

A sad sight greeted us a short distance further along Westferry Road. One of the oldest buildings we'd seen so far today, once The Anchor and Hope pub opened in 1829, was all boarded up. It may have been living on borrowed time at its demise in 2008, but I hate seeing pubs die away. Give me one of those over a plastic coffee shop any day.

According to the 'Island History' website, a planning application was granted in 2011 to convert the property into retail units and first floor flats, but, as of our visit in August 2013, nothing appears to have changed.

There's plenty of evidence of the name Millwall around this area; we walked past Millwall fire station, Millwall Park, and our circuit of the Isle of Dogs on Westferry and Eastferry Roads had Millwall Dock behind the buildings to our left. Like Shadwell Basin, this is now a centre for water sports, allowing people to learn to sail without the risk of being cut in half by a tourist boat on the Thames.

Leaving the prestige of Canary Wharf behind, it was striking how quickly the area changed. Whilst not scruffy, the buildings were not as grand, shops sold halal meat, an international supermarket multitasked by combining dry cleaning with selling cheese, newspapers and fruit and veg, and the suits had been replaced by turbans and burkas. This was clearly a community that had existed long before the corporate powerhouses moved in a few hundred metres down the road, giving the impression that Canary Wharf had been dropped out of the sky and had little connection with those who live around it. A contentious point has always been that the employment brought to this area mostly goes to people who either commute from elsewhere, or move in to take up jobs they've been offered, with comparatively little benefit to those whose doorstep One Canada Square and the other huge buildings cast a shadow across.

Westferry is a road that sees industry, community and residential property mingle along its length, blocks of flats, an Islamic centre and the printing press for Northern & Shell - that's the Daily Star and Daily Express to you and me. We pass their offices later in this book.

Among the most eye-catching of buildings is a former church, now a theatre called The Space. Describing itself as a "performing arts and community centre", The Space hosts theatre, comedy, music and dance, plus workshops giving those living in the area the chance to experience the thrill of creativity. Theatre productions are both developed in-house and from visiting companies. When Abi, who helped me research Deptford and Surrey Quays, and I worked together we visited The Space as a potential venue for a theatre production we were seeking funding for. The money never came, and we ended up working on other things, but I remember rather liking The Space.

London's diverse theatre scene means you can find something to like, no matter how obscure your taste might be, and as long as you're willing to travel. I've seen plenty of enjoyable shows in the West End, but for me the real excitement is visiting a venue for the first time, optimistically, and with an open mind, taking a chance that what I'm about to see might be brilliant, because 'you never know unless you try'. If, as sometimes happens, it turns out to be a stinker, at least I've got something ready for the "worst theatre I've seen" pub conversation.

Just before the left turn from Westferry into Eastferry Road, a blue plaque on the wall of Burrells Wharf caught our attention. It told us that the Great Eastern, the largest steam ship of the 19th century, was built here by J. Scott Russell & Co, to the design of Isambard Kingdom Brunel. This was the ship you'll remember from my Brunel boat trip that was too large to launch in the conventional way. At the time of her taking to the water - sideways - in 1858 she was by some distance the largest ship ever built with the capacity to carry 4000 passengers around the world without refuelling.

If you've ever been to Berlin you'll know that walking round the city centre gives you the opportunity to play 'spot where the bombs hit'. Lines of uninspiring 1960s concrete lumps will be broken up by far more attractive older buildings, and areas, which at first look to have survived relatively unscathed, will have a blatant reminder that explosives landed indiscriminately across the city as a gaping hole was filled by a construction that was understandably built with speed and function as their main aims over architectural style.

Walking the streets of the Isle of Dogs it's easy to spot the bits the Germans missed. Just after you turn into Eastferry Road is one such occasion, for, on the left hand side is a row of Victorian houses. Their very presence makes them stand out from the rest as a reminder of how much of this part of London was either flattened during the Blitz, or demolished in the second half of the twentieth century as industry moved elsewhere. The contrast between the Docklands then and now is complete because, once again, Canary Wharf has appeared on the horizon.

I found East to be the more appealing of

the two 'Ferry Roads, not least as there's a reasonable amount of open space to be found along it.

The origin of the name Mudchute comes from the dumping of soil from hollowing out land to create Millwall Dock. As the land was fertile it quickly became a wildlife haven and is now a park, allotment site, and the home of one of London's inner city farms (the largest urban farm in Europe), riding stables and an education centre. You can also see the remains of the anti aircraft defences which were built here during the Second World War.

After a short walk around part of Mudchute Park we returned to Eastferry Road and caught sight of a branch of Asda. Nothing special about that you might think, until I remembered the Monopoly board from the Docklands Museum, which highlighted this as one of the Isle of Dogs' most important locations.

Barely able to contain our moderate interest in finding such a prestigious local landmark, the opportunity for a drink stop was very welcome. The George pub was offering 'a kaleidoscope of cast ales and continental coffee all day', so in we went to be eyed suspiciously by the half a dozen Monday lunchtime locals. This didn't spoil my enjoyment of it one little bit, as there's lots to like about this pub. The walls had oak panelling, with pictures of the docks from days gone by, including one taken from the air at what looked like war time. Opposite the sofa we sat on was a fire place that suggested it would be real rather than fake during the winter; above it David Gower looked out from the TV screen introducing the beginning of the afternoon session at the cricket. Most excitingly, behind where we were sitting was a dart board. I've noticed that the gastrofication of pubs has meant this important fixture is becoming less common. Although down a side road, The George does offer a good viewing point on London Marathon day.

Chapter 15: 'Morning Glory' - Isle of Dogs to Poplar

Our walk continued along Eastferry Road before turning into Marsh Wall, where we spotted the rather odd sight, at number 197, of the University of Sunderland's London campus. It turns out this was one of those strategic moves that managerial types like to make, in this case designed to encourage international students to study at the University without the inconvenience of having to go to Sunderland.

Further along, the International Hotel was taking bookings for Christmas, in the middle of August! Meanwhile Field & Sons were claiming to be London's oldest independent estate agents. "We've been here longer than Tower Bridge," they boasted, leaving them open to pedantry as Tower Bridge was nowhere to be seen.

We're approaching Canary Wharf once again, having almost completed our circuit of the Isle of Dogs. A noticeboard highlights the line where the City Canal used to cut across this area, creating an island. The City of London Corporation opened the canal in 1805, hoping to make large profits from charging ships a toll to take this shortcut, rather than follow the long bend in the river around the bottom of the Isle. Unfortunately for them, ship operators didn't see the value in paying for such a convenience, so the canal became a financial disaster and was sold to the West India Dock Company within thirty years.

The World War II stats for South Dock

are just as striking as everywhere else I've read about. For 76 consecutive nights the area, where I now stood, was bombarded. Fifty eight bombs landed in just one night on April 19th 1941. With these destruction numbers in mind, and with the noticeboard continuing the story up until the closure of the docks, to look around is a reminder of how far this part of London has come in such a short period of time, something which marathon runners will have seen, year in, year out.

Runners leave Canary Wharf for the second time and head along Trafalgar Road. As we walked I felt a noticeable change in surroundings. Gone was the claustrophobic feeling of tall buildings crowding round, creating a breeze-free microclimate. Out in the relative open, a stiff wind was blowing from the tidal Thames, bringing with it the strong scent of fish. Crossing a bridge we located the source of the smell which, were I running would probably make me want to be sick - the modern-day Billingsgate Fish Market.

Once a major part of the Pool of London, on what is now Lower Thames Street just upstream from Tower Bridge, the market relocated in 1982. Despite being close to the river and easily reached from the sea, the majority of fish sold here arrives by road from ports as far apart as Cornwall and Scotland.

Blackwall Basin and Poplar Dock lie ahead, and in the distance on the other side of the Thames stands the O2 Arena. Its former life as the Millennium Dome now seems such a long time ago. In the late 1990s that place was the definition of knee-jerk over ambition, with little thought given to the 'what next' question. The Dome's transformation, from empty shell to world class entertainment venue, has in part led to the demise of the Earls Court Exhibition Centre, and significantly hit the pulling power of Wembley Arena.

Crossing the road which serves the Blackwall Tunnel, we're soon away from the roar of traffic, walking down Poplar High Street. Approaching from the south a domed roof appears ahead, under which stands St Matthias Church. Now a community centre, this building boasts the impressive claim to fame of being the oldest in the Docklands.

St Matthias is yet another reminder of how this part of the London Marathon route has changed since 1981. A history of 320 years of worship was brought to an end in 1976, five years before the first running of the marathon. The building was declared redundant in 1977. Lead from the roof had been nicked, inviting the rain, as well as vandalism and theft.

For the first decade, runners would have passed a decaying heap of a place. Discussions over the church's future use were, as you might imagine, protracted and ultimately unsuccessful. Plans for an arts centre, music venue and squash courts came and went. It wasn't until 1990 that English Heritage and the London Docklands Development Corporation stepped in, concerned for the welfare of this important historical site.

So why did they care? It certainly sounds as if the building was in a pretty sorry state. A leaflet produced by English Heritage describes the building's story, its importance to the area and tale of survival; yet by the end of the 1980s, before English Heritage got involved, the church was being left to slowly rot away, a symbolic reflection of the entire dockland area.

If St Matthias' recent survival has been its biggest challenge, coming into existence runs it a close second. Dr Roger Bowdler of English Heritage takes up the story:

"Originally known as Poplar Chapel, it had two purposes: it served as a chapel for the inhabitants of the hamlets of Poplar and Blackwall, who had previously been obliged to travel several miles to the overcrowded parish church of St Dunstan's, Stepney, and desired a more local place of worship; secondly, it served as the chapel for the East India Company, which had an almshouse and a dockyard hard by. It is their coat of arms that is carved upon the ceiling boss inside the church, and their history that is central to the story of the Poplar Chapel.

"In 1600 a Royal Charter was granted which formed 'A Company of Merchants of London Trading into the East Indies'. Trading with the East, and above all with India, was seen by London merchant venturers as a profitable, if risky, area of vast potential: a similar company based in Amsterdam had already been set up in 1594. The Company had been granted a monopoly on all English trade with the Far East which consisted primarily of spices, fabrics and, in later years, tea. The East India Company retained such a monopoly until 1813 and was not wound up until 1858. It became Britain's most powerful trading body and was responsible for the administration of vast stretches of her empire, including all India."

St Matthias is the second significant

reminder of the legacy of the East India Company on the London Marathon course. They operated the Cutty Sark, built to be the fastest ship at sea in the competitive tea trade. Whilst many who explore the route of the marathon will know, or be able to draw the connection between Cutty Sark and the East India Company, far fewer will see the church from Poplar High Street and realise the link. Dr Bowdler writes:

"The East India Company purchased a house on Poplar High Street in 1627 for use as a hospital for disabled company seamen, their widows and orphans. It did so in bizarre circumstances. A jeweller named Hugh Greete had worked for the company in India buying diamonds; he was sent back to England in 1618 for purloining the best stones for himself, and died a prisoner in 1619. However, his will directed that a school or hospital be founded out of his estate. The Company had no choice but to honour this, but understandably insisted that the foundation be made in their name and not that of the fraudulent Greete. A shipyard at Blackwall had been bought by the Company in 1614 and this made Poplar an obvious location for their almshouses. In 1627 Captain Thomas Styles, a director of the East India Company, reported that "behind the house there is a faire field, and a dainty row of elmes, and a private garden, wherein a chapple may be built of 90 foote in length and 32 foote in breadth". The fair field is now Poplar recreation ground; the elms have gone, but the chapel remains.

"The inhabitants of Poplar and Blackwall in 1633 requested that the Company build a chapel that they might use, but it was not until the Lord of the Manor of Poplar, Gilbert Dethick, died in 1639 leaving £100 towards the building of the chapel, that the project began to gather momentum. Dethick had stipulated that this money would only be paid if work was commenced within three years of his decease. Since the money was paid, it must be presumed that work began on laying foundations in 1642."

So the people of Poplar had their location, their money and the will to build their own place of worship; then came the outbreak of the English Civil War, certainly not the ideal point in history to be trying to build a new church. Both the Archbishop of Canterbury and the head of the Church of England, Charles I, had their heads removed during that decade.

A second dose of good fortune would come Poplar's way in the late 1640s, following the death of former East India Company director and Lord Mayor of London Sir John Gayer in 1649. Money was left for the glazing of the Poplar Chapel, but, as with the previous donation left ten years earlier, this could only be claimed if the work began within three years. The chapel was finally completed in 1654.

London Marathon runners in need of a pit stop, and prepared to sacrifice time in favour of decent facilities, are welcomed at St Matthias for a comfort break. I took advantage of the annual Open House London weekend to pay this historic site a visit. When I mentioned my marathon connection, both as a runner and researcher, it was clear London Marathon day is a highlight of the year for the people of St Matthias. A reminder of how the atmosphere on this part of the course has changed beyond recognition.

Those that ran early marathons would have found this section a far tougher experience than those taking part today. I've already referred to descriptions I've heard of the Docklands stretch being a ghost town. But with the support of the folk at St Matthias, who are joined by the local fire service band which performs on the pavement throughout the day, the atmosphere is vibrant in this corner too.

Whilst researching this book I discovered that my Grandad was born in Poplar - I'd known of the East End link in my family but not the specific area. The tower block he once called home was one of hundreds which took a direct hit from a bomb during World War II. Fortunately for my bloodline, he was by then living elsewhere.

I've written a lot about the damage done during the Second World War, but what is often overlooked is the destruction inflicted from the sky three decades earlier. As many as 1,413 people lost their lives as a result of air raids during World War I. These began at night, but one of the most devastating happened in broad daylight, just before midday on June 13th 1917. That day 104 people died in Poplar, with the Upper North Street Primary School taking a direct hit.

Chapter 16: 'The Road Goes on Forever' - what it's like to hit the wall

Even if you've never intended to go anywhere near running a marathon, you may well have heard of the term 'hitting the wall'.

The scientific explanation is that your body uses carbohydrate in the form of glycogens as fuel for marathon running. When supplies of glycogens run low, you run slow. The general guide given is that a well-trained individual can run for around 2 hours, or for approximately 15 miles, before their natural levels of glycogen stores run out. Given that even the men's marathon world record holder cannot, and won't for some time, break two hours, refuelling at some point is absolutely essential for all of us.

You may well also have heard of the term carbo-loading. To the untrained eye this is where someone prior to a marathon pigs out on pasta-based meals to the point where the non runner would feel extremely bloated. This is done so that the runner's store of energy is higher than normal when they're standing on the start line of their marathon and, in theory, will help them avoid 'the wall'.

The non-scientific description of hitting the wall is to simply say it hurts - a lot!

Hitting the wall is as much a mental challenge as physical one. In the first half of a marathon it's easy to think about anything you wish, admiring the view (or imagining it in my case), soaking up the atmosphere, chatting to other runners, checking your pace against the plan you'd set at the start of the race, wondering how the runner in the dog costume you've just passed will be feeling about life in an hour or so, or something completely unrelated to running.

I sometimes play travel games in my head. A to Z goal keepers - I always get stuck on E, I and O, and have usually given up by the time I reach the impossible Q.

A to Z bands is too easy, so I make that more of a challenge by only allowing myself ones I can name an album by. You might think that's still straightforward, but you try naming XTC albums ten miles into a marathon.

All this is do-able, and a good idea if it helps you enjoy the experience. Meanwhile the legs keep on turning, the glycogen stores keeps on burning and the blood and oxygen keep on working their way round the body until, somewhere in the third quarter of the race, suddenly you feel completely different from how you did five minutes ago.

That comfortable pace you were running at just now feels a struggle, the legs may start to wobble as they desperately try to get the last little bit of stored-up energy out of the muscles. You become aware of parts of your body working hard that you'd normally never notice such as a pounding heart, and even the act of breathing feels a struggle. This is because oxygen is needed by the bits of the body that are doing the majority of the work and, as a consequence, less oxygen is heading to the brain, meaning you lose the ability to control your thoughts. The act of ignoring discomfort becomes so much more difficult. Whereas half an hour ago you were happily trying to decide between Messrs Schmeichel, Seaman or Shilton, now negative

212

thoughts start ganging up on you, elbowing positivity aside, and turning a rational runner into one who would happily quit if offered the chance for a sit-down.

I have a very patchy memory of the second half of the London Marathon. I remember Canary Wharf, as one of the guys I was running with spotted my Dad who had hopped on the tube from Bermondsey, where we'd seen him earlier. I also remember running back along The Highway and thinking how glad I was to be going west having done the Isle of Dogs loop. The stretch in between may as well never have happened, for all I could tell you about it. I don't believe I hit the wall as such, more that I sat at the top, slid down and landed in a heap at the bottom; a slow draining of energy, over about half an hour, as if inside me an energy balloon was being deflated. A gradual build-up of fatigue, as the furthest I'd run prior to London was 21 miles. Once I reached the bottom, I was at an exhaustion point of no return. The only thing which kept me going was the thought that I didn't want to have got this far and not to be able to say I'd completed a marathon.

My second and third marathons, Loch Ness and Berlin, whilst tough, were wall-free. Number four in Chester had a definite collision.

The day was hotter than expected for the first weekend in October and running on country roads for the majority of the race meant little shade or protection from the sun. I also believe I may have had a lingering bug picked up from over-exposure to sniff/cough/sneeze/splutter on public transport.

On course for a personal best time at half way, I was still running strong at 18 miles having taken a Lucozade gel at the 14 mile point. This was at the same time which had worked well in previous marathons, the purpose of which was to top up the glycogen levels in my body which would by then have been running low. By mile 19 my body temperature had rocketed; at 20 miles, the 3 hour 30 minute pacer we'd overtaken 15 miles earlier had caught us up. At mile 21, as the pacer disappeared into the distance, my motivation had completely gone and I didn't care if I never made the finish line. Andrew, my guide runner, was forced to use his amateur psychology skills, otherwise known as "I've not run this far to stop, so you won't either", and somehow I made it.

As I have never run for charity, and had no friends waiting for me at the finish, the desire to push through the pain barrier temporarily left me. Who would care if I walked back or, at the first opportunity, I snuck off the course and crept back to our B&B? I was anonymous, being watched by a crowd who didn't know me from the next runner.

At the point when you hit the wall all sorts of strange ideas go flashing through the mind. As I struggled to complete the last few miles into Chester I became very self conscious of being guided, with the contradictory thought that, whilst nobody knew who I was, I still stood out from the rest of the runners as if I had a fancy dress costume on. Somewhere in my subconscious was the thought that there are people who give me more credit for running a marathon than a sighted runner and, consequently, might be more sympathetic if I did step off the road. I could handle the thought of failing to finish - to really push yourself to achieve beyond your limit requires an acceptance that you might not succeed. What I couldn't handle was the idea that people might feel sorry for me and I might be given more credit for trying than my fellow runners who were suffering just as much as me. One thing which forced me to carry on running was the paranoia that somebody watching me might think my guide was helping me to the finish. In truth, the only time this could be said was during a bout of dizziness in the last couple of miles, when all he was doing was preventing me from falling over.

No sooner had I crossed the finish line than I realised that quitting would have been a stupid thing to do. A couple of days later I read this quote from Thomas A. Edison (the American inventor of the phonograph and motion picture camera), tweeted by Runner's World magazine:

"Our greatest weakness lies in giving up. The most certain way to succeed is always to try just one more time." A better mantra for the final quarter of a marathon you couldn't wish to find.

But it would be so easy to stop, to step to the side of the road, to convince yourself that the cramp which is building up is a genuine injury. After all, if you're not being sponsored, who are you letting down other than yourself? And if you don't care, who else will? All these, and many more, are questions that push to the front of your mind when you hit the wall, clouding your judgment and allowing you to kid yourself that giving up is the right thing to do. Andrew's firm but fair approach, whilst never suggesting I would be letting him down, did give me something to focus on, even if I did argue saying "what's 33 marathons when you've already done 32?"

The answer to that question is that it's not about the numbers. Whether me completing my fourth marathon, or Andrew almost thirty more than me, it's about here, right now, this moment, not then, not anywhere else. As I found in Chester, and in the days and weeks afterwards, the feeling of knowing I overcame that challenge is immeasurably more satisfying than having to explain why I didn't.

In the aftermath of Chester I got a lot of credit from other runners, people who have been there, done it - and in some cases not done it through quitting - many reminding me that to run 3 hours 37 minutes is still an impressive performance, even though I was hoping to go at least 8 minutes quicker. As runners, we can sometimes focus too hard on arbitrary targets which run the risk of unjustifiable disappointment if we fall short. One supportive Facebook message came from someone who, three weeks later, was disappointed to only just break 3 hours in the Frankfurt Marathon when she'd been hoping for 2:54. Seems illogical when written like that, but for some of us, to push ourselves to the limit and beyond, requires an all-or-nothing desire.

One of those to show her support through Facebook did so by highlighting two of her friends, both of whom had difficult marathons that day, and saying that to achieve when running well is good, but to tough it out when there are significant physical or psychological hurdles to overcome is what really inspires her in others. The word 'inspire' is one which usually makes me recoil, but since the friend in question, Jess Draskau-Petersson, competed for Denmark in the 2012 Olympics, I'll gladly take that compliment. Plus, she's right, sticking at it when things aren't going as you'd hoped is a test of character which should be admired.

Inspiration is a much over-used word, especially when referring to people who have a disability. It's a word I often hear people use to describe me, something which I've never been very comfortable with.

I'm quite willing to accept that other runners might be inspired by my approach to training, my determination to first push through the 3 hour 30 barrier for a marathon, then attempt to consolidate that. As runners, we take inspiration from each other and are free to be motivated by the achievements of whoever we choose, be that a friend, a stranger you see training in your local park or Mo Farah. If someone happens to use me as motivation, and it helps them get to the finish line of a race, it's a heart-warming thing to hear.

However I'm often told that my running achievements are even more impressive because I can't see, and this is the part I'm less comfortable with.

As a person with a disability the reality is that in many people's minds I am one of society's unlucky ones and they are therefore impressed by the fact I overcome my lack of sight in order to

217

run at all. Whereas what's important to me is getting credit for my athletic achievement. Apart from organising guide runners to be available when I need them, it takes very little effort to overcome the perceived barrier of having no sight. For people to focus on that as the achievement, rather than my times over 5K or a marathon is missing the point of what the real challenge is: training week in, week out, in everything the weather feels like throwing at me, and completing training sessions which might at the time push me to the physical limit. In short, what other runners do.

This might appear to be a bit dismissive, unappreciative of human nature's desire to be impressed by each other's individual achievements, and I accept this may be the case. The problem I have is that, so often I hear praise in day-to-day life for what I do, it's difficult for me to figure out if it's justified or not, and whether it's born out of sympathy, or genuine empathy with the achievement I'm being praised for. When I first started school my parents were warned by a very switched-on local authority special needs advisor to question whether my teachers were telling them I was achieving 'well' when they actually meant 'as well as could be expected'.

Too often I'm complimented in the street for the achievement of simply leaving the house in the morning and catching public transport. It's not unusual for a stranger to follow me for a short time, probably watching what I do as if I'm some kind of street performer (it's an uncomfortable feeling when I realise it's been happening), then say "I think you do very well".

I'd charge them for watching; only I know some people would actually give me money!

The sight of a white stick seems to make people forget that all I'm doing is what I do every day. As a result of this my brain is programmed to be suspicious of praise if I don't know the person well, and therefore I'm less able to enjoy it when there is real cause for me to be basking in my own glory.

Marathon running has allowed me to appreciate praise, up to a point. When you're part of a field of nearly 40,000 competitors you're surrounded by people, all of whom have their own story as to how they've reached the start line and why they're there. The fact that there are so many of us makes me more comfortable to accept the credit when it comes my way - my own personal success as part of a shared experience. Even with everything I've said, completing marathons is an impressive achievement and I do understand why it might be inspiring to the non runner. I finished in the top 5,000 in a field of over 37,000 the year I ran the London Marathon, which statistically means I was actually pretty good.

Blending in, or not standing out for who you are, but instead being noticed for what you achieve is something disabled people seek, and I'm no different. Give me credit for doing my job well, but it shouldn't be necessary to give me credit for having a job in the first place. The fact so many disabled people don't is society's fault, not that of the individual.

And away from the day job, I'm a runner, not a blind person who runs.

As shown by my ability to push through

'the wall' in a marathon, and my day-to-day demonstration that having a visual impairment is not something to be considered as a life barrier, the body, with or without disabilities, does what the mind tells it to. I may at times need some help along the way, but who doesn't? The inspirational part should be that we can all think like this.

Chapter 17: 'A13, Trunk Road to the Sea' - Poplar to The Highway

Close to Poplar High Street is the Lansbury Estate, so-named in recognition of one time Mayor of Poplar and Labour MP George Lansbury. His story, one of the most historically significant for the area of Poplar, comes courtesy of a book titled 'A People's History of London' by Lindsey German and John Rees. The extract I am using to support this next section was reproduced on the eastlondonhistory.com website.

At the beginning of the 20th century the Labour movement was gaining power and political representation. Whilst the majority of Labour MPs elected in 1910 served constituencies in Scotland, Wales and the north of England, areas of London, in particular the East End, saw a strong presence for the colour red. Bow and Bromley's long standing Tory MP was defeated by George Lansbury.

Pre-war strikes broke out across the UK, with the London Docks playing a vital part in the campaign, given how much of the UK's trade could be restricted through workers walking out. By the end of the war, Poplar was a trouble spot for both Labour's enemies and elements of the party wishing to appeal to the middle class vote.

George Lansbury was a figurehead for the working class East Londoner. Even though his support for the Suffragettes saw many voters desert him in the 1912 election, he went on to become Mayor of Poplar. This ultimately put him in a strong position to fight for what he believed was right.

By 1918 the Labour party under Herbert Morrison, controlled half of London's councils. Whilst Morrison was one who wanted Labour to move away from its traditional ideals, Lansbury had other ideas. He and his fellow councillors in Poplar set about trying to create a mini welfare system, building council houses and repairing roads (let's not forget Poplar received air raid bomb damage in World War I). All council workers who joined a trade union were given additional money, and there was even equal pay for men and women.

Poplar councillors took a strong stance against workhouses which didn't stop receiving London council's funding until the 1930s. The Labour party in Poplar, instead, decided to pay the unemployed something not unlike dole money, which was funded through property rates. The rates system in London was worked out based on rent value. If your rent was low you paid more, meaning the poorest people contributed the most. Money received would ordinarily go into a London-wide pot in order to fund public services, but in a radical move designed to force a government change, Poplar's council withheld the money meant for public services in order to fund their ambitious welfare plans.

Thirty Poplar councillors were summoned to the High Court and sent to prison, but were out within weeks with the Conservative government fearful of a backlash from those who supported them. On their release, thousands gathered for a huge demonstration in Victoria Park.

222

And the result of all this? Additional funding for Poplar, increasing from £50,000 to £300,000, outdoor relief (the dole) for the unemployed, controlled by the Ministry of Health, and better living conditions for the poorest people living in Poplar and its surrounding areas.

Leaving Poplar High Street runners take a side road up to the West India Dock Road, to be greeted by flats, flats and more flats. It's only when you walk around the Isle of Dogs, and neighbouring parts of the East End, that you realise how London Marathon day must equal virtual lockdown for those who live here.

Westferry DLR can be seen across the road, and we pass the confusing road junction which stumped us as we tried to find our way into Canary Wharf a few miles back.

Where West India Dock and Commercial Roads join, on the runner's left, stands a building which has the continents of the world inscribed on the front wall. Sailors' Palace was built in 1901 as the headquarters and hostel for the British and Foreign Sailors' Society. It was funded by philanthropist John Passmore Edwards, a self-made man who rose to the position of editor of The Echo, the first halfpenny newspaper. One of his greatest legacies in East London is the Whitechapel Art Gallery.

We're on the A13 now, a road immortalised in music by Billy Bragg. On a 1991 compilation of his songs recorded for John Peel's BBC Radio 1 show, is one titled 'A13, Trunk Road to the Sea', Bragg's 'Route 66' - ode to this major highway. In a Radio 4 documentary

223

'Lyrical Journeys' (February 2013) Billy Bragg followed the A13 looking at the stories to be told about this road. He talked of how growing up in Barking it was the route to better worlds. Go east and you headed for the seaside at Southend; west took you to the bright lights and the opportunities of London. As he writes in an article included in the Victoria and Albert Museum's 'Memory Maps' project:

"For as long as I can remember, whenever my father and uncles spoke lovingly of their motorbikes, of speed and the wind in their hair, the road they spoke most of was the A127, the Southend Arterial, with its three-mile straights, out beyond Gallows Corner. It was where they could push their Nortons and Triumphs up to 100mph, 'doing the ton' down to the Halfway House roundabout and back. For their sons, the Boy Racers in their two door Ford Capris and jacked-up Escort Mk1s, the road to ride was one of sharp bends and swift change-downs, of New Towns and land fills - the A13. This was the main drag out to the Promised Land of the Goldmine Discotheque on Canvey Island, caravan capital of the world. This was the route to the Kursaal at Southend and a plate of cockles or a cup of whelks. This was the road to the paradise of the Kiss-Me-Quick Never Never Land of the Essex Coast."

Whilst lyrically Bragg works from west to east, "It starts down in Wapping; There ain't no stopping", today we're heading for the bright lights of the west under a clear blue sky. It makes such a difference as the last time I was here, the day I visited St Matthias Church during London's Open House weekend, it was chucking it down with rain. Then, the area seemed grim and devoid of life, apart from those in cars hurtling past on the way to one of Billy Bragg's better places.

Two of the area's most significant buildings stand close to one another on the left hand side of Commercial Road. The church of St Anne's Limehouse is another of Hawksmoor's creations. Remember the 'Commission for Building Fifty New Churches' in the early 18th century? This was one of them. They never got near fifty, building just twelve.

Further along at number 646, looking a bit sad and neglected is the former Limehouse Town Hall. The National Museum of Labour History was once here before its relocation to Manchester.

On July 30th 1909 David Lloyd George, then Chancellor of the Exchequer, came to Limehouse Town Hall to make his famous speech attacking the Conservative-dominated House of Lords who were opposing his People's Budget. A landmark moment in British political history, the Budget was the first of its kind with the expressed intent of redistributing wealth amongst the British public. It contained revolutionary plans to tax the rich and an extensive social welfare programme. Lloyd George and Winston Churchill (the latter was, like Lloyd George, a member of the Liberal party at the time, and a vocal supporter of the People's Budget), were labelled as the 'terrible twins' by right-wing Tories.

Lloyd George famously told his audience in Limehouse, and I think this is a wonderful line, that a "fully equipped Duke costs as much to keep up as two Dreadnoughts (battle ships) but were far less easy to scrap".

An immense political battle followed with the Lords refusing to back the Budget, but agreeing they would do so once the Liberals had an electoral mandate. In other words, they dug their expensive heels in the ground for as long as they could get away with it. The Liberal Party didn't gain an overall majority in the election of January 1910 resulting in a hung parliament. Only with the support of Labour and the Irish Nationalists and the removal of a land tax, was the Budget eventually passed in April 1910.

As a result of this, and further squabbling which saw a second general election in December of that year, the Parliament Act 1911 was passed which prevented the House of Lords from being able to veto money bills. A term of parliament was also shortened from seven years to five.

Alongside the Town Hall, steps lead down to the Limehouse Cut which connects the River Lea and the Limehouse Basin. On the opposite side of the road is an eye-catching grand yellow stone building with two huge columns and an archway over the entrance. In blue letters is written 'The Mission' - it did look as if it might have once been a church and, as I discovered afterwards, used to be the home for the Sailors' Mission. A banner tied to the railings outside read "DIY and builders centre now open".

On the left, the Limehouse District Public Library, another building to receive financial support from John Passmore Edwards, looked long since shut. Anyone who still has one of their books they'd forgotten to return can probably keep it now.

Underneath a huge tower is another church, this one Our Lady Immaculate. Further along, past a bridge carrying the DLR, is a reminder of how Commercial Road has changed in recent times, a hoarding for "the new face of East London - Concierge, residents' gym, landscaped garden and private roof terrace". All it needed was someone to cook your meals on demand and that sounds like a hotel to me.

The builders at 'posh flats are us' have been busy here. I soon realised the attraction, for a bridge crosses the Regent's Canal and steps lead down to a path which runs around the Limehouse Basin. We went down for a break from the road and found, with the sun shining on the water, an oasis of serene calm, albeit one with drilling to repair lock gates on the canal, and a DLR train rumbling past what seemed like every thirty seconds. With a water view, and such a regular rail service from Limehouse into the City, it's no wonder this is a 'posh flats' part of town. If you grew up in Limehouse and have since moved away, coming back must be a weird culture shock.

A handy information board told of the history of the basin, or the Regent's Canal Dock as it was originally known.

"Between 1820 and 1969, thousands of ships arrived here from Scandinavia, America, Canada, Germany, Holland, Belgium and Mediterranean ports."

Barges would also arrive from elsewhere in the UK, bringing coal. Before the introduction of hydraulic cranes apparently it took a week to unload.

Of all the cargo which passed through

here the one which caught my imagination the most was the arrival of fifteen ice ships each year from Scandinavia. The ice would be transferred onto barges that would travel to ice wells near King's Cross, where the Canal Museum now stands. The ice would be prepared for distribution to butchers, fishmongers and ice-cream makers.

Back on Commercial Road, The White Swan pub stands on the corner of Butcher Row, the road into which runners turn in order to return to The Highway. During the 19th century the pub had the local nickname Paddy's Goose as it was a popular haunt for Irish workers who flooded into the London docks to escape the potato famine at home.

As you turn west onto The Highway The Shard stands smack bang in the middle of your view. With Canary Wharf competing for attention to the east the two skyscrapers could be the modern day equivalent of homing beacons. Reaching The Highway is an important moment for the London Marathon runner. It's that point where you're running back to Tower Bridge, circuit of the Isle of Dogs complete, and a stream of humanity heading in the other direction across the road, with the section you've just run still to do.

Roughly half way along The Highway, on the right, stands St George's Church. Stepping away from the road we found a well-kept churchyard which provides a cut through to Cable Street. At the far end, on the wall of St George's Town Hall is an enormous piece of public art, a mural depicting the 1936 Battle of Cable Street.

The accompanying description told of how "On the 4th of October 1936 the people of the East End halted a march by fascists in what has gone down in history as the Battle of Cable Street. Members of the Jewish community, communists, trade unionists, Labour Party members, Irish dockers and labourers joined forces to oppose a march through Stepney planned by Sir Oswald Mosley, leader of the British Union of Fascists and thousands of his followers known as the Blackshirts. Their uniforms echoed those used by their counterparts in Italy and Germany and the arm-raised salute was a symbol of their political allegiance.

"The planned route was through an impoverished area with a high concentration of Jewish residents and was seen as a deliberate provocation. The government of the day refused a request by Jewish locals and community groups to ban the march and on the day over 250,000 East Londoners took to the streets to bar the way to British Fascism. The Spanish Civil War had begun a few months earlier and opposition to Mosley's Blackshirts was seen as the same struggle being fought by Spanish Republicans against Franco's German and Italian backed Nationalists. The slogan used by Republicans in defence of Madrid was adopted at the barricades in Cable Street - they shall not pass.

"The ensuing action ensured that Mosley's marchers were turned back and political history was made. One resulting legacy was the Public Order Act of 1936, banning the wearing of political uniforms in public. More importantly on the day itself the fascists 'did not pass' and the people of the East End played an important role in the defeat of organised British fascism for decades to come."

The mural shows in fantastic full-coloured detail the events of that day. Anti-fascist protestors carrying banners, bottles being thrown, a blockade across the street made from furniture, marbles being thrown under the hooves of horses carrying baton-wielding police officers. One of the stand out parts of the mural is a startled-looking man in his pants with a Hitler moustache, designed to represent a fascist who is realising the game may well be up.

Artist Dave Binnington began work on the mural in 1976, carrying out extensive research and conducting numerous interviews with local people in order to create a piece of work which best reflected the events of July 1936. The process of creating the work was lengthy, not helped by several acts of vandalism, and intimidation from far-right activists.

Binnington was unable to finish his work, and three other artists saw it through to completion in 1983. The mural suffered further damage resulting in Tower Hamlets Council's promise to repair any acts of vandalism inflicted on the work.

London has many places for the public to view some of the best art in the world, and this mural in Shadwell should be high on everyone's list. Striking in its detail, impressive in its creation, and vital, not only for telling the story of the history of the East End but also how a community joined together to fight against those who sought to divide it

Chapter 18: 'Towers of London' - Tower of London and the Ceremonial City

As a school child in London, the trips I remember were to the Science Museum and the Tower of London. Disappointingly, the former doesn't appear on the marathon route; the latter does and provides memories of coaches, lunchboxes and trying to make enough notes to knock some sort of history project together. Today I've taken the tube - those coach journeys through Central London were no fun at all - and I don't have a packed lunch; perhaps I should have asked my Mum to make me one for old times' sake.

As I exited Tower Hill tube station, crossed the road and headed for the ticket office, it occurred to me I'd not been to this famous London tourist attraction in over twenty years. Were it not partly a research trip, and partly to entertain my cousin Jess who was visiting from Sheffield, I may not have got round to going for yet another twenty years. This is not something I'd usually do with a Thursday afternoon. One thing that writing this book has forced me to do is to become a tourist in my own town. I spent eighteen months commuting through Tower Hill tube station and would hear the helpful lady who announces the stops reminding passengers that they could "alight here for the Tower of London and river boat services from Tower Pier". Every morning, I would think how that would be a far better way of spending the day than sitting in an office just off Whitechapel Road. Of course I never did, and I expect there's a tourist attraction near where you live or work that you've never visited, not been to since childhood, or which you would only go to if people come to stay. Don't wait for that as you'll only end up going to the pub up the road instead. Make a list of five places you've always wanted to go to, or haven't been to for years, and aim to cross them off. True, entry fees can be a barrier, The Tower of London is not the cheapest day out; we paid around £35 for a group of three - my brother Ed came with us - which included student and disabled concessions but, as the leaflet informed us, your guide will "entertain with tales of intrigue, imprisonment, execution, torture and much more". Our guide was a Beefeater called Bob, and he did all of that.

Beefeaters, otherwise known as Yeoman Warders, are the Queen's official guards. They must serve twenty-five years in the Armed Forces before they can apply for this role. As Bob explained, Beefeaters are so called because, due to their significant security responsibilities, they were required to be as strong as possible. They were fed beef to help bulk them up; those envious of their ability to jump the roast beef and Yorkshire pudding queue adopted the name by which they're now most commonly called.

The Tower of London's name is a misleading one, for there's not one, not two, not three, but twenty of the things. There's the White Tower in the middle, with thirteen towers in the inner wall, and another six around the edge. As a child I was rather taken by the Bloody Tower, although I don't remember if this was due to stories of imprisonment, death and gore, or because I'd recently learnt that bloody was a swear word.

The White Tower is the original, built in the 1070s for William the Conqueror. Whilst the castle has been lived in by numerous monarchs since the days of William, its primary function was as a fortress stronghold, a role which remained up until the late 19th century. The last time The Tower of London was used as a prison was in the early 1950s. Among the last to be held here were the Kray twins in 1952 as they both refused to do National Service.

Another noteworthy building is the Queen's House. This was meant for Anne Boleyn, but since she was beheaded before it was finished, she naturally never got to use it. Queen's House is said to be one of the most haunted buildings on the site, the most infamous of ghosts is Arbella Stuart, a cousin of James I.

The Royal Palaces' website has a ghost stories section, and the account for Queen's House tells of how Arbella married William Seymour (Lady Jane Grey's nephew) in 1610, without King James I's permission.

"This marriage of heirs to the throne was regarded as a threat; Arbella was put under house arrest in Lambeth, while William was sent to the Tower. Arbella, spirited and rebellious, escaped, and disguised as a man plotted to get William released so that they could travel to France. William was smuggled out of the Tower, but unfortunately missed their rendevous.

"Arbella had to set sail alone, but she was recognised and sent back, this time to the Tower. William made it to France, and freedom, but he never saw Arbella again. She died at the Tower in what is now the Queen's House in 1615."

The story goes on to quote Major General Geoffrey Field, Governor of the Tower of London from 1994 to 2006, who lived in the building with his family.

"Soon after we'd arrived in 1994, my wife Janice was making up the bed in the Lennox room when she felt a violent push in her back which propelled her right out of the room! No one had warned us that the house was haunted – but we then discovered that every resident has experienced something strange in that room. The story goes that the ghost is that of Arbella Stuart, who was imprisoned and then possibly murdered in that bedroom. Several women who slept there since have reported waking in terror in the middle of the night feeling they were being strangled."

Queen's House is the last remaining Tudor building in this part of London. The rest were destroyed during the Great Fire, but Queen's House, protected by the Tower's walls, was never under threat.

The moat was a stand-out part of the Tower of London's design, filling up with the rise of the Thames tide, emptying out as the water receded. With thousands of people living on the site, and long before Tower Hamlets Council enforced an exciting rubbish collection and recycling policy, with a range of different coloured bins where no one could quite remember what was supposed to go where, a considerable quantity of waste was dumped into the moat. With some hint of poetic licence, Bob the Beefeater took great pleasure in pointing out how tons of crap, including actual crap, would be sucked downstream into the sea, and sent off across the English Channel to France. In reality it was probably dumped on the opposite bank at the first bend in the river.

Bob drew our attention to Trinity House, a building which can be seen from inside the Tower. On the site of the infamous Tower's gallows now stands the headquarters for the organisation given a royal charter by Henry VIII in 1544, to oversee the safety of shipping and the well-being of seafarers.

On execution days, hundreds of thousands of people would gather. The beheading of a criminal was a major show, with music and dancing as part of the pre-chop build-up. This event was for the masses of the day what football is now. With an hour to go, a bell inside the Tower would sound, and the prisoner would be dragged up the hill to the waiting platform. With the sombre, intimidating reality of the bell tolling, the roughness with which the prisoner would have been treated, perhaps even signs of fear from the condemned; in all its brutality this must have been quite a spectacle. On the platform, the executioner would kneel before the prisoner and ask for forgiveness for the act he was about to carry out. This would of course be given, after which the prisoner would address the crowd. Speech over, the prisoner would place their neck on the block and down would come the axe. No doubt a retired executioner would then analyse the action in great detail to a 16th century equivalent of Jeff Stelling!

Usually the chop would result in a clean

cut, although this wasn't always the case. One such occasion saw a part-time butcher, part-time executioner, full-time drunk in charge of proceedings. Taking a swig of brandy before the vital moment, he brought the axe down hard, slamming it on to the shoulder of the convicted. Again and again he missed the important bit, eventually pulling out a butcher's knife and going for the kill in the crudest of ways.

In the 21st century the death penalty sounds like an act from a different time, or something they do in other less humane parts of the world, but there are members of the Conservative Party who think a return to this form of punishment would be a splendid idea. One such group of MPs tabled a Private Members' Bill in June 2013 as part of "the alternative Queen's Speech", with Parliament required to debate the matter which the group of Tory backbenchers described as "popular" and what the "British public really want".

Those in favour no doubt argue they're only calling for a less barbaric method of death such as fatal injection, which obviously makes no difference at all when trying to correct the inevitable miscarriage of justice. How would, say, the Birmingham Six have been brought back to life?

Inside the walls of the Tower is a private execution site away from the baying mob on the hill. This was reserved for significant figures, friends or associates of the king or queen of the day. These included Anne Boleyn and Catherine Howard. The Tower of London website explains that "all three queens" (for Lady Jane Grey was also beheaded here) "were treated with respect right up until the end. For Anne Boleyn's execution, an expert swordsman was imported from France to make sure her death was quick". So that makes it all fine then, conscience clear Henry.

The Yeoman Warder tour ends with the Chapel of St. Peter ad Vincula. As this is still a place of worship serving as the parish church for HM Tower of London used by the 150 residents, on entering, we're requested to switch our phones off and those who can, to remove headgear. Unsurprisingly there was one guy who strolled in, making no effort to take his baseball cap off. Whether or not you subscribe to, participate, or have any interest in a religion, to completely ignore a request such as that is just rude.

In 2012, the Chapel marked its 500th anniversary. As well as the three queens, the bodies of disgraced royal favourites, bishops, rebels and Lord Chancellors were disposed of beneath the floor.

Once the tour was over, we were free to continue exploring the Tower of London and its various exhibitions for as long as we wished. For the vast majority this meant heading straight for the Crown Jewels made up of cases and more cases of diamonds, rings, jewel-encrusted plates and of course, numerous crowns.

Perhaps it's because I can't see to appreciate their breathtaking beauty, or maybe it's because I'm a bloke and would rather look at weapons, but either way, the Crown Jewels did little to enthuse me. That said, it's worth fighting your way through crowds of drooling females just to see a punch bowl measuring over one metre in width; this thing could hold 144 bottles of wine, which is one hell of a house party by anyone's standard.

The original Crown Jewels were melted down at the request of Oliver Cromwell following the English Revolution in 1642. All that remained were a couple of swords and a spoon. Why a spoon you may ask? I certainly wouldn't want to be the one sent into battle with that. The spoon plays an important role in the coronation ceremony as it's used to put oil on the head of the monarch, so not a trick to try with a sword then.

Walking around the grounds we passed the famous ravens. Legend had it that should the six ravens leave, the kingdom would fall, so a great vote of confidence in the army given the job of protecting the nation. Charles II was the paranoid monarch who first insisted the birds should be protected. Today there are seven, six plus a spare, just in case one should flap away into Shoreditch and Britain gets invaded from all directions.

The ravens are the only wildlife remaining at the Tower. The menagerie, a collection of wild animals, was moved out in the early 19th century to form what is now London Zoo.

In 1811 a bear called Martin became the first grizzly bear seen in the UK when he came to live at the Tower. On looking round the gift shop, I certainly felt there was a missed merchandising opportunity to market Martin as a character for kids; no, make that a character for people like me who would buy into that sort of thing. If I were designing their product range I'd have Martin on absolutely everything. That's not to say the shop wasn't packed with people gleefully loading themselves up with cuddly ravens, chocolate Beefeaters, London bus-shaped pencil sharpeners and jars of Tower of London lemon curd: because of course, think Tower of London, think lemon curd. But where was the 'Martin the Bear' toy, T shirt, mask, lunchbox, colouring-in book or pencil case?

I bought an ice cream instead.

On the way out we spotted a sign that told us how, in the 14th century, archery was considered so important to national security that it was compulsory for every male from the age of seven to sixty. Had we kept that up we certainly wouldn't have lost in the 2012 Olympics to a partially sighted Korean.

A board across the road from the gate to the Tower of London welcomes people to the London Borough of Tower Hamlets - although from the marathon runner point of view, Tower Hamlets, with its never ending circuit of the Docklands, is at last behind them. All that remains is a run by the river, through the City and along the Embankment. Just a few short miles up to Westminster; you can do that in eleven minutes on the District Line, how far can it really be?

Further than you could possibly imagine!

At least the reversal of the route, which I've already written about, means runners no longer have to cross the cobbles immediately in front of the Tower. Friends of mine who did London before 2005 tell me that part of the course was hell!

London 2011 was my first attempt at

completing a marathon. Prior to that, the furthest I'd run was 21 miles, so as I passed the Tower of London for the second time, 22 miles, I was at the point at where every step would take me further into the physical unknown.

Australian runner Rob de Castella, winner of the World Championships' marathon in 1983 and a two-time Commonwealth Games marathon winner, once said of the 26.2 mile distance: "If you feel bad at 10 miles, you're in trouble. If you feel bad at 20 miles, you're normal. If you don't feel bad at 26 miles, you're abnormal". So we're now at the point on the course where pain and suffering are a given.

This is where the role of the guide runner becomes so much more than just making sure I run in a straight line and don't bump into things; a challenge that should not be underestimated if they too are doing the full distance. Although they should be able to cover the 26.2 miles more quickly than the blind runner in order to be a suitable guide, it's still a long time for them to be on their feet, and longer than they might usually expect to run for. At the point when I'm fighting fatigue I need my guide to be calling out mile markers, and keeping track of how long it takes to complete each mile so that I can be given an idea of how far away the next one is, even telling me about the runners who are around us, within reason of course. I'm not sure if I'd want to laugh or cry if a cabbage came past looking relaxed and full of running. One of my friends, with more than ten marathons to his name, regularly talks of feeling confident, relaxed and running well, even though he was some way past the halfway point in the London Marathon one

240

year, only to be overtaken by a courgette.

It was at about this point during my marathon debut where tiredness took its hold on me to the point where, despite the best efforts of Simon my guide runner, I still managed to completely lose track of where we were.

There's a community running initiative called parkrun, where every Saturday in parks across the UK, plus many more around the world, a free, timed, 5K run is held. It has taken off to such an extent that broadsheet journalists will often use their columns to tell readers of their visit to one such event, with runners lining up for their weekly 5K in locations as diverse as Poland, Australia and Camp Bastion. As each event is managed by a team of volunteers parkrun relies heavily on sponsorship to exist. The London Marathon are one of a number of brands to lend their support to this initiative which sees participants as wide-ranging as Olympians Mo Farah and the Brownlee Brothers, to those who wish to walk round the course in over an hour.

The birth place of parkrun is Bushy Park, close to where I live in South West London. I'm fortunate enough to have several of these parkrun events within easy jogging distance of my house. As I'm approaching 100 runs on various parkrun courses, the familiarity of the 5K distance (3.1 miles) is one I can easily call to mind in longer races. It's not uncommon for a distance marker sign which is three miles from the finish of a race to trigger the motivating thought of "just a parkrun to go". In other words, all I have to do is the same distance as a lap of one of the courses in Bushy or Richmond

Parks that I know I can comfortably jog round in under twenty-five minutes.

During my marathon debut, I had fixed my mind on this thought a few miles before the moment arrived. As each mile was ticked off and the fatigue increased, my thoughts became less clear and more focused on significant targets. So driven was I by the line "just a parkrun to go", which would bring the 23 mile point and, in theory, less than half an hour to run, that I became convinced this would be the next mile marker to come. The closest I came to quitting was the moment when Simon announced the arrival of 22 miles and I realised I was a mile further away from the finish line than I'd thought.

If, or when, I run London again, I hope I don't repeat that mistake. I'd say it's unlikely to happen as I'm now much more experienced at running 26.2 miles than back in April 2011. A bigger problem might be the knowledge that, for the two years I've been a spectator not a runner, we have retired from our viewing point on The Highway to a pub, just off the course close to the 22 mile point called The Minories. Nor will the memory of pie and mash from the excellently-named Hung Drawn and Quartered pub, a short distance on from the Tower of London, be a spirit-lifter. There's a hangman's noose behind the bar, which is one way of dealing with any rowdy customers. The online reviews are almost unanimous in their praise, the only grumble appears to be that, if you head there early evening on a week night it's full of 'pretentious banker types'.

On the other side of the street from the

Hung Drawn and Quartered stands the oldest church in the City, All Hallows by the Tower. It predates the Tower by over 300 years as it was founded by the Abbey of Barking in the year 675AD. On display in the church crypt is a Roman pavement, showing evidence of city life on this site for nearly 2000 years.

Due to its location, the church was often used as a temporary resting place for beheaded bodies as they were prepared for burial.

The church survived the Great Fire of 1666, Samuel Pepys watched London burn from its tower. The tower also survived the Blitz, although most of the rest of the church was destroyed, being rebuilt once the war was over.

There's another reason for drawing your attention to the boundary line between Tower Hamlets and the City, aside from it being a significant sign to runners that the end is getting near. All Hallows church is involved in maintaining certain ancient customs of the area, such as Beating the Bounds which is still observed at this point, as it is in many English parishes. In mediaeval times boundaries were ceremonially reaffirmed during Rogation week. A beating party would walk the boundary edge, beating each boundary marker with wands and praying for protection for the land. Rogation week, for those who didn't pay attention during RE class, ahem, was traditionally a period of four days of solemn procession to invoke God's mercy, and takes place on the Monday, Tuesday and Wednesday before Ascension Day each May.

This tradition still takes place at All Hallows today. The All Hallows' Beating Party is made up of students from St Dunstan's College,

Catford, who return to their roots in the parish of St Dunstan-in-the-East to take an active part in the proceedings. The south boundary of the parish is mid-stream of the Thames, and the Beating Party, together with the clergy and the Masters of the Livery Companies associated with the parish, board a boat which takes them out onto the river where one of the students beats that boundary mark. No doubt straws are drawn beforehand to find out who gets the dubious honour of sitting next to them as they smack a stick on the surface of the river. They then return to shore and the procession moves around the parish, stopping at various points for the beating party to mark the boundaries with canes as they go.

Excitingly, every third year the ceremony includes a 'confrontation' with the Resident Governor and Yeoman Warders of HM Tower of London at the boundary mark shared by the Tower and the Church. During the middle ages the boundary was always in dispute, and this meeting commemorates an occasion in 1698 when a riot took place between the people of the Tower and those of the parish.

I have a particular interest in the concept of a beating the bounds ceremony, for we in the Stragglers Running Club in South West London, where I am a member, have one of our own.

Bushy Park, where the parkrun concept first saw light of day, is one of the areas we use to train, and each year we celebrate the park's existence as public land, for this was not always the case.

In 1734 the Earl of Halifax built a new wall which would completely surround Bushy

Park, thereby impeding traditional local footpaths and obliging residents to obtain tickets for entry. This situation created much resentment and it was a humble local resident who brought the matter to a head. Timothy Bennet was a shoemaker in Hampton Wick located on the north side of the River Thames opposite Kingston. The story tells of how Bennet was incensed that the villagers had to walk around the wall in order to reach the church in Hampton. It just so happened that the new route to and from Kingston Market did not take people past his shop.

Bennet told Halifax: "When I was a young man, sitting at my work, the people cheerfully passed my shop to Kingston Market but now my lord, they are forced to go about, through a hot and sandy road, ready to faint beneath their burdens and I am unwilling to leave this world worse than I found it". (This story comes courtesy of 'Hampton and Teddington Past' by John Sheaf and Ken Howe.)

Under growing pressure Halifax reopened the gates and footpaths, and each July, I, and a number of my running friends, mark this victory for the common man over the establishment in the only way we know how. Our Beating of Bushy's Bounds begins at a pub called The Swan by Kingston Bridge, said to be the approximate location of Timothy Bennet's shop, from where we run the full circuit of the park, a distance of seven miles, stopping for a pint at seven pubs on the way.

A number of the Kenyan distance runners are based in Teddington and use Bushy Park to train. We sometimes see them as we set off and, on exchanging greetings; we wonder if they're impressed to see us at the beginning of what might appear to be the definition of dedication, training on a Saturday night. If only they knew what we were really doing.

Beating the Bounds isn't the only ancient tradition connected with the City of London which caught my eye.

The Knollys Rose Ceremony is held in June each year and is organised by the Company of Watermen and Lightermen of the River Thames. On this day one red rose will be plucked from a garden in Seething Lane and taken to the Mansion House, carried on the altar cushion of All Hallows by the Tower, where it will be presented to the Lord Mayor.

The ceremony commemorates an ancient City judgment dating from 1381. Sir Robert Knollys owned a house on the West side of Seething Lane. He was sent abroad to war and, while he was away, his wife is reputed to have become annoyed with the chaff dust blowing from threshing ground opposite their house, so she bought the property and turned it into a rose garden.

Trouble came when she built a footbridge over the lane to avoid the mud, but failed to get the equivalent of planning permission, and you know what fun that can cause at the local council office. The penalty was that rent of a red rose from the garden had to be paid annually to the Lord Mayor. The rose payment was no more than a symbolic fine upon Sir Robert, a leading citizen and a successful and respected soldier. You can bet your life that the neighbours would have grumbled about "one rule for one, another for the rest of us".

For this payment permission was given "to make an haut pas of the height of 14 feet" across the lane - in other words, "it's OK Sir Robert, your wife can keep her bridge". The footbridge has long since disappeared, but the legal requirement for the payment of this rent has been established as one of the City's traditions.

Chapter 19: 'I'm on Fire' - climbing the Monument to the Great Fire of London

As you head along Lower Thames Street, away from the Tower of London, peeping above the buildings on the right hand side is the famous guilded urn at the top of the Monument to the Great Fire of London. Further along the road, level with the former Billingsgate Fish Market, if runners look half-right and ahead of them they will see the Wren-designed column towering proudly at the end of a side street. We don't pass directly by it, but where the Church of St Magnus the Martyr stands on the left hand side close to London Bridge, Fish Street Hill climbs away to the right, and it is on the corner of this and Monument Street where the Monument itself is to be found.

Its location is important, were you to lay down the 61 metre (202 feet) tall stone column, it would stretch to the point where, on September 2nd 1666; a fire broke out in a baker's house in Pudding Lane. Three days later, the City of London was almost entirely wiped out.

As well as Samuel Pepys, who watched events unfold from the All Hallows Tower, his contemporary the diarist John Evelyn, who gave his name to Evelyn Street in Deptford which runners follow during mile 8, chronicled events as the day by day horror unfolded.

In a brief entry dated Sunday September 2nd he writes of going to the southern bank of the Thames in Southwark and watching as the "dismal speectaccle" developed across the water. The following morning he returned to the same spot where the fire had raged all night, "…if I may call that night, which was as light as day for ten miles round about".

He describes seeing the fire take hold of St Paul's Church, and devour the streets, buildings and wharves of the city. His entry of September 3rd also gives us an indication of the helplessness of those whose homes and livelihoods were being destroyed.

"The Conflagration was so universal, & the people so astonish'd, that from the beginning (I know not by what desponding or fate), they hardly stirr'd to quench it, so as there was nothing heard or seene but crying out & lamentation, & running about like distracted creatures, without at all attempting to save even their goods; such a strange consternation there was upon them, so as it burned both in breadth & length, The Churches, Publique Halls, Exchange, Hospitals, Monuments, & ornaments, leaping after a prodigious manner from house to house & streete to streete, at greate distance one from the other, for the heate (with a long set of faire & warme weather) had even ignited the aire, & prepared the materials to conceive the fire, which devoured after a[n] incredible manner, houses, furniture, & everything. Here we saw the Thames coverd with goods floating, all the barges & boates laden with what some had time & courage to save, as on the other, the carts carrying out to the fields, which for many miles were strewed with moveables of all sorts, & Tents erecting to shelter both people & what goods they could get away. O the miserable &

calamitous speectacle, such as happly the whole world had not seene the like since the foundation of it, all the skie were of a fiery aspect, like the top of a burning Oven, & the light seene above 40 miles round about for many nights. God grant mine eyes may never behold the like, who now saw above ten thousand houses all in one flame, the noise & crakling & thunder of the impetuous flames, the shreeking of Women & children, the hurry of people, the fall of towers, houses & churches was like an hideous storme, & the aire all about so hot & inflam'd that at the last one was not able to approch it, so as they were force'd [to] stand still, and let the flames consume on which they did for neere two whole mile[s] in length and one in bredth. The Clowds also of Smoke were dismall, & reached upon computation neere 50 miles in length."

The fire was finally extinguished on September 5th, three days after it began. Thousands of houses, streets and even the city gates were destroyed; the only buildings to survive were the few made of stone such as the Guildhall. The present day St Paul's Cathedral was built between 1675 and 1710 as the church which stood here was destroyed by the fire. Many of the churches we've found around the marathon course such as St Alfege's Greenwich and St Paul's Deptford were either built or rebuilt from money left over from that which was raised from a coal duty to fund building a new St Paul's.

As part of the rebuilding of the City, and to symbolise its rebirth, Sir Christopher Wren was given the task of designing a permanent memorial to the great fire. The Monument took six years to construct and was opened in 1677. As presumably there was still much work to be done in resurrecting the City around it, was this a symbol of great hope and inspiration of what could be achieved? Or did people then, as they would no doubt do now, complain about time and money being wasted faffing about with needless vanity projects when people needed homes to live in?

On the closest Saturday to the date on which the Great Fire began, I stood at the bottom of the 311 stairs; the extra step into the ticket office doesn't count by the way. For the small sum of £3 you can climb to the viewing platform 150 feet above ground. With Tower Bridge close by, you can buy a combined ticket, giving you access to two of London's most iconic landmarks for a mere £9. If you exclude the capital's parks and free museums, of the things you have to pay for, I'm not convinced there's much better tourism value to be found anywhere in this city. On a clear, warm and sunny Saturday afternoon, plenty agreed, as I and my friend Geraldine, who had also visited the Tower Bridge exhibition with me, joined the steady stream of people winding their way up the spiral stairs.

I'd had it in mind that the steps would be exposed to the elements, but you're actually climbing up inside the column. It put me in mind of a mediaeval castle tower, especially as there were occasional narrow windows that looked just wide enough to point a bow through to shoot an arrow into a neighbouring office block window.

Just as I was saying how I thought an interesting challenge would be to see how fast I could run from the bottom to the top, someone must have tried it. Geraldine went quiet and sat down on what passes for a ledge. As low blood pressure-induced nausea took its hold, we were treated to the public's ability to show no concern whatsoever in the wellbeing of their fellow citizens. Not one person asked if she was ok as she vomited into a cardigan which became an emergency sick bag, instead awkwardly squeezing by, casting disapproving or inconvenienced "you should know better than to come up here if you can't hack it" or "had too much to drink last night young lady" looks in our direction.

After a few minutes, composure was recovered almost as quickly as it had gone away, and with sick-covered clothing safely hidden in a bag, we resumed the climb and were rewarded at the top with an unbroken view of everyone's favourite London landmark, the Crystal Palace TV mast.

It's a much more rewarding climb than that though. The platform runs full circle, with a health and safety cage in place - one too many 19th century suicide attempts were successful from up here.

The height of surrounding office blocks does impact on what can be seen. Oddly, Big Ben is hidden, but you get a great view of Battersea Power Station. What a great vantage point this must have been one day in 1977, to observe a 40 foot helium-filled pig being launched for a photo shoot for Pink Floyd's 'Animals' album. The viewer would have watched as a gust of wind caused Algie to break free from his ropes and rise up into the sky, causing flights from Heathrow to be grounded. The pig was eventually found some hours later having crash-landed on a farm in Kent.

One of the most striking things, which isn't so obvious at ground level, is what a huge number of churches there are in and around the Square Mile. A list on the City of London website totals fifty. As we stood on high, the bell ringers at St Magnus the Martyr were exercising their arm muscles. Geraldine pointed out they were playing different tunes but it all sounded the same to me.

Sermons were held here following London's 1640 fire, giving thanks for the church's survival. Twenty-four years later it was one of the first to be destroyed by the Great Fire. A church has stood on this site, where people entered the City via London Bridge, for 1000 years; apparently there's a four metre long model of the bridge inside. St Magnus the Martyr, like the Monument, is the work of Sir Christopher Wren.

We descended the spiral stairs without incident. Excitingly at the bottom you're given a certificate to "certify that" insert name "has climbed the 311 steps of the Monument", signed by David Right, Tower Bridge Director.

As we left the attendant called after us, warning me to "be careful of the step". Perhaps a little unnecessary given she'd just handed me a piece of paper confirming I'd successfully climbed up and down over 300 of them.

253

Chapter 20: 'Run For Home' - Tower of London to Upper Thames Street

When I was 12 years old I spent a half-term holiday walking the Thames Path, over 150 miles from the source to Richmond, with my Dad. So it seemed a logical choice to do this stretch of the marathon course with him, something we did on a couple of occasions.

It is an April Monday lunchtime in the City and the sun is making a lame attempt at coming out, but to quote Terry Pratchett, it was doing so "slowly, as if it wasn't sure it was worth all the effort". As the days draw longer and the temperature rises signalling that winter is giving way to spring, the prospect of evenings in beer gardens and weekends in one of London's many parks becomes a realistic dream. But for many, there's something big blocking their route to the barbecue. A large, or should that be long, 26.2 mile-sized thing. How the hell has that marathon appeared so quickly?

I say this at this point in my marathon exploration for the lunchtime in question is the Monday immediately before the London Marathon. Having had lunch I've decided to walk to Westminster, something many will be forced to do post lunchtime this coming Sunday. On the subject of food, I know we're in the City but who knew fish fingers in a roll could be so expensive? Clearly, if pricey menus are sustainable in the Square Mile not everyone is living in financially tricky times. As it turned out what was advertised as 'posh fish fingers' didn't taste any different from what I'd expect to be served up at 'the Captain's table'.

There are numerous sights and points of interest along this stretch, which sees runners work their way, painfully in most cases, along Lower and Upper Thames Streets and the Victoria Embankment. A good number of these runners won't be remotely interested in trying to spot the Monument or St Paul's Cathedral, or looking at the ships moored along the North bank of the river. The existence of the London Eye on the South Bank will mostly serve the purpose of being a target to run towards, and every pub they pass, no matter how interesting a name it may have, is more likely to make them long for a sit down and a drink.

As I set out for my afternoon walk to remind myself of exactly what can be found on this part of the course a number of runners passed me, squeezing in a few miles during their lunch hour. I wondered how many of them were making final preparations for Sunday's race?

March and April is one of the times of year when a number of marathons take place. I had been due to run in Brighton the day before, but a knee injury at the beginning of March put an end to that. Paris, Barcelona and Rome are some of the major cities to have staged their marathons in recent weeks. Boston, the oldest and perhaps most prestigious of them all, was taking place that very day. It's a 'must do' for thousands of runners; it is one of the World Marathon Majors alongside London, Berlin, New York, Chicago and Tokyo, and this despite the IAAF (International Association of Athletics Federations) not recognising times run there for world records due to the hilly nature of the course.

Later that night, marathon running was making headlines around the world as news broke of two explosions close to the finish line in Boston. There will have been those who questioned why BBC and Sky News went to rolling coverage. I did read views expressed about disproportionate attention being given in favour of this over other acts of terrorism; the often-used accusation of British media being more interested in what happens in the US than anywhere else in the world wasn't difficult to find.

This was a major story for the UK because of the number of British people potentially caught up in the blast. As you have to run a qualifying time in order to secure a place at Boston, running clubs across the UK would have been mindful that some of their own members were competing. Mine certainly was. Fortunately for the Stragglers Running Club the news was good, as one of my training partners for my Brighton campaign was two blocks away at the time of the explosions.

Thoughts in the media quickly turned to security at the London Marathon. The road I walked along that Monday afternoon would be packed come race day as the Embankment is one of the most popular viewing points. Reassurances were given by the race organisers; security plans were reviewed and adjusted accordingly and police numbers were increased, although this was as much for public reassurance as a reaction to any genuine threat. As race day drew closer, developments in Boston showed that London should not be considered a target. The motive appeared to be a domestic one; the suspects were known, with one already dead and the other in hospital seriously injured with the police awaiting their opportunity to question and potentially charge him.

The worry from a runner's point of view was whether people might be put off coming out to show their support, especially relevant for this part of the course. For these last few miles present one of the most physically demanding experiences you could imagine.

As it turned out this was an unnecessary fear. Once the initial shock of events in Boston had subsided, a noticeable feeling of defiance grew from the people of London, something this city is known for in challenging times. This determination to show that marathon running, and London itself, would rise above the threat of terrorism, were helped by the added bonus of a perfect sunny morning, and the 'Farah Effect' with Mo running the first half of the course ahead of his anticipated debut at the full distance in 2014. On the day, record crowds lined the streets with the marathon organisers estimating a turnout of 700,000 spectators - an event record.

In the aftermath, Hugh Brasher, new race director for the London Marathon, reflected on his first time at the helm on the big day by saying "overall we are really, really pleased with the support London showed us. People said the atmosphere has never been better. It was an outstanding success".

At times such as this, it's worth revisiting the six objectives drawn up by Chris Brasher and John Disley when planning for the first London

257

Marathon in 1981. Alongside the aims to improve the standard of British marathon running, to raise money for the capital's sporting and recreational facilities, to demonstrate that Britain can host major events and show off London's tourist attractions, were two aims which were of particular significance in 2013: to show mankind that, on occasions, they can be united, and, to have fun and provide some happiness and sense of achievement in a troubled world.

Those values which underpinned the original dream stood firm at the end of what must have been one of the most challenging weeks in the London Marathon's history, which saw marathon running caught up in the most unwanted of media storms.

On returning from his first visit to the New York Marathon with John Disley, Chris Brasher wrote an article in the Observer titled 'The world's most human race'.

It began: "To believe this story you must believe that the human race can be one joyous family, working together, laughing together, achieving the impossible".

Whilst staging the London Marathon post the Boston bombing was far from impossible, the response of the public to turn out in the numbers they did showed we very much 'believed'.

Brasher concluded his article by wondering if London could stage an event like New York.

"We have the course, a magnificent course, but do we have the heart?"

On Sunday April 21st 2013, hundreds of

thousands of people did. London did itself proud that day.

So to return to that "magnificent course", the one which served to boost London tourism, with the Tower of London and Tower Bridge now behind me, I set off that Monday afternoon to walk the three or so miles to Westminster, past many of the most eye-catching sights on the route: St Paul's Cathedral, the Monument to the Great Fire of London, the London Eye and Cleopatra's Needle are all in view at one point or another. The tower which houses Big Ben acts as a target to run towards and, as in so many places around the course, the Shard rises above the rest.

This was also a personal trip down memory lane, reminding me of how tough I found the latter stages of my debut marathon, as much of those last few miles are little more than a hazy collection of random flashbacks.

The section of the course between Tower and London Bridges is the site of the original Pool of London, part of the Port of London.

The area became known as Legal Quays as this was where cargo was brought into London to be checked by Customs Officers. Trade via the Pool expanded dramatically during the second half of the 1700s. The river became so congested during the latter part of the 18th century that it could be possible to cross the Thames by stepping from ship to ship.

Smuggling and theft were widespread. This was one of the contributing factors, along with limited space for larger ships, which led to the development of the docks further downstream.

In 1796 the City Corporation, along with

the owners of the wharves and warehouses in the Pool of London, sought ways in which to win back trade by redeveloping the profit-hit Legal Quays. These ranged from simple schemes such as extending the quays into the river, to huge riverside warehouses with dock basins for barges within. Their expansion ambitions were significantly restricted by the position and design of London Bridge which meant ships could not travel any further upstream. Many new designs for the bridge were produced, but it wouldn't be until the 1820s that a new bridge was built.

We've entered the Ward of Billingsgate, of fish market fame. Now the market is a few miles further back down the course close to Canary Wharf and Poplar. The Lower Thames Street building which used to house the market is now a prestigious events and conference facility where the only sign of fish comes in the form of canapés.

Further along the street, on the left hand side, is the headquarters for Northern & Shell - Channel 5, Daily Express, Daily Star et al.

I've always had a bit of a soft spot for the Daily Star, although I've lost interest in recent years with its saturation coverage of Big Brother. It was always worth buying on a Saturday for its extremely difficult football quiz. As they print the answers the following week I've spent many a Saturday desperately trying to find that week's paper to see how well, or badly I'd done.

As a student I did a few days' work experience at the Express and the Star, then in a different building south of the river. The highlight of my week was the day I spent with the Star's sports team, at the end of which the

Sports Editor opened a drawer in his filing cabinet and handed me eight cans of beer saying: "We give these to people we like". That was the end of my national newspaper career; I like to think I quit while I was ahead.

Tabloid journalism has been dragged through the gutter in recent years, often deservedly so, and of their own doing, but the people I met at both papers all seemed genuinely keen to help and make time for someone with an interest in their industry.

You can walk in off the street and pick up a free paper from the Northern & Shell reception; I duly paused for my 'ooh ah Daily Star'; sadly there was no football quiz on a Monday.

As runners pass underneath the road which leads up to London Bridge, *Lower* Thames Street becomes *Upper*. A short distance further on is the railway line into Cannon Street, the beginning of the line to Kent via Deptford and Greenwich - the route of the oldest railway in London.

Another historical sight greets those who look left down a street called Angel Lane, by the large glass offices of Nomura (Japan's largest investment bank). The Golden Hind, a replica of the galleon built for Sir Francis Drake to circumnavigate the globe in the 1570s, rests in a dry dock next to Southwark Cathedral.

The small park on the right of Upper Thames Street is Whittington Gardens. The church behind is St Michael Paternoster Royal, the church for the Mission to Seafarers. The building is also the home for the Dunkirk War Memorial Trust.

We discovered a couple of interesting statues on the right of Upper Thames Street.

The first was of two stylised hooded men on horseback, given to the City of London by the President of Italy in 2003.

Then, further along, outside the church of James Garlickhythe and across the road from the Vintners' Livery Company, was a barge master in a very smart-looking uniform, with a swan looking up at him. If I were the swan I'd get out of there for the pole over the man's shoulder was to be used in the odd practice of swan upping, which my Dad explained to me as we walked.

Swans are either owned by the Queen or they're not. If you're a swan, who owns you depends on which county you live in: the Crown claims swans on stretches of the Thames in the counties of Middlesex, Surrey, Buckinghamshire, Berkshire and Oxfordshire.

Swan Upping is the annual census of the swan population and once a year, a group of brightly-coloured boats carrying people dressed like the bloke depicted in the statue row up the Thames. When they find cygnets they corner them, do a health check and mark their beak by way of proving that the Queen owns them. Should you wish to see this ceremonial occasion it takes place in the third week of July.

Chapter 21: 'Light at the End of the Tunnel' - Upper Thames Street to Temple

There's a light at the end of the tunnel, but unlike in the Half Man Half Biscuit song, this one isn't the 'light of an oncoming train' but spirit-lifting lights in the 'Tunnel of Yes'.

In its day job the 'Tunnel of Yes' is the Blackfriars Underpass, close to Blackfriars station, which runs under what look to be mostly office buildings. In 2013 London Marathon organisers decided to make this a less bleak part of the course by plastering inspirational slogans on the wall and playing motivational music designed to put a spring in the weary step. Sadly although the name suggests it should, there were no 20 minute 'prog rock' epics. Who wouldn't want to hear songs with titles like 'Gates of Delirium', 'The Revealing Science of God' or 'The Ancient (Giants Under the Sun)' in their hour of need? Nor was grumpy old man himself Rick Wakeman standing at the end, keyboard at the ready to serenade participants as they painfully stagger by.

The crowds are huge by this point and they make a lot of noise. As Upper Thames Street dips down into the tunnel there's no pavement for people to watch from, so runners leave the vibrant, inspirational atmosphere outside. All you have for company is the sound of footsteps and the groans of other runners as they wearily drag their bodies towards the promised land of The Mall.

In here, away from the eyes of those enthusiastically cheering from the sidelines, tears might be shed, prayers may be said, pledges to "never run one of these bloody marathons ever again" are likely to be made. With only other runners to see them, people who have forced themselves to keep to something resembling a jog now slow to walking pace, gulp the air, stop to stretch their aching muscles and gather their thoughts for that final effort. It's so much harder to stop and walk when there are thousands of eyes looking at you, even though you're not the only one doing it. In here, with only your fellow warriors for company, your secret is safe.

The year I ran the London Marathon, by the time I reached the tunnel, the sun was burning on to my face. Twenty two degrees is lovely for watching, but brutal for running. All I remember of the tunnel was relief. I was out of the sun for a few minutes, the break from its unrelenting glare actually gave me a small lift. I'm sure running marathons in the dark would be a lot easier.

At the entrance to the tunnel is a church tower, which appears to have lost its church, once St Mary Somerset. At the other end is the old Mermaid Theatre, now a conference centre. The theatre was opened in 1959 and is noteworthy for being one of the first to move away from the traditional design, seating the audience in one tier on three sides of the stage. The venue hosted an annual production of 'Treasure Island' and in later years was used for the BBC Radio 2 concert programme 'Friday Night is Music Night'.

One of its most famous productions was

the premiere of 'Whose Life is it Anyway' in 1978. The play, which had already been seen as a TV drama, focuses on sculptor Ken Harrison who was paralysed from the neck down in a car accident. The action is played out in his hospital room, with Harrison determined to have the right to end his own life. Given that this is a controversial subject in the 21st century, I think it would have been fascinating to have been around at the time of the play's London debut, to see how it, and the issues raised, were received over thirty years ago. As campaigners like Terry Pratchett have discovered, even now there's plenty of room for improvement in public understanding of the life experiences of severely disabled people.

In 2008, with no production having been staged at the Mermaid for ten years, the City of London Corporation Planning Committee stripped the venue of its theatre status. In doing so, they saved any potential developer £6m which would have been the original sum required had the theatre been closed. Whilst this decision was deeply unpopular in the theatre world, £6m does have the appearance of a deal breaker from a developer's point of view. The Mermaid may have been an iconic venue, but, and I say this as a keen theatre goer, London's theatrical landscape doesn't appear to be worse for its absence.

My Dad and I walked this route a couple of times, and on the second visit - another Monday but this one in October - the rain was never far away. With drizzle falling and beer calling, we stopped at a triangular-shaped pub called The Black Friar, which my Dad was keen for me to go to. I'd recommend you do too, although given its location two pints, a sandwich, admittedly one with smoked salmon in it, and a packet of peanuts did come to the eye-watering total of £15. Despite that it is one of my favourite pubs I've visited around the marathon course.

In the bar they were blowing up balloons for a beer festival. We headed through one of three small arches to the room at the back which had mahogany framed mirrors set in walls of orange, green and black marble. The ceiling had a gold and earthy-coloured mosaic, with hanging lamps that feature figures such as milk maids incorporated into their design.

Above the arches a number of life-enhancing phrases were written such as "haste is slow", "finery is foolery" and, as if inspired by the social media era, "don't advertise it, tell a gossip".

The leaflet we picked up told us that "The historic Art Nouveau Grade II masterpiece of a pub was built in 1905 on the site of a Dominican friary. The building was designed by architect H. Fuller-Clark and artist Henry Poole, both committed to the free-thinking of the Arts and Crafts Movement. Jolly friars appear everywhere in the pub in sculptures, mosaics and reliefs."

The pub was threatened with demolition but was saved thanks to a campaign led by Sir John Betjeman.

And art is but a short swim away, or walk across the Millennium Bridge if you don't fancy a dip, as the Tate Modern stands on the South Bank. Marathon runners won't see the bridge as they pass it whilst in the Blackfriars tunnel.

Shakespeare's Globe can be reached that way too, a venue I've visited several times but I've yet to see any actual Shakespeare performed there. As good value nights out go, you'll have to work pretty hard to find better than the 'two tickets for £5' offer at the Globe. You will have to stand though, and it's uncovered, but that's better than you think for the stage is designed in a C shape, with the theatrical equivalent of a pit down the front. With the action happening in front and on either side you're certainly in the thick of it. Fans of tourist tat, as I am, will be excited to know you can buy a gingerbread Shakespeare head from here.

As you pass Blackfriars Bridge you see the columns of Brunel's original still standing in the river between the railway and road crossings. Beyond the Blackfriars Road bridge we're now on Victoria Embankment where thousands gather every New Year's Eve to watch millions of pounds go up in flames in the form of the Mayor of London's fireworks. I'm not a big fan of New Year, the changing of the date has never struck me as something to get excited about, but the fireworks on the river are now one of the 'must see' things in London unlike that disastrous River of Fire at the turn of the Millennium. As BBC News reported at the time:

"Up to three million people who gathered in the capital and millions of television viewers had hoped to see 200ft flames rising above the water and shooting along the river. The fiery display had been due to travel at 775mph from Tower Bridge to Vauxhall Bridge in just 10.8 seconds after being launched from a string of barges", which does sound spectacular.

They quoted spectators who had wondered if they'd missed it, which would seem an achievement given the suggested scale of the thing. Spokespeople for the organisers lined up to say words to the effect of: if you didn't like it that's your fault for expecting it to be great.

"There is no doubt that it did happen - the River of Fire was lit and it did travel down the Thames as planned. Unfortunately, it may not have been as people had presupposed," shrugged one.

"Maybe the television pictures didn't do it justice," blamed another.

One of the undeniable trophies of the Millennium is the London Eye. It's hard to imagine the South Bank without it now, such is its success.

It's a landmark which, along with the recent addition of the Shard, many runners will focus on in the way they've always looked for the Big Ben clock tower which has been dwarfed by both of them.

A variety of large ships are moored along the riverside here which have been converted into bars, entertainment venues or party boats: HMS President, HMS Wellington and PS Tattershall Castle. On the right hand side is the Temple, which isn't a temple at all, but what look to be stately houses, many built around gardens, which have been converted into offices for legal eagles of every description. I imagined behind those walls Sherlock Holmes or Rumpole of the Bailey-like characters, pipe in mouth, working through files of evidence trying to spot some tiny detail that would lead them to clear the name of a client framed for a gruesome series of murders which, on the face of it, they seem certain to have committed. In reality, neighbourly disputes over loft conversions and garden sheds that are two inches too tall, and marriages which looked doomed from the start were probably being resolved. Real life is boring.

London is the greenest city of its size in the world. Green space covers almost 40 percent of Greater London, equivalent to 173 square kilometres (stats from London Councils). In addition to the parks, heaths and commons are numerous small public gardens such as those of the Temple. Much of the Embankment is flanked by open space, and as we walked, we wandered in and out of Victoria Embankment Gardens.

On either side of the road stands a silver dragon. Each one at seven feet tall and mounted on six foot plynths, they're impressive landmarks. The dragons hold a shield with a red cross on it, matching a cross on their wings, the symbol of the City of London.

In 1849 both dragons were positioned above the entrance to the Coal Exchange building which used to stand on Lower Thames Street. When the building was demolished the statues were preserved and moved to their new home on the Embankment. There are many other smaller dragons marking the boundary of the City including at the southern ends of London Bridge and Blackfriars Bridge, on Fleet Street, High Holborn and Aldgate High Street.

The dragons which towered over us mark the boundary between the City and Westminster, the final borough we run through and, the location of the finish line!

Chapter 22: 'Waterloo Sunset' - Somerset House to Westminster Bridge

When you pass through Temple tube station you're encouraged by the automated announcement to "alight here for Somerset House". Temple is also the station where, in 'Skyfall', James Bond begins his underground chase of Silva, first getting off at Embankment before running through tunnels to Westminster. We're taking a more conventional route, continuing to walk along Victoria Embankment.

Somerset House is without doubt one of the finest music venues in London, be that a regular venue, or one which has been created within another space. The annual Summer Series, a two week run of gigs every July is one of the highlights of London's summer.

This historic building in its current guise stands on the site of a palace built in 1545 for Edward Seymour, Duke of Somerset. It fell into disrepair and was demolished in 1775, making way for what we see today. Many organisations and societies have occupied space at Somerset House throughout its long and intriguing history; HM Revenue & Customs still use parts of it today, the Inland Revenue first moving there in 1789. In the centre is a giant courtyard which hosts concerts and film screenings in the summer, and is the home for one of London's most popular ice rinks during the winter.

Now one of London's most eye-catching entertainment and arts venues, a programme of exhibitions runs all year round, Somerset House has been at the heart of English history throughout its existence. The riverside and Strand, due to their location, had been popular spots for London residences of those seeking influence at Westminster since the 12th century. The bishops of Chester, Exeter, Norwich, Worcester and Durham all had homes here. Like when one footballer buys a house in Cobham and the rest all move in next door, by the 1500s these bishops' homes had been joined by houses belonging to the King and Queen, plus the Dukes of Norfolk, Suffolk and Richmond.

When Henry VIII died in 1547 his son, Edward VI, was still too young to become King. Edward Seymour, Edward's ambitious uncle, jumped at the chance to have himself created Lord Protector and Duke of Somerset. Realising he wasn't wanted, Edward VI ran away to the New Forest and spent some years hanging out with a skunk and a warthog, to return some time later to reclaim his Kingdom in heroic style, prompting Elton John and Tim Rice - you had no idea they were that old - to write the 'Circle of Life'!

Seymour decided that, as Duke and Protector, he needed a house which was right for his newly-found status. In 1547 work began on Somerset House. Seymour already owned the land, however, clearing the site meant the demolition of a number of churches and chapels, something which didn't exactly please his religious neighbours. To say that this was an extremely unpopular and provocative move is an understatement; it caused a clash with the ruling Privy Council and was the subject of the indictment that led to the Duke's arrest and brief imprisonment in the Tower of London in 1549. You don't have the sort of power Seymour had gained for nothing, and he soon obtained his release and reinstatement.

Somerset House was virtually completed by 1551. Although he had commissioned one of the most influential buildings of the English Renaissance, the Duke had little opportunity to enjoy the place, for another brush with the authorities came in the same year. His opponents had him arrested again and tried for the much more serious crime of treason. This time there was no escape and the Duke of Somerset, Lord Protector of England, was executed on Tower Hill in January 1552. His house became property of the Crown.

Somerset House got its first real taste of the entertainment world during the 1600s. Anne of Denmark and Norway, the wife of James I of England and VI of Scotland, found life north of the border rather dull and was given Somerset House. It's very convenient, if your wife is unhappy, to just happen to have grand houses lying around unused. She renamed it Denmark House, and encouraged the development of the English masque - a form of dramatic and musical entertainment, employing Ben Jonson to write and Inigo Jones to design the sets for a series of extravagant productions.

The 18th century saw Somerset House host the extremely popular masked ball which would either be an 'invitation only' event, or one where any member of the public who could afford to attend was able to buy a ticket. Fancy dress was an absolute requirement. The Somerset

House website has a couple of interesting descriptions of the masked ball from the media of the day, The Spectator talked of how "people dress themselves in what they have a mind to be, and not what they are fit for", while this unaccredited snapshot of the occasion described one woman's appearance as "Iphigenia for the sacrifice, but so naked the high priest might easily inspect the entrails of the victim".

I've been to Somerset House twice, and on both occasions seen the same band, Super Furry Animals, as part of the annual Summer Series. One of the reasons why Somerset House is such a popular venue is that, despite being right in the centre of London, once you've walked through the gate and left behind the Strand, you can easily forget about the world outside. Something which for many was more than welcome the first time I came to this venue, thirty-six hours after the bombings on public transport in July 2005. It was a surreal evening having a beer in the riverside bar in the sunshine, while police helicopters circled overhead. They were still there as we walked back to Waterloo at midnight, and had our route home required getting on the underground so soon after three trains and a bus had been blown up, it wouldn't have concerned me at all. People from elsewhere in the UK, in the weeks after the bombing, often asked me, "so are you nervous about using the tube?" The answer, for me at least, was a resounding 'no'. Because the tube is such an integral part of how this city functions, it was important for London to dust itself down and carry on as soon as possible. There was talk that the Super Furry Animal's gig might have been cancelled; the R.E.M show I was due to go to in Hyde Park the following night was moved back a week.

Opposite Somerset House on the south side of the river, looking like it has been built out of black and white LEGO, is the headquarters of ITV, and further along, just before Waterloo Bridge, is the National Theatre. The year before Danny Boyle captivated Britain with his Olympic opening ceremony he'd been directing a version of 'Frankenstein' at the National. This is also the venue that developed 'War Horse' which has gone on to take the West End, Broadway and the world of cinema by storm. I once went on one of the public backstage tours at the National Theatre where I learnt my favourite fact about the 50 year old venue. They showed us a series of pulleys used to move props into place during a production. We were told they have the ability, should it ever be needed, to make a double-decker bus appear to fly.

I have friends who believe Waterloo to be the bridge which provides the best view of London, the bend in the river giving an excellent vantage point to see the tall buildings of the City to the east and the Houses of Parliament to the west. I obviously can't back this up, but watching London life from here was good enough for Ray Davies. London culture completes the picture from the bridge. As well as the National Theatre, both the Royal Festival Hall and National Film Theatre which are legacies of the 1951 Festival of Britain, are located at the southern end; the latter has the bridge running above it.

Continuing our walk, the Houses of Parliament and Millbank Tower are ahead, with political offices and posh hotels like The Savoy on the right. One of my life ambitions is to stay in one of those. It would be a ridiculous use of money and I'd need to have more of it than sense, given that I live in London, but it might be fun to see how the other half lives. There's a Savoy Pier where I imagine guests from the hotel board fancy boats for fine dining on the river.

Victoria Embankment has many war memorials. Conveniently they're on both sides of the road so if, like me, you are interested in reading the inscriptions on them all, you have to play several games of chicken with the traffic. Alongside Cleopatra's Needle, on the river side of the road, is one such inscription which reads: "To the British nation, from the grateful people of Belgium 1914 -1918".

Behind it are descending steps which, with the tide high, look as if they've been built to give people an easy way to get wet. Waves crashed against the wall, occasionally one with extra force would splash over the top spraying anyone who got too close.

Cleopatra's Needle is an ancient Egyptian obelisk, with a sphinx on either side of it, which has stood here since 1873. It is part of a pair, the other standing in New York. A further needle can also be found in Paris. They're thought to date from the Eighteenth Dynasty of ancient Egypt (c. 1550-c. 1292 BC) around 1000 years before the time of Cleopatra. The Eighteenth Dynasty was the period during which the Pharaoh Tutankhamun reigned.

So how did it come to be standing on the side of a busy road in London?

It was a gift to the British government

275

from the ruler of Egypt and Sudan, interestingly called Muhammad Ali, following Lord Nelson's victory in the Battle of the Nile. The thank you letter to the donor read something along the lines of:

"Dear King Muhammad, thank you very much for this kind gesture, but if you think we're paying to have that thing shipped over here then think again."

So it remained in Egypt until the 1870s when a dermatologist called Sir William James Erasmus Wilson with money to burn, paid the large sum of £10,000 to have it transported to London. To achieve this the obelisk was encased in an iron cylinder named Cleopatra, designed as a floating pontoon, complete with deckhouse, mast and two keels, which was towed behind another ship. The journey was a disaster, with six men drowning while trying to prevent Cleopatra from sinking in a severe storm in the Bay of Biscay. Eventually it was left drifting, to be found four days later. It finally arrived in London via Spain and a major repair job.

When it was erected, a time capsule was concealed in the front part of the Needle's pedestal containing, among other things, a set of 12 photographs of the best looking English women of the day, a box of hairpins, a baby's bottle, a map of London and 10 copies of daily newspapers.

Hungerford is the next bridge, which serves as the pedestrian crossing and railway line into Charing Cross station, and was originally a Brunel bridge until the railway was built in 1859.

Before the bridge is Embankment station, behind which is 'Gordon's', London's oldest wine bar. Entering through a narrow door, visitors descend a steep flight of stairs which must be fun to negotiate after a bottle or two. It's like being in a cave, as the bar is narrow and mostly lit by candle light. The occasional drip falls from the ceiling, and regular rumbles reverberate through the floor as tube trains pass underneath. Samuel Pepys had lodgings here and a plaque further up Villiers Street marks the spot where Rudyard Kipling once lived, close to what is now an excellent German sausage take away shop.

Just past Embankment station is Northumberland Avenue which runs up to Trafalgar Square. On its corner stands the National Liberal Club (NLC). The building dates from 1887, with the Club having been founded five years earlier with three objectives:

- To provide an inexpensive meeting place for Liberals and their friends from across the country;
- The furtherance of the Liberal cause;
- The foundation of a political and historical library as a memorial to the work of William Gladstone.

George Bernard Shaw, Bram Stoker and H.G. Wells are among the legendary authors to have held membership of the NLC, as is the creator of one of my alltime favourite books 'Three Men in a Boat', Jerome K. Jerome.

Next is Whitehall Gardens, behind which are offices where armies of suited civil servants attempt to run the country. The Ministry of Defence is one of them. I'd advise any runner not to look right at this point as down a side road you get a glimpse of Horse Guards Parade -

home to the ceremony of Trooping the Colour and the 2012 Olympics beach volleyball - which deceptively suggests the finish is closer than you think. "Are we nearly there yet?" Yes, yes we are, just not as nearly as you'd like.

The bend in the river means we're now looking London Eye full in the face. I wonder how many runners are so tired they never even notice it?

On the left is a column of Portland stone with a bronze eagle on the top, in memory of all those in the RAF and Commonwealth Air Forces who lost their lives during the First and Second World Wars. Across the road stands a sculpture of a man in flying gear complete with life jacket and wings strapped to his arms, a memorial for the Fleet Air Arm - the aviation branch of the Royal Navy.

Victoria Embankment runs parallel to Whitehall, and through another gap in the buildings you can see through to the gates of Downing Street. We crossed the road yet again to take a look at the Battle of Britain Monument - I wonder how many people make the effort to stop at all these memorials?

This one is the most striking of the lot. It's an oblong-shaped sculpture which, when you walk around it shows representations of life during the Battle of Britain. People are looking through binoculars, their job being to pass any message back the moment they spot enemy aircraft on the horizon. A pilot pats his dog whilst waiting by the phone. Civilians prepare by putting on their gas masks. An air raid warden looks up at the sky, hand over his mouth in horror. People rescue those trapped in the rubble of buildings which have been struck. On one corner a German plane emerges from the clouds but with a British plane appearing over its left shoulder. The impression I got was that the German pilot doesn't know he's been spotted.

A lady pours tea for an exhausted pilot; the thorough detail in Paul Day's sculpture includes tea cups and a milk jug. Meanwhile a team of female engineers either build or repair aircraft.

Around the memorial are the names of everyone who flew during the Battle of Britain, listed alphabetically and by country, emphasising the global contribution to this victory. One name is from Barbados, a few are from Belgium, three columns list thirty or so names from Canada and Czechoslovakia. France, Ireland, Jamaica, Newfoundland and New Zealand all had nationals who fought.

As you might imagine, one whole side of the memorial is given over to British names, but another long list, with well over 100 names, is of those from Poland. Initially their contribution was lauded, but by the time of the 1946 victory parade, the political landscape had changed. Poland now had a Soviet-backed communist government and it was to them that the British government sent an invite for a flag-bearing party to represent the country. No specific request was made for members of Poland's armed forces to attend. Those who had fought felt that this not only undermined their own efforts but in particular the endeavours of those who had lost their lives during the war. Last-minute invites were made to the heads of the Polish Army, Navy and Air Force, as well as to twenty-five

Polish airmen who had fought in the Battle of Britain. All refused, with the Polish government also declining their invitation because of the last-minute additional requests. In the end Poland, who contributed around 200,000 people to the war effort, was not represented by anyone.

Westminster Bridge spans the river ahead. For a number of years the finish line was here, before construction work in the early 1990s saw it move to The Mall. Portcullis House is on the right hand side, just before runners do a right turn to run round past the Houses of Parliament. The building is very new in comparison to many around here, and was commissioned in 1992 but didn't open until nine years later. It was built to provide office space for Members of Parliament and their staff, and is where visitor groups gather for parliamentary tours. In the next chapter, I'm going in.

Chapter 23: 'At the Chime of a City Clock' - Big Ben

"What have you done today to make you feel proud?"

I'll tell you Heather Small, I climbed the stairs of the Palace of Westminster Clock Tower, all 334 of them!

I know I'm an occasional marathon runner, but I still lazily use the lift rather than the stairs at work, so that was a lot of steps, all the way to the top, where Big Ben lives.

It's one of the great misunderstandings of London, the false assumption that the tower is called Big Ben. This came to a head in 2012 when news emerged that consideration was being given to rename the tower in honour of the Queen's Diamond Jubilee. The indignation was quite hilarious: angry newspaper columns were written, Facebook and Twitter went crazy, as they do. Then someone pointed out that the bell is the bit called Big Ben, and everyone looked a little embarrassed that they'd been drawn into that one without doing their research. In the end the Elizabeth Tower was formally named in September 2012 with minimal fuss, and everyone got on with their lives as if nothing had happened. It was all rather logical since the other Palace of Westminster tower was named after Queen Victoria on the occasion of her Diamond Jubilee; so, 'Much Ado About Nothing' as a bloke called William once wrote.

As tourist trips in London go, this one's pretty prestigious - you can't just rock up and pay an entry fee. Partly as it's free, but also, to secure a place on one of the tours you have to write to your MP or a member of the House of Lords should you know one. As I do, it was as simple as arranging to meet for lunch. We did that too, although not in the really posh bit of the House of Lords so luckily I didn't have to try and remember how to do a tie knot.

Tours of the Tower happen three times a day. Our group, who met inside Portcullis House, was taken through a walkway under the road and up a couple of steps. These don't count towards the 334, our fantastically enthusiastic guide, a lady called Catherine, points out. Through a door with Elizabeth Tower in large letters written on it, and we're at the base of the spiral staircase. Look up and you can see the winding black rail snaking away as it's swallowed up by the hole above.

The climb was broken up into three parts, as much to give people a breather as to talk us through the history and workings of this famous old clock tower. After 114 steps we pause in a side room and wait for those at the back to come panting in, and hear about the building of the tower and the making of the bell. As our guide spoke we heard the distant chime of 11:15 being announced to London.

A large fire destroyed much of the Palace of Westminster in 1834. Construction of the current clock tower began in 1843. The project fell five years behind schedule and wasn't completed until 1859, presumably accompanied by grumblings about how "we don't do major building projects in this country".

As a result of the faffing about getting

the tower finished, the bell was delivered before its new home was ready. The equivalent of leaving the sofa in the garden while the decorating is completed was to hang the bell in New Palace Yard where it was tested every day. It was thought the bell didn't sound quite right, but when they tried a larger hammer it caused a massive crack to appear.

The Whitechapel Bell Foundry came to the rescue producing a second bell. This was not without incident either, for it was too tall to fit through the door, so had to be turned on its side.

The final act of a project, that has all the characteristics of one which the Chuckle Brothers were involved in, saw the bell winched by eight men over ninety metres to the top, a job which lasted thirty hours

On the next level we were able to walk around the edge of the tower behind the iconic clock faces. On one wall is a picture of a group of window cleaners in reddy-orange boiler suits. Imagine having to abseil from the top with bucket and sponge; it's no wonder this is a once every five years job.

11:45 thundered above us, followed by an intriguing noise made by the clock's mechanism which sounded more like someone dropping a load of metal poles down some stairs.

The final 53 steps climbed and, blimey, it's cold up here!

The belfry is a square platform right at the top of the tower. A walkway runs around the edge with the mighty thirteen ton Big Ben sitting in all its splendour in the centre. Forming a square around it are the four smaller quarter bells.

283

It's a strange feeling to be standing the best part of 100 metres up in the air, with the wind howling round you and ear plugs in position, blocking out the traffic noise coming from far below. It goes without saying it's a fantastic vantage point to look out over the city, with Westminster Bridge, once the finish line for the London Marathon immediately below, and the London Eye and the Shard looming over it, and us.

At 11:59 we were warned to brace ourselves. From this position, you can watch as the hammer lifts up, strikes, then that famous booming bell tune pummels the rib cage, followed by bong! bong! bong! …

We hear it so often on the news and as the soundtrack to the birth of a new year that it's easy to lose appreciation for what an iconic sound it really is. Experiencing the clock strike twelve a few feet from my head, New Year's Eve will never sound the same again. As each bong died away, I felt the air begin to be sucked from within my ears.

Perhaps I was lost in the moment for a few seconds as I tried to count to 12, only to be surprised when the bongs stopped at 10 - News time. Numbers never were my strong point. Whether the reverberations after the final bong rolled around that little bit longer, or my ears have never rung like that before, it was hard to tell, probably both.

Back on the ground I visited the Parliament Gift Shop (I've become quite a victim of over-priced tourist traps during the writing of this book) and left the proud owner of Big Ben-branded chocolate. Later that day I took it out of its box with the intention of taking a bite, only to discover it was actually shaped like the clock tower and put it back again.

As well as Big Ben, the Whitechapel Bell Foundry cast Philadelphia's Liberty Bell, and designed the bell which Bradley Wiggins (before he became a Sir) rang at the beginning of the opening ceremony of the London Olympics. Although Whitechapel produced the design for this 23 tonner, Europe's largest bell, the manufacturing took place in Holland, something which rival company John Taylor & Co were none too impressed with. The Loughborough firm, who have the original bell at St Paul's Cathedral on their CV, claimed they could have cast the Olympic bell in the UK.

The Whitechapel Foundry have been trading since 1570, although bell-making can be traced as far back as the 1420s, but what's an extra few decades when you've already got an entry in the Guinness Book of Records as Britain's oldest manufacturing company to your name?

Casting bells was a monk's job, but as the church grew wealthier, this dirty work was outsourced to the poorer folk. In the days when bellfounding happened within the walls of London, this rather smelly occupation took place on the eastern side of the city as it was believed the wind generally blew from west to east. Any marathon runner will tell you that this is not true; the wind actually always blows in the opposite direction you're running in.

Originally in Aldgate, the Whitechapel Bell Foundry arrived in 1670 at its current location which was then in the middle of the countryside on the site of a coaching inn called the Artichoke. Over the centuries the East End has grown around it, immigrant workers have crowded into the neighbourhood, Jack the Ripper walked the streets nearby, Oscar Wilde sent Dorian Grey to sample the local entertainment, and millions have reluctantly bought the road it stands on as part of the cheap set in Monopoly.

Miraculously the bell foundry survived the Blitz in one piece. The nearby Church of St Mary's, the 'White Chapel' which gives the area its name was one of many buildings to be destroyed. In its place is a small park, first named after the church, but then, in 1998, renamed Altab Ali Park twenty years after a local textile worker was murdered in a racist attack on Whitechapel Road.

Now the foundry stands in the shadow of the impressive golden fibreglass domed East London Mosque and has the Whitechapel Art Gallery close by. Anyone walking along Whitechapel High Street is more likely to catch the scent of curry from Brick Lane than the production of bells.

As with the Elizabeth Tower tour, booking months in advance is essential for the Whitechapel Foundry, although for this one a simple phone call will do to part with £24 in return for 90 minutes of company history, and a behind the scenes look at this centuries-old craft.

We're given a thirty minute window of opportunity in which to arrive, and late comers will not be admitted under any circumstances. The woman on the door had the air of someone who wouldn't think twice about enforcing that rule. As most of those on the tour were early we whiled away half an hour in a small courtyard in the centre of the building. The sound of call to prayer came drifting across the roof from the Mosque.

Our tour took us through a series of dusty rooms where the process of casting or repairing bells takes place. It's definitely a good plan to take your own water as by the end of the tour the throat is raw from the heavy air. Whilst some technological developments will have undoubtedly been made, the practice of bell founding isn't that different from hundreds of years ago. Perhaps no better example of this is the loam which is used to cast the bell mould, which even now is made from the very medieval sounding mixture of sand, clay, water, goat's hair and horse manure. So next time you hear the sound of Big Ben, just remember that bell was cast in poo. When you consider Big Ben is 13 tons, that's a lot of horses going for a lot of curries down Brick Lane. What do the Dutch feed their horses with if the Whitechapel Foundry believed the Olympic bell, Europe's largest, needed to be cast in Holland?

Ever wondered what happens to Big Ben when the clocks go back or forward? Just as you're desperately trying to remember which of the countless items you own that have the ability to tell the time, adjust automatically and which ones don't, a team of clock operatives are hard at work up at the top of the tower. Big Ben is stopped for a few hours, the lights are dimmed and the manoeuvring of hands takes place. Whilst it's a shame we can't all watch this, imagine what a disorientating experience it would

be to stumble out of a nearby pub and see time
speed up in front of your eyes.

Chapter 24: 'Home Town Glory' - Westminster Bridge to The Mall

Have you ever been so tired that you lose sense of what's going on around you? That was me in the last couple of miles of my first marathon.

Since doing London in 2011 I've completed marathons at Loch Ness, Berlin and Chester, lowering my time to under three and a half hours. In each of these I have clear memories of approaching the finish line, crossing the River Ness, running through the Brandenburg Gate, even along the river Dee to Chester Racecourse when I was at an exhaustion point I've rarely experienced, but not in London. By the time I was on the Embankment I'd run further than ever before. All I knew was noise, fatigue, heat, how badly I needed water, and that the finish line was close, but not close enough.

Somewhere along the Embankment, Simon, my guide runner, got cramp in one of his calf muscles. Fortunately our friend Jim, who had his own race place and who trains with me regularly, had decided he'd run the course with us as moral support, as much for Simon as for me.

Had I needed to stop to let Simon stretch, I'm certain starting to run again would have been a very painful experience for both of us. This sounds an obvious thing to say but the key to keeping going in the latter stages of a marathon is just that. Fortunately for me Jim and Simon did a baton-style changeover that Great Britain's sprint relay team could learn from, passing the guide band from one to the other without me needing to break stride.

We weren't convinced we'd see Simon again before the pub, but after he'd taken a bit of a stretch on the side of the road, and the fact he can run considerably quicker than me even with 24 miles in his cramping legs, meant that as we approached Parliament Square he was alongside us again.

I remember Jim shouting "come with us", or words to that effect, but at first I thought he'd recognised someone else as Jim is a guy who knows pretty much everyone in our local running community. Eventually I realised that Simon had put in a massive effort to find us again. What I have no recollection of is the two of them doing a second smooth handover and Simon taking control once again. The first time I had any idea that I'd crossed the line with Simon attached to me, rather than Jim, was when we looked at the finish line photos a couple of months later.

I do remember Simon and I, both broken and shadows of our former selves, staggering through the finish area. Meanwhile Jim, fresh from having run a marathon well within his comfort zone, was announcing that it had been "a good training run" and that he would "jog over and collect our bags". Neither Simon nor I had the energy to laugh, cry or punch him.

The London Marathon would only allow me one guide, so for Jim to decide to run my race rather than his own was a great personal sacrifice, to support both me and Simon in a challenge that we anticipated would take an enormous amount out of both of us, and to share the guiding if Simon needed it. I completed Loch Ness, Berlin and Chester with just one guide; the chance of them getting injured and that being a reason for me not finishing is a chance I'm quite happy to take. London was different though, an iconic race in which it is very difficult to secure a place. With London being my home marathon and my first attempt at this distance, there were many people around the course keen to see me run well. Jim and Simon were determined nothing would stop me that wouldn't be experienced by a sighted runner. If my body broke down that would be one of those unfortunate things, if my guide runner picked up an injury we considered that a potential risk we could plan for and avoid, something which came true on the Embankment.

Other events I've entered since have been open to two runners supporting me, something I plan to try in the future. An idea we're all keen to experiment with is for one guide to run with me until half way, and then hand me over to another who is waiting to do the second half. As I will hopefully become a faster runner, and, as the three guys quoted in chapter two keep reminding me, they are not getting any younger, it's important I don't rely on one person to assist me in getting round the full 26.2 miles. We'd planned to try a two guide strategy at the Brighton Marathon in April 2013 only for my left knee to break down during a race six weeks before. Although he's still very capable at running shorter distances, Simon has knee problems the like of which I can only have nightmares about, and so is unlikely to do a full marathon anytime soon. Jim and Andrew who still have ambitions of their own, both ran London in 2013. Had I made the start line in

Brighton, Andrew was to have done the first half by way of a final longish run seven days before the London marathon (he doesn't think twice about knocking out a steady half marathon that close to a full one), with Simon taking over at the midway point.

The Rules of the International Paralympic Committee permit up to four guides to assist elite runners over the 26.2 miles. Perhaps if I get really stuck in the future, a 4 x 6.5 mile relay might be a fun thing to try (I know that leaves us 0.2 miles short but I'm sure the last runner could manage that final little bit). It's certainly something which would break up the race in my head, but whoever takes over at 20 miles would have a tough job on their hands given everything I've written about my experiences brought on by fatigue in the closing miles of a marathon.

With the Embankment behind us, by now the only landmark a London Marathon runner cares about is The Mall. The original marathon finishing point was Constitution Hill. A year later, in 1982, this moved to Westminster Bridge due to construction work. It remained here, in what must have been a fantastic location, before moving again in 1994, due to roadworks, to the current point on The Mall.

Were Parliament Square in the first half of the race, the statues may well be as celebrated a landmark as the Cutty Sark and Tower Bridge are, but most runners probably don't even notice them as they run past with the Square on their left. There are ten statues forming a ring around the green of British and overseas statesmen. Winston Churchill faces the Houses of

Parliament. When the Square was being redeveloped in the 1950s he pointed out the spot where he'd like his statue to be. Next to him is David Lloyd George, maker of that famous 1910 speech at Limehouse Town Hall, and prime minister between 1916 and 1922. The circle also includes a number of 19th century British prime ministers, plus Abraham Lincoln and, the most recent addition in 2007, Nelson Mandela. I wonder who will be next and what sort of media, political and public fuss will be kicked up when they're chosen?

Birdcage Walk connects Parliament Square to The Mall. London Marathon runners, you're not hallucinating, the roads around Buckingham Palace really are red. This is to give the impression that The Mall is a giant red carpet leading to Buckingham Palace.

If I had been making a TV documentary I'd have gathered together everyone who has helped me research this book, a bit like at the end of one of those charity concerts where all the performers come back to join Sir Paul McCartney for one final song.

My group could have met in Parliament Square and walked to Buckingham Palace, down the tree-lined Birdcage Walk, maybe singing 'Chariots of Fire' or 'Keep on Running'. We could have turned the final corner on to The Mall and broken into a jog, which would have been awkward as someone would have been wearing the wrong kind of shoes. Bemused tourists would have watched, meanwhile Londoners would ignore us thinking we were another one of those stupid flashmobs, and not a very well attended one. Then someone would have asked me if I knew where the finish line was and I'd have admitted I didn't, because the last time I ran down here I was so tired I didn't even know who I was attached to. This revelation would have curbed any half-hearted enthusiasm in trying to run, and we'd wander off in search of a photo opportunity with Buckingham Palace in the background, whereupon any Londoner walking by would probably grumble because we were blocking the pavement.

I could have done that, but as it's hard enough getting some of the people you've read about out to the pub I didn't think it was worth the effort. Plus, it would have looked silly.

Instead, almost a year to the day after I stood on Blackheath my Mum and I got off the tube at Westminster on our way back from somewhere else and walked the short distance which feels like a never-ending one when you're running it.

Having refreshed my memory of the final section of the course we walked back to the tube via St James's Park. I do remember this part of the day as Simon and I limped our way in search of the agreed family meeting point. Trees are given letters of the alphabet and logically we'd picked S, without realising it would be about as far away as possible.

If the last few miles of a marathon are one of the toughest experiences I've had, then the time immediately after crossing the finish line is one of the best.

An often quoted line in the world of running is this one from Czech runner Emil Zátopek: "If you want to win something, run 100 metres. If you want to experience something, run a marathon".

Zátopek is the winner of four Olympic gold medals, three of them in the same Olympiad - 5K, 10K and marathon in 1952 - so some might point out that he can make statements like that, but as I've competed at both the 100m and marathon, I believe that sentiment to be correct.

It could be argued that my greatest sporting achievement is representing England at the 2002 Commonwealth Games in Manchester. For a few weeks I had a glimpse into the life of the international, professional athlete. I conducted TV, radio and newspaper interviews, was named Athlete of the Year by my University, and received an award from Leeds City Athletic Club where I'd been based in the two years prior to the Manchester Games. All that was fun while it lasted, and provides me with many good memories and a feeling of great satisfaction, but without doubt the most fun I've had as a runner has been training for marathons.

The planning, commitment, routine and physical challenge that comes with completing a 14 week programme in order to stand on the start line in the best condition possible is an enormously enjoyable experience. If it wasn't I wouldn't be doing it, given that part of the challenge is the life/training balance.

I'm lucky to have friends who also love the marathon challenge, and as most people find training in groups more productive than on their own, others benefit from running with me. On a cold, wet, dark winter's evening, after a long day at work and an energy-sapping London commute, it would be so easy to stay indoors, leaving the miles scheduled for that evening to another day. Admitting you don't fancy it to someone else is so much harder than telling yourself. In my case it would be rude to skip a session when someone else has made that commitment to come and run with me, and, for their part, if they whimp out then I miss out too.

Whilst some will be lucky enough to have the opportunity of travelling to compete on a track - I ran a few times in Dublin and I don't think you'd be surprised to learn that those weekends were about much more than just a couple of races. In general, though, distance running presents much more potential for the non elite runner to see the world. Running tourism has taken me to the Scottish Highlands, the Welsh coast and the streets of Berlin. It's also allowed me to discover so much about my home city I never knew, and would probably not have bothered to find out, were I not looking for ways to pass the time when running the London Marathon.

Before the race I merely scratched the surface when researching the route, but as I've since discovered in far greater detail, and as I suspected, it's impossible for 26.2 miles of London road to be dull.

Chapter Names Explained

The following is a list of the song titles I have used as chapter names.

Chapter 1: Elbow - 'One Day Like This'

If only for the lyrics: '... it's looking like a beautiful day, so throw those curtains wide, one day like this a year would see me right'. This is Elbow's best known song, written by Guy Garvey. It appears on the album 'The Seldom Seen Kid'. It's often heard at sports grounds and the band performed it during the closing ceremony of the London Olympics as the athletes were arriving in the stadium.

Chapter 2: Canned Heat - 'Let's Work Together'

This seemed the most appropriate title for a chapter on guide running. The original blues song, written by Wilbert Harrison in 1962, is titled 'Let's Stick Together'. Canned Heat's version was released in 1970 and can be found on the album 'Future Blues'.

Chapter 3: The Stills-Young Band - 'Long May You Run'

Song from an album of the same name released in 1976.

Chapter 4: Squeeze - 'Up the Junction'

Chosen because Glenn Tilbrook, Squeeze vocalist, was born in Woolwich. The 1963 Nell Dunn novel, 'Up the Junction', was adapted into a TV play and film, from where Squeeze took inspiration. Whilst the junction Chris Difford refers to in his lyrics is Clapham, I'm relating it to John Wilson Street in Woolwich where the marathon routes meet.

Chapter 5: Yardbirds - 'Stroll On'

A song included in the film 'Blow Up' with scenes filmed in Charlton. The Yardbirds are seen performing this song in a Central London nightclub, and is an updated version of the Tiny Bradshaw 1951 song 'Train Kept A-Rollin'.

Chapter 6: Lemonheads - 'It's About Time'

A 1993 single from the album 'Come on Feel the Lemonheads'. Song written by Evan Dando and Tom Morgan.

Chapter 7: Alternative TV - 'Fun City, SE8'

Alternative TV (ATV) was one of a number of bands to emerge from the music scene of Deptford in the second half of the 1970s. ATV is the band of Mark Perry, famous for the fanzine 'Sniffin' Glue'. 'Fun City, SE8' appears on their 1981 album 'Strange Kicks' and is about a night out on Deptford High Street.

Chapter 8: Dire Straits - 'Let's Go Down to the Water Line'

Another band with a Deptford connection, this song is the opener of their 1977 self-titled debut album.

Chapter 9: Underworld - 'Caliban's Dream'

Featuring Dockhead Choir, Only Men Aloud, Elizabeth Roberts, Esme Smith and Alex

Trimble with percussion by Dame Evelyn Glennie. Caliban's Dream is the speech from Shakespeare's 'The Tempest' (act 3, scene 2) which was delivered by Kenneth Branagh, in character as Isambard Kingdom Brunel, during the opening ceremony for the 2012 Olympic Games. The song was performed as the Olympic cauldron was lit. In this chapter I go in search of Brunel's London thanks to a walking tour organised by the Brunel Museum.

Chapter 10: Bob Dylan - 'Watching the River Flow'

Chosen for the chapter about Tower Bridge, both for being able to actually watch the river flow, and as this bridge is one of the most popular places for people to gather to watch the flow of runners pass. Released in June 1971 its first album inclusion was on Dylan's 'Greatest Hits Vol 2' compilation later that year. For what it's worth this is probably my favourite Bob Dylan song.

Chapter 11: Jimmy Eat World - 'The Middle'

Once over Tower Bridge we're at the halfway point, or 'middle', on the course. This is Jimmy Eat World's best known song. It appears on the 2001 album 'Bleed American' which the band self-financed after being dropped by Capital Records.

Chapter 12: AC/DC - 'Highway to Hell'

This is the title and opening track of AC/DC's 1979 album, and the last to feature vocalist Bon Scott who died early the following year.

Chapter 13: Django Reinhardt - 'Limehouse Blues'

One of the numerous early 20th century cultural references to Limehouse and its mysterious double 'Chinatown'. A jazz song written by Douglas Furber (lyrics) and Philip Braham (music). Django Reinhardt recorded five versions, his first in 1935.

Chapter 14: Stone Roses - 'I Am the Resurrection'

Having focused on historical Docklands in the previous chapter, including a look at how 'Chinatown' came to be so notorious, during this next part it is clear for all to see the transformation the area underwent from being industrial wasteland to a commercial, corporate and financial powerhouse. To illustrate this I took the title of one of the Stone Roses' most loved songs, released as a single in March 1992, and to be found on their self titled debut album.

Chapter 15: Oasis - 'Morning Glory'

If you look closely at the opening shots of the video to this song you will see the One Canada Square tower at Canary Wharf between two blocks of flats. One of these is the Balfron Tower in Poplar, an 84 metre tall, 27 floor block in the social housing Brownfield Estate where the video for this single from the '(What's the Story) Morning Glory Album' of 1995 was filmed.

Chapter 16: High Contrast - 'The Road Goes on Forever'

Chosen because, at this point in a marathon, the road really does. This track was used in the one minute countdown film before the London Olympics opening ceremony and features a sample of The Who's hit 'Baba O'Riley'. Welsh DJ High Contrast put together the music for the Athletes' Parade during the opening ceremony.

Chapter 17: Billy Bragg - 'A13, Trunk Road to the Sea'

A song to be found on a 1991 John Peel sessions album, and is Bragg's ode to the A13 in the style of Bobby Troup's 'Route 66'.

Chapter 18: XTC - 'Towers of London'

From their 1980 album 'Black Sea', a song inspired by the hard labour which went into constructing London's landmark sites: blood, sweat and, in some cases, death. 'Towers of London, when they had built you, did you watch over the men who fell?'

Chapter 19: Bruce Springsteen - 'I'm on Fire'

One of seven singles released from Springsteen's 1984 album 'Born in the U.S.A' which has sold over 30 million copies worldwide.

Chapter 20: Lindisfarne - 'Run For Home'

We're on Lower Thames Street now in the final few miles towards the finish in Westminster. 'Run For Home' was a Lindisfarne single, written by Alan Hull, to be found on their 1978 'Back and Fourth' album. A UK top ten success, it would be the band's first hit in the US.

Chapter 21: Half Man Half Biscuit - 'Light at the End of the Tunnel'

A song from their 2002 album 'Cammell Laird Social Club'. The album takes its name from a working man's club near Birkenhead and also features fantastic song titles: 'If I Had Possession Over Pancake Day', 'The Referee's Alphabet' and '27 Yards of Dental Floss'. The significance of this chapter title is that runners pass through the Blackfriars underpass, a notoriously tough section of the course.

Chapter 22: The Kinks - 'Waterloo Sunset'

I chose this title for the 'Waterloo' bit. If you see the sun setting during the London Marathon you're likely to have had a very long and tough day. Written by Ray Davies, the song was released in May 1967 and was included on the album 'Something Else by The Kinks'. Time Out magazine called the song the "anthem of London".

Chapter 23: Nick Drake - 'At the Chime of a City Clock'

A song found on Nick Drake's second album 'Brighter Later' released in 1970. It features the sax playing of Ray Warleigh, a session musician who performed with Mike Oldfield, Humphrey Lyttelton and Ronnie Scott. Beach Boys drummer Mike Kowalski, and Fairport Convention bass player Dave Peg make up Drake's backing band on this song.

Chapter 24: Adele - 'Home Town Glory'

Adele's debut single, first released in October 2007 as a limited run of 500 copies, and then re-

released a year later following download demands. As London is my home town, this seemed the obvious choice to conclude this list.

Acknowledgements

I would like to thank everyone who has assisted me with the writing and publication of this book.

Anna Cooper: *Cover design*
Becky Thurtell: *Copy Editor*

Research and other Assistance
Ellie Baugh: *Greenwich research*
Simon Brazil: *Guide runner*
Will Cockerell: *General research*
Jess Culbert: *Tower of London research; Website design*
Jim Desmond: *Guide runner*
Stewart Henderson: *Publishing and other general advice*
Abi Knipe: *Deptford to Tower Bridge research*
Graeme Knuckey: *Rotherhithe/Bermondsey research*
Andrew Lane: *Guide runner; General research; Proof reader*
Geraldine Quaine: *Tower Bridge and Monument research*
Jodie Sadler: *Rotherhithe/Bermondsey research*
Hannah Storm: *Proof reader*
Tim Thomas: *Brunel Museum tour guide*
Edward Webb: *Blackheath, Somerset House, Tower of London research*
John Webb: *Big Ben, Blackheath, Charlton, Docklands Museum, Embankment, Lower and Upper Thames Street research*
Sarah Webb: *Big Ben, Blackheath, Charlton, Docklands Museum, Highway, Isle of Dogs, Limehouse,*

Poplar, Whitechapel Bell Foundry, Woolwich research;
Proof reader/editor

Additional Thanks

Baroness Dee Doocey OBE
for getting me on the Elizabeth Tower tour

Dr. John Seed
for help writing the chapter on Limehouse and Chinatown

Becky Swift and the Literary Consultancy
for her publishing advice and guidance

The Stragglers Running Club
for providing guide runners to support my training and racing.

About the Author

A former sprinter, Simon represented England in the Elite Athletes with Disabilities 100 metres at the 2002 Commonwealth Games in Manchester. As well as running the London Marathon, Simon has completed the Berlin, Loch Ness and Chester Marathons and has a personal best time of 3:29:36.

Simon was born and raised in South West London. As a former Deputy Editor of the online music magazine www.roomthirteen.com, he covered festivals including Reading, Isle of Wight and the Edinburgh Fringe. His review of the Foo Fighters in Hyde Park was published in the Review Section of the Independent. He has also contributed articles to Disability Now Magazine, Gapyear.com and the New York-based alternative arts publication Knight.

'Running Blind: An Alternative View of the London Marathon' is Simon's debut book.

Printed in Great Britain
by Amazon.co.uk, Ltd.,
Marston Gate.